THE EARTH IS THE LORD'S

EMORY UNIVERSITY STUDIES IN LAW AND RELIGION

John Witte Jr., General Editor

This series fosters exploration of the religious dimensions of law, the legal dimensions of religion, and the interaction of legal and religious ideas, institutions, and methods. Written by leading scholars of law, political science, and related fields, these volumes will help meet the growing demand for literature in the burgeoning interdisciplinary study of law and religion.

RECENTLY PUBLISHED

Thomas C. Berg, *Religious Liberty in a Polarized Age*

Douglas Laycock, *Religious Liberty*, 5 vols.

Steven D. Smith, *Pagans and Christians in the City: Culture Wars from the Tiber to the Potomac*

For a complete list of published volumes in this series, see the back of the book.

The Earth Is the Lord's

A Natural Law Theory of Property

Liam de los Reyes

William B. Eerdmans Publishing Company
Grand Rapids, Michigan

Wm. B. Eerdmans Publishing Co.
2006 44th Street SE, Grand Rapids, MI 49508
www.eerdmans.com

© 2025 Liam de los Reyes
All rights reserved
Published 2025
Printed in the United States of America

30 30 29 28 27 26 25   1 2 3 4 5 6 7

ISBN 978-0-8028-8520-3

Library of Congress Cataloging-in-Publication Data

Names: Reyes, Liam B. de los, author.
Title: The earth is the Lord's : a natural law theory of property / Liam de los Reyes.
Description: Grand Rapids : Wm. B. Eerdmans Publishing Co., 2025. | Series: Emory university studies in law and religion | Includes bibliographical references and index. | Summary: "Drawing on scholastic canon law and theology, the author develops a natural law theory of property, arguing that all things belong to God and that God has given human beings the power to use the things of this world for their own flourishing"—Provided by publisher.
Identifiers: LCCN 2024030517 | ISBN 9780802885203 (paperback) | ISBN 9781467469739 (epub)
Subjects: LCSH: Property (Canon law) | Property—Religious aspects—Christianity. | Property—Religious aspects—Catholic Church | Christian sociology—Catholic Church.
Classification: LCC KBR3410 .R49 2025 | DDC 346.04/011—dc23/eng/20240714
LC record available at https://lccn.loc.gov/2024030517

Contents

	Introduction	1
1.	Property in Gratian and His Patristic Sources	13
2.	A Natural Law Framework for Property	55
3.	The Principles of Property	95
4.	Critiquing Locke	135
5.	Reception and Innovation in Catholic Social Teaching	176
	Acknowledgments	215
	Works Cited	217
	Index of Names	229
	Index of Subjects	233

Introduction

WHY CAN ANYONE OWN ANYTHING AT ALL? After all, the world and all that is in it precede humans. At some point, no one owned anything. Now, it seems that whatever one sees is owned by someone. The question has occupied philosophers and theologians because when nothing is owned, then everyone can use anything. As soon as someone claims something, like a beautiful stretch of oceanfront land, it seems that person has prejudiced everyone else. Before, everyone could use anything. Now, everyone can use almost anything, but not that beautiful stretch of sand. Everyone might reasonably ask, "What gives him the right?" Indeed, what gives anyone the right?

At the most general level, philosophers and theologians have given two answers to this question. Some scholars are sincerely committed to defending a natural right to claim things for private ownership. Many of these propose some variation of a Lockean or "no harm" theory of property. If I exert labor on something that is unowned, like turning an unowned stretch of beach into a resort, then it becomes mine. Or, at least, in claiming it as my own I have done no harm to anyone else. No law, no political order, no social sanction is necessary. In fact, this argument continues, I have done more than not harm anyone else. I have made a positive contribution to humanity by bringing forth more value than was there before I labored, increasing the amount of stuff available to society, in this case a secluded spot to listen to the waves with fences, perhaps, to limit those intruding on my seclusion and decks for comfortable relaxation. Importantly, once something is owned, nobody may simply exert their labor on it without first making some agreement with the owner. Labor on owned things, like cleaning and smoothing the sand at the resort, does not necessarily transfer ownership. Rather, labor on owned things only transfers whatever the laborer and the owner agree upon, like a wage.

INTRODUCTION

The second set of approaches begins from the premise that each person receives the right to claim things only from society, either by custom or by law. There are important varieties of this claim, but all who fall into this category think of property as a social or legal convention. In this view, a person may only claim something on the terms agreed by her society. No one may say "this is mine" on her own authority, even regarding things she has developed—it would be neither natural nor just. A person may legitimately say "this is mine" only because society permits it. In Anglophone political philosophy, this idea has typically been associated with utilitarian philosophers like Hume, Bentham, and Mill. These utilitarian theories, though, are but one example of a broader tradition that conceives of property instrumentally.[1] What justifies property in this view is its usefulness for achieving some set of societal goals. For Hume and Bentham, this was the general welfare or happiness of society, aided by the efficient exploitation of resources that property facilitates. One need not be utilitarian to take this approach, though. For instance, another approach might suggest that whatever property laws a society adopts, they ought to be useful for the achievement of principles of justice. Property can be useful to secure general happiness, or a set of principles of justice, or perhaps other ends that are valued by political society, but it is always a product of society.

One of the most astounding aspects of recent philosophical and theological discourse around property is just how little this latter approach has been theorized. Lockean and "no harm" theories of property have been articulated and defended by libertarian philosophers.[2] Any alternative theory of property, however, often remains implicit and presupposed in the literature. When John Rawls renewed interest in political justice with *A Theory of Justice*, he had a great deal to say about economic principles of justice but little to say about the explicit theory of property underlying his argument. Among those who follow him and develop their own theories of justice, from Ronald Dworkin to Amartya Sen and others, only Robert Nozick develops a theory of property, and his fits squarely within the libertarian "no harm" approach.[3] At least one way of interpreting the approach to property in many of these theories of justice is in this second manner, that property is a convention that should be structured to achieve principles of justice in society. Liam Murphy and Thomas Nagel are

1. Alan Ryan, *Property and Political Theory* (Oxford: Blackwell, 1984).
2. Jeremy Waldron has suggested a Hegelian theory of private property as a natural right. I engage extensively with Waldron in this project, but his adoption of Hegel is in the minority, at least in Anglophone political philosophy and theology. See Jeremy Waldron, *The Right to Private Property* (Oxford: Clarendon, 1988).
3. Robert Nozick, *Anarchy, State, and Utopia* (New York: Basic Books, 2013).

among the few contemporary philosophers who have made explicit what is presupposed here: "Private property is a legal convention."[4]

Theological discourse is no clearer on alternatives to Lockean theories of property. Apart from Anthony Parel and Ignacio Ellacuría, the idea that property is a convention goes almost entirely unarticulated.[5] As with the literature on theories of justice, theology has developed a robust literature rethinking capitalism and the economy without explicitly developing the theory of property presupposed in it.[6] With a few exceptions, these analyses have focused on the market, consumption, commodification, and the theological and moral significance and liabilities of these phenomena. Economic theory, though, suggests that rethinking capitalism means addressing private property, especially over the means of production—the theoretical, juridical, and practical heart of the economic system on which the free market, commodification, and consumption are structured.[7] Though recent work in economic ethics has focused more concretely on problems adjacent to property, like need, sufficiency, and inequality, property itself remains largely presupposed here as well.[8] Theological studies that do engage the question of property tend to focus on a single data point, often either the patristics, Aquinas, or the disputes between the Franciscans and John XXII.[9] Connecting these traditional sources with contemporary questions of capitalism and property, though, necessitates situating

---

4. Liam Murphy and Thomas Nagel, *The Myth of Ownership: Taxes and Justice* (Oxford: Oxford University Press, 2002), 8.

5. Anthony Parel, "Aquinas' Theory of Property," in *Theories of Property: Aristotle to the Present*, ed. Thomas Flanagan (Waterloo, ON: Wilfrid Laurier University Press, 1979); Ignacio Ellacuría, SJ, *La lucha por la Justicia: Selección de textos de Ignacio Ellacuría (1969–1989)*, ed. Juan Antonio Senent (Bilbao, Portugal: Universidad de Deusto, 2012).

6. Kathryn Tanner, *Christianity and the New Spirit of Capitalism* (New Haven: Yale University Press, 2019); Kathryn Tanner, *Economy of Grace* (Minneapolis: Fortress, 2005); D. Stephen Long, *Divine Economy: Theology and the Market* (New York: Routledge, 2000); William T. Cavanaugh, *Being Consumed: Economics and Christian Desire* (Grand Rapids: Eerdmans, 2008).

7. Robert Heilbroner, *The Nature and Logic of Capitalism* (New York: Norton, 1985).

8. David Cloutier, *The Vice of Luxury: Economic Excess in a Consumer Age* (Washington, DC: Georgetown University Press, 2015); Christine Firer Hinze, *Radical Sufficiency: Work, Livelihood, and a US Catholic Economic Ethic* (Washington, DC: Georgetown University Press, 2021); Kate Ward, *Wealth, Virtue, and Moral Luck: Christian Ethics in an Age of Inequality* (Washington, DC: Georgetown University Press, 2021).

9. Charles Avila, *Ownership: Early Christian Teaching* (London: Sheed & Ward, 1983); Helen Rhee, ed., *Wealth and Poverty in Early Christianity*, trans. Helen Rhee (Minneapolis: Fortress, 2017); Drostan MacLaren, *Private Property and the Natural Law: A Paper Read to the Aquinas Society of London on March 10, 1948* (Oxford: Blackfriars, 1948); Parel, "Aquinas'

them synchronically and diachronically. This sort of historical approach allows one to understand the development of theories of property across this span of time as part of a coherent and compelling tradition, one whose principles can speak as much to the political and economic situation of today as to that of antiquity, the high Middle Ages, and the early modern period.[10]

So, why can anyone own anything at all? Or, at least, what does the Christian tradition have to say about this? The most significant and consistent answer to this question across the Christian tradition, which I re-present in this study, is that property of whatever form is indeed a convention, something humans create for the sake of something else. The establishment of property regimes is an expression of the social and creaturely nature of humans. As such, that it is a convention does not mean humans are free to create whatever kind of property regime they might fancy. Property regimes of whatever form must respect humanity's social and creaturely nature, as well as the nature of the world itself, which this tradition distills in a number of theological and moral principles: all things belong properly to God; God has given each person the power to use the things of the world for his own flourishing; property as a convention ought to govern and distribute the things of the world in accordance with this divine purpose.

What this means in practice is even more distilled and concrete. If God has given the earth to everyone but societies may licitly divide it by instituting property regimes, then some things must remain true in that division: namely, that the equity, equality, sufficiency, and liberty that characterize the divine intention must be in some sense preserved and even fostered in the establishment of property regimes. These convictions are held across many of the most important patristic, scholastic, early modern, and contemporary theological sources. This book explores how this Christian tradition presents a coherent and compelling answer to the question of property from that second, undertheorized line of thinking. I call this a natural law theory of property—it is general enough to support a wide array of philosophical and theological theories of justice and concrete enough to support and clarify many of the related critiques of capitalism and markets.

Theory of Property"; Mary L. Hirschfeld, *Aquinas and the Market: Toward a Humane Economy* (Cambridge, MA: Harvard University Press, 2018).

10. Exceptions to this narrow focus are Daniel Finn, *Christian Economic Ethics* (Minneapolis: Fortress, 2013), and Ulrich Duchrow and Franz J. Hinkelammert, *Property for People, Not for Profit: Alternatives for the Global Tyranny of Capital* (London: Zed Books, 2004), though Finn is less focused on property and works in broader strokes to outline consistencies rather than systematize general principles across the tradition.

Theoretical Considerations

To draw together such a long line of thought, one that stretches from antiquity to today, I make use of several theoretical terms and concepts. Introducing them briefly here will provide a précis of the argument while also forestalling any misunderstanding about their meaning and provenance. The first is a terminological note: *property* is not simply private property but any form of managing access to things (material or otherwise) that contrasts with what is known as *open access*. In an open-access regime, there are no rules structuring access, development, transfer, or use. In any property regime—communal, collective, or private—society has instituted some set of rules and regulations that govern the way individuals and groups exercise those and related powers over the things of the world.[11] Because private property has been and remains an important question for the Christian tradition and other traditions of thought, my discussion frequently will focus on it, but the tradition I discuss does not justify private property alone among the various forms of property regime. Indeed, at the center of my argument is that this tradition's justification of property is general enough to accommodate a variety of ways of organizing property regimes.

This generality connects with the way that I understand the *natural law*. A "natural law theory of property" will undoubtedly raise concerns about a hegemonic Christian moral system that imposes one (western European) way of life—in this case, one way of arranging property relations—and undermines the autonomy of other ways of life. I hope the opposite becomes clear in the course of my argument, but at the outset I should note that natural law as I understand it underdetermines morality. In recent research, this approach to natural law has been associated with the recovery of scholastic theories of natural law, in contrast to other recent articulations like the "new natural law" theory.[12] Scholastic natural law is "natural" because it is grounded in what might be termed the givens of human life—both biology (the importance of health, access to material goods, the reality of bodily vulnerability, etc.) and reason (the power of abstraction, of articulating principles of logical thought, of recognizing and developing ideas of goodness and what is good, etc.). It is not natural because there is only one way in which the biological and rational

---

11. Waldron, *Right to Private Property*, 31–33.

12. For a developed articulation of scholastic natural law, see Jean Porter, *Natural and Divine Law: Reclaiming the Tradition for Christian Ethics* (Grand Rapids: Eerdmans, 2013), and *Nature as Reason: A Thomistic Theory of Natural Law* (Grand Rapids: Eerdmans, 2005).

exigencies of human life can be legitimately expressed. For example, the human need to join in and organize society is ubiquitous but can be legitimately expressed in a tribal confederation, a representative democracy, or a direct democracy, among others. Where the natural law approach shows its teeth is in the way it rules out certain forms of government, like a tyranny. Since human society is a response to human exigency, and so for the sake of the well-being of the members of that society, a tyranny in which society becomes for the good of one and not the good of the members runs afoul of the very logic of society itself. It is unreasonable and, to the extent it also violates other aspects of the equal regard due to its members, like their access to material goods or respect for their bodily vulnerability, it is unjust. In this book, I refer interchangeably to a scholastic theory of property and the natural law theory of property. Both refer to a theory that systematizes what different scholastic approaches, as well as patristic and more contemporary approaches, hold in common.

This brings me to a third key concept for both this approach to natural law and this book—a *convention*. "Convention" is a term used to distinguish between what is natural, in the sense of what precedes human societal and institutional arrangements, and what is established by human custom and legal enactment.[13] Nature includes the exigencies of human biology and reason, like the importance of bodily integrity and the moral equality of each person, and natural law contains the general principles that are intrinsic to this conception of nature, like a principle of nonmaleficence. Convention is what proceeds from the exercise of reason to establish various customs, institutions, and ways of life that build on those natural exigencies and general principles, like specific laws codifying what constitutes maleficence, modes of enforcing those laws, and punishments for their violation.[14]

Characterizing an institution as a convention does not imply a moral judgment about the institution itself. Some conventions are obviously good, like marriage, while others seem ambivalent or outright problematic, such as servitude and, for some of the thinkers I discuss, property. When I refer to property as a convention, I mean simply that it is not given by nature. Rather, property is a product of humans reflecting on themselves, their needs, the material world, and what is morally salient about each. Through this process of reflection, human societies establish rules—either tacit (in the form of customs) or explicit (in the form of legal agreements)—that structure access, use, and division

---

13. For a detailed analysis of the distinction and relationship between nature and convention in scholastic natural law, see Porter, *Natural and Divine Law*, esp. 76–85.
14. Porter, *Natural and Divine Law*, 51–52.

of the material world. That is, through this process of reflection, humans institute property regimes. And it is precisely the conventional status of property, its status as something not given but constructed to respond to more basic exigencies, that makes it, in scholastic thought as well as much contemporary political thought, instrumental or something "for the sake of."

This brings me to a term I develop to group together the theological and moral principles this tradition articulates around the topic of property: the "natural law of common dominion." If the first pillar of a natural law theory of property is the conventionality of property, the second is that what it is "for the sake of" must always include the divine intention in the creation of the earth and the grant of dominion to all in common. However humans divide the things of the world in the establishment of property regimes, they must in part aim to realize the equity, equality, sufficiency, and liberty that characterize the divine donation. My phrase "natural law of common dominion" collects these points together.

The underdetermined nature of these principles with respect to the division of material things means there are various ways to determine property relations. Patristic theologians, for instance, stressed the equity of the divine donation: no one is unduly favored, all are granted open access to use the things of the world. And each person is granted access precisely to have enough to live well, free of servile dependency on or subordination to others. Given the present fallen condition of humanity, open access regimes are more likely to lead to inequity than equity, as the powerful seize what belongs to all in common. Laws that structure access to the things of the earth are one way of protecting the vulnerable, and so seem to accord with the intention of the divine grant of dominion, even though they inevitably entail a shift in what equity looks like. This is one example of how property laws must be for the sake of the natural law of common dominion. In the prelapsarian state, equity could reasonably entail open access; in the present historical state, equity demands laws that divide and distribute the things of the world in a manner that does not unduly favor some, threaten the sufficiency of anyone, etc. In accordance with the vision of the natural law just outlined, the natural law of common dominion remains normative but open to specification.

The final concept to introduce is the idea of *dominion* itself. Just what is granted in God's grant of common dominion to all? It would be easy and, indeed, is common to equate dominion with property, given the historical and contemporary association of the terms. The theologians and philosophers in the tradition I present, though, are primarily concerned with powers of self-direction, and the importance of the ability to use the things of the world to exercise that self-direction. On these terms, dominion describes powers of directing and ordering parts toward the good of the whole. The parts can be a person's own faculties—reason, will, and body—directed and ordered into acts that serve the good of the whole individual. This is what Aquinas refers to when he writes that each person has dominion over her own acts. Dominion over the things of the world is just an extension of this primary sense: one directs and orders the things of the world toward one's conception of the good. That dominion over other things is granted in common does not mean the world is owned in common, but that each person shares in the responsibility of ordering the world toward each one's best conception of the good, which is always a conception worked out in society. The implications of this idea of dominion become clear throughout the project, but bear in mind that references to dominion are not primarily to a proprietary sense of dominion but to its political or directive sense.

I can now restate the most significant contention of this study in terms that reflect these theoretical considerations. Both in its normative dependency on principles of justice and in its indeterminacy, property is an expression of the political nature of humans. When it is instituted well, property gives expression to core principles of justice regarding how humans order and govern the material order. The rational norms intrinsic to interpersonal relations find expression in how those relations are mediated by access to and control over the things of the world. Since these norms underdetermine legitimate modes of governing the material order, property further expresses the properly social and political self-determination of peoples to pursue some set of values or another. These might be economic values like efficiency, productivity, and development, but they might be others as well, like sustainability or more egalitarian or common governance regimes. The pursuit of diverse communal goods leads societies to institute diverse property regimes, "natural" to the extent that they foster principles of justice that reflect what it means to be human, but conventional in their openness to a plurality of ways of instituting those principles and other meaningful values. Hence, a natural law or, since it achieves its most systematic expression in scholastic thought, scholastic theory of property.

Implications

The clearest statement of this theory of property is given by the canonists and theologians of the twelfth and thirteenth centuries. Though I show how this theory remains relevant in theological thinking today, it is almost always implicit, and so, undeveloped as a theory. Recovering a theory of property from the high scholastics entails several significant implications. As premodern and, perhaps more importantly on the topic of property, pre-Lockean, they can offer ways of thinking about property that are foreclosed by the presuppositions of contemporary thought. As I discuss in more detail in a later chapter, Locke responds to the same tension the scholastics inherit: that God has given the world to all in common, and yet now many things are owned privately. Locke's response is such a powerful articulation of a natural right to private property, drawing on the prevailing notions of improvement through enclosure contemporary to sixteenth- and seventeenth-century England, that even today it is hard to think outside of property as a natural phenomenon. This certainly seems to be the case popularly, and the prevalence of libertarian political philosophy in the academy, which is essentially founded on this natural right, testifies to its significance across multiple spheres of contemporary public life. The complacency with which the idea of property as something natural is held is perhaps one reason for the provocative title of Murphy and Nagel's *The Myth of Ownership*. By studying closely scholastic thought, I can inhabit a viewpoint that holds many of the same contemporary political principles but a radically different conception of property.

Despite the apparent historical submergence of this approach to property, the fact that the theological and moral principles of this tradition remain operative makes contemporary thought ripe for the kind of systematization that the scholastics provided to patristic thought. By applying the logic of a natural law theory of property to Catholic social teaching (CST), I offer a stronger and clearer interpretation of that tradition than secondary sources that either fall back on the natural right to private property to interpret it or focus almost exclusively on the social mortgage or dual character of property. To a lesser extent, I bring the same lens to analyze the thought of Ignacio Ellacuría, one of the clearest liberation theologians on the topic of property. My analysis brings CST and at least some iterations of liberation theology under the same, general natural law theory of property. Though scholars have long recognized the convergences between CST and liberation theology on the political regulation of property, I show how this convergence rests on the same moral and theological principles that animated patristic and scholastic thought. Whether through Aquinas (for CST) or the Spanish scholastics (for liberation theology), a natural law theory of property remains latent within these two contemporary traditions and remains the best way to understand and bring order to them.

INTRODUCTION

Finally, a systematic account of property provides the means for bringing this Christian tradition of property into comparison with other contemporary theories. By bringing the natural law theory of property into conversation with contemporary political philosophy and economy, I can demonstrate what I consider to be broad convergences on the question of property between the Christian tradition and the work of Rawls, Murphy and Nagel, Dworkin, and Elinor Ostrom, among others. Despite these convergences, the natural law theory I present also generates space for critical discourse with many of these same authors and others like Jeremy Waldron, raising questions about the appropriate level of specificity of theories of property, the interaction of various normative principles, and the manner in which conventional property rights can still be insulated from arbitrary and even simple utilitarian exercises of political authority.

Structure of the Argument

There are other answers to the question of property from within the Christian tradition. Nonetheless, this project illuminates the foundations, development, and influence of the most significant answer to that question from within the tradition. The foundational principles of property that develop from patristic scriptural exegesis and theological reflection are received and systematized by scholastic canon lawyers and theologians in the twelfth and thirteenth centuries. This synthesis informs the way early modern Spanish scholastic theologians and canonists think about property and colonization explicitly and continues to inform the way liberation theologians and Catholic social teaching treat the question of property. It is broadly compatible with other ways of thinking about property but is foundationally incompatible with Lockean theories of property. Lockean and similar theories of property, then, form the foil for the natural law theory of property throughout this book.

The first chapter examines this patristic tradition to show that scholastic thought on property is constituted primarily by a reception of prior tradition, the enunciation of that tradition's principles, and an attempt to resolve tensions latent within it. This chapter is structured by the scholastic reception of the patristic theologians through four key texts in Gratian's *Decretum* that formed the backbone of scholastic reflection on property through the thirteenth century. The following two chapters examine the key principles and implications of the scholastic development of this tradition. Chapter 2 articulates the theoretical pillars of this theory: that property is a convention normed by the natural law of common dominion. This chapter also demonstrates how these pillars are systematized in part by utilizing the principles and attempting to resolve the tensions inherited from earlier Christian thought. The result is that for the scholastics property is indeed a product of human reason, the legitimacy of which depends on its intelligibility as fostering and protecting the moral principles enshrined in the idea of common dominion: equity and equality, sufficiency, and liberty. Chapter 3 presents an overview of both historical and contemporary implications of this idea of property.

Chapter 4 develops a critique of Lockean theories of property as a contrast with the natural law theory of property set forth in the first three chapters. This is particularly relevant for a book in theological ethics, since interpretations of property in Catholic social teaching, when they do not rely explicitly on a Lockean theory, fall short of explicating an alternative theory of property that can make sense of the trajectory of papal teaching. Locke's theory is part of a very influential stream of early modern thought on property that deserves a full treatment, both on account of its power and on account of its potential to wreak havoc in colonial, neocolonial, and neoliberal contexts. Locke's theory also, however, contains both promise and legitimate concerns, and I highlight each at the end of the chapter to show how the natural law theory of property can attain to the same level of promise while avoiding the liabilities Lockean theories present.

The final chapter demonstrates not only that the scholastic theory remains relevant today but that it is also very much a living tradition. I show how the theory undergirds many of the convictions regarding property in Catholic social teaching and provides a coherent framework for interpreting the trajectory of CST's treatment of property. The progenitors of CST receive the natural law tradition, though it is not always clearly or even coherently presented in individual encyclicals and remains unsystematized and implicit in CST. More than just receiving this tradition implicitly, though, CST also innovates within it, introducing the conduciveness of property to moral self-development as a new criterion of evaluation. Though this certainly connects with the criterion of property's conduciveness to liberty in the prior tradition, it also emphasizes opportunities to develop capacities, responsibilities, and a public presence in a way that is new to the tradition, and likely occurred in dialogue with Hegelian approaches to property. Nonetheless, while a Hegelian approach may construe private property as a natural right, CST ultimately resists this characterization of property. In this way, CST achieves what according to Alan Ryan was one of Locke's significant accomplishments—holding instrumental and self-developmental accounts of property in tension. In light of my arguments regarding the superiority of this tradition's approach to property over Locke's, the natural law theory of property shows itself as a theory as comprehensive as Locke's but preferable in a number of crucial ways and deserving of close examination as a theory with significant implications for contemporary political theology and philosophy.

ONE

Property in Gratian and His Patristic Sources

THIS CHAPTER EXAMINES THE FOUNDATIONS of a Christian approach to property that is rooted in patristic sources and comes to be perhaps the most significant tradition of Christian, or at least Catholic, thinking on property up to today. In the twelfth and thirteenth centuries, scholastic canonists and theologians synthesize earlier sources to develop the first systematic expression of this approach to property as part of a more general renewal of medieval society as well as its legal and political thought. The canonists and theologians of this period hold no single, systematic theory of property. They do, however, hold a common set of commitments across their diverse theories of property, allowing me to place them under a general approach to the question of property and its political and legal significance. Like their forebears, these authors consistently invoke key theological and moral principles, a shared sense of the salient questions regarding the emergence and legitimacy of property, and agreement about the relevant texts and authorities for resolving those questions (as well as moral, legal, and social questions in general).[1]

One of the greatest forces unifying scholastic theories of property is Gratian's *Harmony of Discordant Canons*, commonly referred to as the *Decretum*, published in its first recension around 1140. Indeed, the *Decretum* was a unifying force for the whole field of canon law, remaining so up until the promulgation of the updated 1917 Code of Canon Law.[2] Gratian's identity remains

---

1. This reflects the diversity and commonality in scholastic thinking regarding the natural law more generally. See Jean Porter, *Natural and Divine Law: Reclaiming the Tradition for Christian Ethics* (Grand Rapids: Eerdmans, 2013), 50–51.

2. See the introduction by Katherine Christensen in Gratian and Johannes Teutonicus, *Treatise on Laws (Decretum DD. 1–20) with the Ordinary Gloss*, trans. Augustine Thompson, OP, and James Gordley, Studies in Medieval and Early Modern Canon Law (Washington, DC: Catholic University of America Press, 1993), ix–xxvii.

CHAPTER ONE

a mystery to historians, but it is evident from the extensive references to the *Decretum* by bishops and the papal chancery, its rapid incorporation into law curricula, and broad dissemination of early manuscripts across the Alps that his work was widely influential.³ At the time Gratian composed the *Decretum*, church law was plagued by contradictions and inconsistencies, a result of the diverse origins of different laws: from the Old Testament through the earliest Christian writings and up to the twelfth century, from ancient Israel to the Eastern and Western Roman Empires to early medieval Germanic kingdoms, and from theological, dogmatic, and legal genres. Previous compilations had been ineffective in bringing order and coherence to church law, a problem that undermined the efficacy of not just ecclesiastical courts but also the training of canon lawyers.⁴ Rather than merely compiling the diverse and discordant canons of church law, Gratian brings together apparently contradictory texts and shows through different interpretive processes how they might be harmonized. His techniques include everything from a simple prioritization of some sources over others to a critical reinterpretation of the key terms.

Though Gratian harmonizes a great deal of the code of canon law, as a result of the sheer scope of the task, many of the *Decretum*'s texts remain unclear, difficult to understand, or still in need of harmonization. At least some of the texts in the *Decretum*, therefore, including texts that reference property, present a set of legal and institutional tensions and questions that continued to challenge the coherence of canon law and its underlying jurisprudence. There is much in the *Decretum* that calls for further explanation, a project that many of the canonists who follow Gratian take up in glosses on the *Decretum* or in their own *Summae* of canon law. Complex and sophisticated conversations among both canonists and theologians on topics as diverse as natural law, penance, and property all find an anchor in the texts of the *Decretum*. Some of these texts provide a clear principle or authority that forms common ground for the participants while others provide a set of common questions and challenges raised by unclear, abstruse, or contradictory canons.

---

3. Michael H. Hoeflich and Jasonne M. Grabher, "The Establishment of Normative Legal Texts: The Beginnings of the Ius Commune," in *The History of Medieval Canon Law in the Classical Period, 1140–1234*, ed. Wilfried Hartmann and Kenneth Pennington (Washington, DC: Catholic University of America Press, 2008), 8; Peter Landau, "Gratian and the Decretum Gratiani," also in *The History of Medieval Canon Law in the Classical Period, 1140–1234*, 48.

4. Stephen Kuttner, "The Revival of Jurisprudence," in *Renaissance and Renewal in the Twelfth Century*, ed. Robert L. Benson and Giles Constable (Toronto: University of Toronto Press, 1991), 310–11.

Property in Gratian and His Patristic Sources

The focus of this chapter is four texts from patristic theologians that form the foundation of Gratian's presentation of property. As a result of their incorporation into Gratian's systematization of canon law, these four likewise come to form a key set of texts from which scholastic canon lawyers and theologians develop more systematic understandings of wealth and property. Familiarity with Gratian's patristic sources offers insight into how scholastic reflection is anchored in the tradition and where the scholastics develop and innovate within that tradition. Since the scholastics extensively reference these texts (indeed, since many of their comments on property are in fact comments on these very texts), a basic familiarity with these texts, and the principles, tensions, and questions they elicit, is a prerequisite for following, let alone understanding, the shape and structure of scholastic discourse on property.

Beyond presenting the letter of the texts, however, I establish the context and background of the authorities upon which Gratian draws. To adequately grasp Gratian (and thus the scholastics) on property, it is essential to understand the sources he draws upon in collating and interpreting the relevant canons, which include texts from Basil, Augustine, Isidore, and a false decretal attributed to Pope Clement (Pseudo-Clement), which was incorporated with many other decretals (false and authentic) in the ninth-century compilation known as Pseudo-Isidore.[5] The texts can be easily misinterpreted outside of their original context, and some of them were not even intended to primarily speak to the question of property. Further, the significance of these texts with respect to the principles they transmit or the tensions and questions they raise is not always perspicuous. An examination of the background of these texts—their patristic authorities and the broader context of patristic thought—will provide a better grasp of the theological and moral principles shaping scholastic thought.

In this chapter, I analyze several of these principles: that the dominion of all things belongs to God; that property is a human convention; that the earth is for the sustenance of each and all alike; and that property is a power of distribution that should be used to alleviate the need of others. I show, further, how these principles are held and ordered consistently across Gratian's four sources on property as well as in Ambrose and Chrysostom. Though Gratian cites neither of the latter in the four central texts that form the foundation of scholastic reflections on property, they are influential sources with whom the scholastics also would have been familiar and are important in other sections

---

5. For more on the proximate source of Pseudo-Clement for Gratian, see Landau, "Gratian and the Decretum Gratiani," 33–34.

of the *Decretum*.[6] I engage their thought to outline the patristic background to scholastic theories of property more fully.

Establishing the immediate context of each text—the purpose it served and its location in the *Decretum*—also draws out more fully the tensions and questions that each text raises with respect to property. I discuss four tensions internal to the text: between the natural and the conventional, between possession and sin, between the common and the private, and between property and theft. The principles and tensions latent within these four texts give this chapter its organization.

I organize this chapter according to the demands of the constructive project of recovering the scholastic conception of property and not according to a historical exegesis of the *Decretum* itself. Rather than organize the principles and tensions in the order that Gratian presents them, I let the theoretical implications of the texts establish their order of presentation. The logic of my approach may only become apparent as one engages the following chapters, but nonetheless I think it will serve the reader better. I begin with a text from Distinction 8 chapter 1 (D. 8 c. 1).[7] I then proceed to a discussion of Case 12 question 1 chapter 2 (C. 12 q. 1 c. 2). I conclude with analyses of D. 1 c. 7 and D. 47 c. 8 and offer synthetic comments on these four texts in the conclusion to the chapter.

What emerges from this examination is twofold. First, I identify the foundations of the Christian tradition that the scholastics systematize. Any conception of property faithful to this tradition will be intelligible as an expression of the scriptural texts, doctrines, and principles that are the touchstones of this set of patristic reflections. Second, I set the stage for the next chapter's examination of the scholastic systematization of this discourse: What are the specific texts they have access to? In addition to a set of doctrines and principles, what questions and tensions do these texts, taken in isolation, convey to the scholastics? This not only provides a clear sense of the issues that motivate scholastic approaches to property—which certainly facilitates understanding—it also helps to situate the scholastics as a part of this longer tradition. The scholastics receive and interpret these texts in a way that transmits the spirit of the

---

6. They are, for instance, central to the related discussion of almsgiving and poor laws in the *Decretum*. Brian Tierney, *Medieval Poor Law: A Sketch of Canonical Theory and Its Application in England* (Berkeley: University of California Press, 1959), 54–58.

7. The *Decretum* is divided into three sections. The first contains 101 distinctions, reconciling difficult or conflicting sources in canon law; the second is a set of 36 cases illustrating the application of different legal principles; the third is a section consisting of 5 distinctions on the liturgy and sacraments. See Hoeflich and Grabher, "Establishment of Normative Legal Texts," 10–11; Christiansen, introduction to *Treatise on Laws*, xii–xv.

patristic tradition even while extending its letter, organizing the principles in such a way as to still bear relevance for Christians today thinking through an adequately theological and moral account of property.

God's Dominion and the Tension between the Natural and the Conventional

The keystone principle of early church and medieval discussions of property is that the world and all that is in it are under the dominion of God.[8] Property, ownership, wealth, and poverty are all thus understood as topics appropriate for theological inquiry. Beyond a few historical donations to ancient Israel, however, Scripture is quiet on the specifics of God's dominion—what and to whom to apportion things, if anything ought to be apportioned at all.[9] Patristic theologians drew on what resources they could from Scripture, but understanding and extending these texts demanded a theological analysis of nature as a created order open to rational inquiry. Of course, nature as such provides little of what human society had already come to employ in its social and political organization—political authority, marriage laws and customs, laws of inheritance, and, of greatest interest for my purposes here, customs and laws of property. A theological analysis of nature is bound to unearth inconsistencies and divergences between the order of nature and the conventions of different human societies. As Gratian notes, "the law of nature differs from custom and ordinance" (D. 8 d.a.c. 1).[10] How and in what way to understand these divergences is what I call the tension between the natural and the conventional.

Though the scholastics rarely use the word "convention" (they often refer to nature), the distinction between convention and nature is an important

---

8. As I noted in the introduction and develop in chapter 3, dominion can refer to powers of directing or to powers of ownership. The primary sense for this study is to powers of directing, but here the idea of "God's dominion" refers analogously to powers of ownership for humans. That God is provident (powers of directing) is likewise undisputed in this tradition.

9. This tradition considers Gen. 1:26 as referring to powers of governing and directing the world. For the patristics, see Morwenna Ludlow, "Power and Dominion: Patristic Interpretations of Genesis 1," in *Ecological Hermeneutics: Biblical, Historical, and Theological Perspectives*, ed. David G. Horrell et al. (New York: T&T Clark, 2010). I discuss Aquinas on dominion in later chapters. Even Ockham has this idea of dominion in mind when he refers to Gen. 1:26 (see chapter 3, note 11).

10. Gratian, *Corpus Iuris Canonici: Pars Prior: Decretum Magistri Gratiani*, ed. Aemilius Friedberg (Graz, Austria: Akademische Druck-U. Verlagsanstalt, 1959). All translations are my own, though where possible I check my translations against Gratian and Johannes Teutonicus, *Treatise on Laws (Decretum DD. 1–20) with the Ordinary Gloss*.

CHAPTER ONE

category for interpreting and understanding scholastic natural law and, in this case, the scholastic reception of patristic thought.[11] For the scholastics, nature refers to exigencies given by biology (plant, animal, and human) and human reason, and general principles that can be inferred from a theological and rational interpretation of these exigencies (e.g., "good is to be done and evil avoided"). It is a category that establishes the framework and orientation of moral action and theory, but which of itself is open to further inference, specification, and addition through the intellectual and social activities of humans. These inferences, specifications, and additions, the products of human reason and society, are collectively referred to as conventions. Conventions are a broad category in scholastic thought and at their most general level simply contrast anything given by nature with anything that is a product of human agency. In its usage here, convention refers to both customs and laws and is broadly referred to as "human law" in contrast with natural law.

In Distinction 8 chapter 1 (D. 8 c. 1), Gratian spotlights a divergence between the order of nature and human convention to provide an example of the distinction between natural and human law, writing that "by divine law all things are common to all; by the enacted law, this is mine and that another's." To prove his point, he cites the authority of Augustine and the principle of God's dominion. In a treatise on the Gospel of John, Augustine writes, "By which [law] does each one possess what he possesses? Is it not by human law? For by divine law 'The Earth is the Lord's and the fullness thereof' [Ps. 24:1 (23:1)]" (D. 8 c. 1). Augustine here takes for granted that what he calls the laws of emperors and kings may diverge from the divine law, but he provides no explanation for such a divergence.

The theoretical questions about property raised by Augustine's argument are sharpened by the fact that Gratian dedicates the next two distinctions to proving that human law (custom and enactments) may not contravene natural law. In D. 8 d.p.c. 1, Gratian writes, "In truth, the natural law prevails simply over custom and ordinance in dignity. For whatever [human laws/conventions], whether they are received through mores or expressed in writing, if they are contrary to the natural law, they are held to be null and void." In Distinction 8 cc. 2–9, Gratian cites a number of authorities to show "that custom is considered secondary to natural law" (D. 8 d.p.c. 9) and, in D. 9 cc. 1–2, to show that "the laws [enactments] of princes should not prevail over natural law" (D. 9 c. 1).

If by the natural law all things are common, then are the various laws of property, which remove things from the common store to make them in some

11. For more on nature and convention, see notes 13–14 in the introduction.

way private, illegitimate? Read in the wider context of the *Decretum*, there is little reason to think that Gratian intends to demonstrate that since property diverges from the natural law of common dominion, it is to be held, in Gratian's words, null and void, but this is precisely the question that Gratian's presentation raises. Not only is property apparently an example of how natural law and human convention differ, it is also the example that directly precedes a long series of authorities denying the legitimacy of human convention when it runs counter to the natural law. Though the presentation of Gratian's text does not directly impugn the convention of property, it does focus the tension between the natural and the conventional squarely on this institution. In doing so, it raises acute questions about the natural law, generally, and the idea of property, specifically. D. 8 c. 1 sets the stage for the development of more systematic theories of natural law and property as the scholastics who follow Gratian attempt to understand the legitimacy of property in its apparent divergence from the natural law.

Before examining the tension that the text presents and the theoretical problems it raises, however, we should examine the substance of Augustine's comments regarding property and the principle of God's dominion that are cited in D. 8 c. 1. The principle of God's dominion is ubiquitous in patristic discourse, especially with respect to questions of wealth and property. Basil, for example, takes up the theme of God's dominion over all things, including the possessions of the wealthy, in the midst of a great famine and suffering.[12] Augustine delivers his thoughts on God's dominion over human wealth and property in a much different context. He is not exhorting the rich in a time of famine but preaching against the Donatists in a time of schism. His whole approach to the question of God's dominion, then, is framed not by the exigencies of hunger but by those of defending the imperial transfer of the schismatics' property to the Catholic Church, which had just been ordered by the emperor Honorius through the Edict of Unity in 405, partly in response to the pleas of the North African Catholic bishops.[13]

---

12. See especially Basil's homily on Luke 12:16–21, labeled Homily 6, "I Will Tear Down My Barns" in *On Social Justice*, ed. and trans. C. Paul Schroeder (Crestwood, NY: St. Vladimir's Seminary Press, 2009), 59–71. Helen Rhee also translates key selections from Basil (and other patristic theologians) on property in Helen Rhee, ed., *Wealth and Poverty in Early Christianity*, trans. Helen Rhee (Minneapolis: Fortress, 2017). Selections from Homily 6 are on 55–60. The context of Basil's preaching is summarized in Justo González, *Faith and Wealth* (San Francisco: Harper & Row, 1990), 173–86.

13. For more about this period of the Donatist controversy, see the section on the Edict of Unity in W. H. C. Frend, *The Donatist Church: A Movement of Protest in Roman North Africa* (New York: Oxford University Press, 2003), 261–74.

In his *Tractates on the Gospel of John*,[14] Augustine addresses the apparent objections of the Donatists regarding the seizure of their property. He first inquires into the source of anyone's property. Do humans possess things by divine law (*ius*) or by human law?[15] For Augustine, the Donatists (and all other humans) can only claim their property through the laws of kings. However, the Donatists had apparently claimed that they possessed their property under divine law, which would put it beyond the mandate or seizure of imperial law. Augustine refutes the idea that property is divinely instituted: "For by divine law: 'The Earth is the Lord's and the fullness thereof'" (Ps. 24:1 [23:1]). Humans hold property under the laws of emperors or kings and not directly through special donations from God, at least not as a general rule. The Donatists, if they wish to claim any property at all, must do so on the basis of those laws. Augustine, for his part, thinks the Donatists are in an insuperable dilemma with respect to their church property: "Do not call those possessions yours, since you have renounced those very human laws by which possessions are possessed" (D. 8 c. 1). The imperial Edict of Unity commands that Donatist church property pass into the possession of the Catholic Church. If the Donatists refuse to recognize imperial law in order to maintain their claims to their property in the face of the Edict of Unity, then Augustine suggests they forfeit the original basis for claiming their property. If the Donatists possess what they do by imperial law, then rejecting that law would seem to undermine their ability to make legal claims for the possession and protection of their property. A natural law theory of property will have to demonstrate its ability to rebut this sort of unwarranted coercion through the seizure of property—no doubt just the kind of example that might have animated Locke's thinking on property. Patristic thinking on the dominion of God and the conventionality of property, though, appealed far more often and widely to arguments that were not aimed at the justification of political and religious coercion.

The patristic theologians that Gratian cites draw on a theology of creation to interpret the biblical text and substantiate their claims about wealth and

---

14. I translate and cite the passages from Augustine's *Tractates on the Gospel of John* as they appear in the *Decretum*. Augustine's tractates can be found in the original Latin in Augustine, *Sancti Aurelii Augustini in Iohannis Evangelium Tractatus CXXIV*, ed. Augustino Mayer (Turnhout: Typographi Brepols, 1954). The passages here are from *Tract. In Ioh. VI* 25–26, pp. 66–67. The relevant sections of the tractates can be found in English translation in *St. Augustine, Tractates on the Gospel of John 1–10*, trans. John W. Rettig (Washington, DC: Catholic University of America Press, 1988), 6.25(2)–26(3) (pp. 152–53).

15. Many translations translate *ius* as "right," but "law" seems to render Augustine's argument more accurately.

property. Basil and Augustine offer examples of this approach with respect to the principle of God's dominion, and Gratian cites key passages of both in the *Decretum*. In a passage Gratian cites in D. 47 c. 8, Basil interrogates Christians who suggest that in not giving alms they merely keep what is their own: "What a shameless thing to say! You say your own? What? From what hidden place in the world did you bring them forth? When you came into the light, when you passed through the womb of your mother, I ask you, with what of these resources and necessities did you come?"[16] In the original homily, not cited in Gratian, Basil goes on: "Where then did you obtain your belongings? If you say that you acquired them by chance, then you deny God, since you neither recognize your Creator, nor are you grateful to the One who gave these things to you."[17] The land, rain, sun, and animals are all the creation of and under the dominion of God. The human can lay no claim to the creation or preservation of the goods of the created order nor any absolute claim to the ownership of these goods. No one is born with even an article of clothing, and no one brings any goods beyond the grave. The body may be buried with what a person claimed, but the person is no longer present to claim it; the soul has departed naked and empty-handed with respect to the goods of this world.

Like Basil, Augustine supports the scriptural text with theological reflection: "The poor and the rich God made of one clay and he supports the poor and the rich by the same earth" (D. 8 c. 1). While Basil points to *creatio ex nihilo*, Augustine makes a more general appeal to something like the natural purpose of the material world. God brings forth the good things of the earth to support each and all alike and has conferred property on no one. As we see below, God tolerates property arrangements and laws as a way of bringing about a variety of goods, but neither in Scripture nor according to the light of reason can one discern that, aside from some historical donations to ancient Israel and certain individuals at that time, God has conferred property on one but not another. Here we can see how the argument about *God's* dominion leads to an argument for *common* dominion: no one can lay claim to any material good, since all is brought forth for the sustenance and use of all. In patristic thought, if there are rich and poor, this is not a part of the divine order of things but a result of human willing and human law. By extension, for

---

16. Gratian, *Corpus Iuris Canonici*, 171. The Latin text that Gratian cites is drawn from a translation by Rufinus of Aquileia in the fourth century and incorrectly attributed to Ambrose. For a more faithful translation of this text, see Basil, "I Will Tear Down My Barns," sec. 7 (p. 69).

17. Basil, "I Will Tear Down My Barns," sec. 7 (p. 69).

Augustine, Donatists cannot claim their property to be beyond the reach of imperial law, since the very institution of property is a product of that law, and not divine law. But Augustine's argument also foreshadows what will become explicit in the following sections: that the human laws of property institutions are conditioned by more basic theological and moral principles, such as God's dominion and the intention of God for the goods of the earth.

Augustine's views on property are more complex than this brief section of the *Tractates* quoted in the *Decretum* can capture. As R. W. Dyson notes, contrary to his elaborate historical explanation for the emergence of political authority, Augustine lacks a correspondingly detailed account of property.[18] Augustine's thoughts on property seem to be framed more in the context of theological polemics than in any systematic fashion. Augustine appeals to Psalm 24:1 (23:1) and a theology of creation in the Donatist controversy. But in an earlier polemic against the Manichaeans, Augustine argues that there is nothing wrong with possessions, so long as one does not love one's possessions.[19] More than Augustine's anti-Donatist argument about the conventional nature of property, it is this belief that forms the core of his thoughts on property. Compared to the other patristic theologians, Augustine has a more benign understanding of property that first takes root in the need to defend the material world and human use of the material world against the Manichaeans. Along these lines, Augustine contrasts *true* possession and *false* possession, the latter of which is no real possession at all, and essentially defines these as *good* possession and *bad* possession. To love one's possessions leads to false or bad possession, whereas to use one's possessions out of love of God and neighbor leads to true and good possession. Though humans possess what they possess by the laws of kings, some possess truly by these laws and others only possess by pretense.[20] For Augustine, lawful possession under imperial law is a simulacrum of true lawful possession: "lawfully implies justly, and justly implies well." Those who use their possessions wrongly "possess them wrongly. You can see then how many people ought in fact to return property that isn't theirs." From this, though, Augustine does not advocate that each person be treated like the

---

18. R. W. Dyson, *The Pilgrim City: Social and Political Ideas in the Writings of St. Augustine of Hippo* (Rochester, NY: Boydell, 2001), 104.

19. Augustine, *Contra adimantum manichaei discipulum* 20.2, cited in A. J. Carlyle, *A History of Medieval Political Thought in the West*, vol. 1 (New York: Barnes & Noble, 1950), 136.

20. Augustine, Letter 153: Augustine to Macedonius (413/414), in *Augustine: Political Writings*, ed. E. M. Atkins and R. J. Dodaro (Cambridge: Cambridge University Press, 2001), sec. 26 (p. 87).

Donatists. Rather, "there is toleration for the injustice of those in wrongful possession, and certain laws have been established among them, known as 'civil laws.' These are not intended to make them use possessions rightly, but rather to make them less oppressive in misusing them."[21]

Evidently, Augustine's aim is not to explore the legitimacy of property as a human institution that derogates from divine law. He presupposes such legitimacy and makes it the basis of his argument: the legitimacy of the discipline that the emperor Honorius enforces on the Donatists by seizing their property (in addition to outlawing the Donatist church) depends on the property institutions of the Roman Empire being licit. Augustine in the *Tractates* seems to have some idea that human enactment of the institution of property was providential and sanctioned by God: "God has distributed to humans these same human laws through the emperors and kings of the world" (D. 8 c. 1). In the end, this providential understanding of property, which sees God as in some way its ultimate distributor, remains a minority position among patristic theologians and medieval canonists and theologians, at least if God's providential action is seen as some sort of command to institute property laws and relations. The scriptural text, at least, does not provide any conclusive support, if it provides any support at all, for this kind of role for God in human institutions of property. The majority view holds with Augustine that property is a legitimate institution, but, contra Augustine, it holds that God makes use of and allows such an institution rather than commanding or ordaining it.[22]

---

21. Augustine, Letter 153, sec. 26 (p. 87).

22. My reading of the patristic tradition agrees with those who find in it this "moderate" position, delivered with forceful and urgent rhetoric, and diverges with those who see in the patristics a radical condemnation of private property, evil at its root and in its outcomes. Charles Avila, one of the radical interpreters, provides an otherwise compelling account of the moral strictures and orientation of private property but takes this to imply a rejection of the institution itself, at least unless it is on its way to common or communal property regimes. Even a critic like Ambrose, though, admits of the usefulness of private property not as a transitory but as a stable element in society. The radical position loses one aspect of the power of patristic reflection, the power of generality, which can accommodate a variety of circumstances, environments, cultures, and mores in the pursuit of the ends of property, a point that another radical thinker, Ignacio Ellacuría, affirms in his more moderate reading of these sources. Charles Avila, *Ownership: Early Christian Teaching* (London: Sheed & Ward, 1983); Ulrich Duchrow and Franz J. Hinkelammert, *Property for People, Not for Profit: Alternatives for the Global Tyranny of Capital* (London: Zed Books, 2004), 164. For representatives of the moderate position: Ignacio Ellacuría, SJ, *La lucha por la Justicia: Selección de textos de Ignacio Ellacuría (1969–1989)*, ed. Juan Antonio Senent (Bilbao, Portugal: Universidad de Deusto, 2012), 262–63; Daniel Finn, *Christian Economic Ethics* (Minneapolis: Fortress, 2013); Martin Hengel, *Eigentum und reichtum in der frühen Kirche: Aspekte einer frühchristlichen*

Augustine's position constitutes one pole on a spectrum of understandings of property in Christianity. Property is a convention, shaped and determined by the laws of emperors and kings and thus by different politics, mores, and legal institutions. But whereas, as we will see below, some Christians hold a deeply skeptical view of property, closely associating it with avarice, sin, and violence and brought about in relation to the Fall, Augustine seems to hold that property could just as well be a part of human social life with or without the Fall. Augustine dedicates little space to reflecting on the state of humanity prior to the distribution of property rights, so we have little access to his explicit understanding of the state of common dominion. While it is possible that Augustine holds that the state of common dominion was merely the primitive state of humanity and bears no normative significance for contemporary institutions of property, what Brian Tierney calls a primitive as opposed to normative understanding of natural law,[23] this is not a necessary conclusion. In any case, speculating about Augustine's view of common dominion is beyond the scope of this project. It is only important that I flag here Augustine's rather sanguine perspective on property since it anticipates what we will later see in Aquinas's own positive view of property as something that could have come into existence without the Fall. It is also worth reiterating that Augustine expresses his views in the context of several heresies that either repudiate the goodness of creation (Manichaeism) or advocate for what he sees as a troubling asceticism (Pelagianism), and so while his rhetorical emphasis differs from other patristic theologians, his underlying views might not diverge as much as they appear to.[24]

Returning to D. 8 c. 1 with the principle of God's dominion in hand, we can inquire further into the tension that Gratian presents between the natural and

---

Sozialgeschichte (Stuttgart: Calwer Verlag, 1973); Peter Phan, *Message of the Fathers of the Church: Social Thought* (Wilmington, DE: Michael Glazier, 1984), 36; Eduardo Rubianes, SI, *El dominio privado de los bienes segun la doctrina de la iglesia*, 3rd ed. (Quito: Ediciones de la Pontificia Universidad Católica del Ecuador, 1993), 36–37; Restituto Sierra Bravo, *Doctrina social y económica de los Padres de la Iglesia: Colección general de documentos y textos* (Madrid: Compañía Bibliografica Española, 1967), 311.

23. Tierney discusses this in an analysis of D. 1 c. 7 and D. 8 c. 1, in *Medieval Poor Law*, 29–32. This resembles what Peter Garnsey, following Samuel Pufendorf, calls a negative community, in which the primeval state is a "rights vacuum" and has no normative implications for the societies that emerge from it. See Peter Garnsey, *Thinking about Property: From Antiquity to the Age of Revolution* (Cambridge: Cambridge University Press, 2007), 115–18.

24. Aquinas, as well, develops his own thoughts on property in the context of the church's battle against the Albigensian heresy, which also held extreme ascetical views and doubted the goodness of creation, which might in part explain some of the similarities between his and Augustine's understandings of property.

the conventional. The principle of God's dominion is in the background not just of the specific question of property but of the normativity of the natural that makes human divergence from it problematic in the first place. As the creation and dominion of God, nature in some way reflects the providential will of God. In both Augustine and Gratian, the conventional institution of property is treated and presented as a legitimate human law that differs from the natural law. Nevertheless, Gratian collates and cites extensive church authorities (including Augustine) that appear to challenge the very possibility that human law may diverge from natural law. The specific challenge for the scholastics who comment on the *Decretum*, then, is to understand the legitimacy of property against the background of the natural law of common dominion. Does the convention of property in fact derogate from the natural law of common dominion? If so, in what way? And, if so, how can the convention of property be legitimate if customs and laws must yield to the natural law when they diverge? If this is true, how should one interpret the natural law? Should the natural law of common dominion be interpreted differently than other natural laws? Or, finally, should the meaning of common dominion be reinterpreted, so that the convention of property can be understood as not deviating from this natural law? All of these questions render more explicit different ways of understanding the tension between the natural and the conventional brought out in Gratian's presentation.

The tension between the natural and the conventional in one sense is a question about the limits of derogation from the natural law. Resolving the tension means providing a theory of natural law that can intelligibly allow for derogations or reinterpret them as something else, something not divergent from the natural law but added to it or permitted under it. In the following chapters, we will see the scholastics address this by finding space for humans to innovate under the natural law or specify the natural law, which must also provide an account of the legitimate scope of derogation, innovation, or specification. If every part of the natural law does not admit of some alteration, a theorist must provide an account of what parts do, and why. Finally, and perhaps most difficult and yet most important, the theorist must provide an account of the limits of legitimate derogation/alteration and whether and to what extent the natural law provides normative guidance and limits for divergence. Responding to these unresolved questions in Gratian, the scholastics develop nuanced and complex accounts of the natural law, which lead them to more sophisticated understandings of the natural law of common dominion and the convention of property. The scholastics respond to the questions and challenges I highlight here in different ways but also with a set of firm convictions held across their diverse approaches. Their response, however, is worked out alongside a set of other concerns, including explicit attention to the principle of the conventionality of property and the tension between possession and sin, which is one of the primary dilemmas to emerge in light of property's derogation from the natural law.

Conventionality of Property and the Tension between Possession and Sin

Without some developed framework to explain how property can legitimately derogate from the natural law of common dominion, the specter of the illegitimacy or sinfulness of property will dwell on the edges of any natural law theory. In C. 12 q. 1 c. 2, Gratian presents the question of possession and sin more bluntly, citing a text falsely attributed to the first-century Pope Clement (hence, Pseudo-Clement): "the common use of all things that are in this world should be for all people; but through iniquity, one said this was his, and another that, and thus division was made among mortals." Instead of taking this claim at face value—that to claim private property itself is sinful—most of the scholastics chose to reinterpret and uncover some more complex meaning to this otherwise blunt and laconic condemnation. The passage points to a genuine tension in Christian thought, though. On the one hand, property is often closely connected with and an occasion for sin. But, on the other hand, both patristic and medieval scholars also conceive of property as a response to sin, in that it alleviates some of the problems created by human iniquity. This tension provides one grounding for the conventionality of property, as a response necessitated by that unnatural phenomenon of sin. More importantly, in negotiating this tension between property's propensity to occasion sin and its usefulness for restraining sin, patristic and medieval scholars adopt an instrumental orientation of property that continues to characterize Christian reflection today.

For this section, I draw on a broader range of theologians than Pseudo-Clement to demonstrate how patristic theologians handled the close connection of property and sin. I conclude by gesturing toward the similar concerns and insights that will animate the scholastics as they handle the same issues. Though some in the early church hold that property was instituted in sin, the preponderance of the early church tradition prefers to discuss not the inherent sinfulness of property but its conduciveness to sin. At the same time, all of these scholars, whether they think property was instituted in sin or simply conducive to sin, talk about possession and sin alongside the usefulness of property for the individual and society. Through their analysis of the uses and hazards of property, the patristics generate something of a virtuous interpretive circle: the divergence of property from the natural law gives rise to the question of sin, and resolving that question reaffirms the conventionality of property. This interpretive circle, in turn, gives rise to a fruitful set of questions and insights into the meaning and significance of property, which I discuss at the end of this section.

For Augustine, property and property laws are conducive to the maintenance and order of society. As Peter Brown discusses, though in his youth Augustine enthusiastically endorsed the Platonic ideal of holding all things in common among friends, when he comes to reflect directly on the question of wealth as a bishop, he fully embraces the legitimacy and indeed usefulness of property for the lay members of his congregation.[25] According to the mode of life he prescribed for the monastic community he founded in Hippo, all things were to be held in common among the brothers, and thus he never relinquishes his ideal for those who pursue monastic life. Private property by the laity had a number of benefits, however, which Augustine proclaimed as one front on his attack on Pelagianism, some of whose adherents held radical views about the sinfulness of property and the demands of the Christian life to live with all things held in common.[26] For Augustine, this view ignores the reality of fallen humanity, makes a selective and heroic calling the norm for all Christians, and, perhaps most direly, threatens the spiritual interpretation and centrality of almsgiving in the church.[27] As we saw above, Augustine argues that part of the good of property and property laws is that they restrain evildoers. Augustine viewed general calls to relinquish property, especially with the ongoing collapse of the Roman Empire, as subversive and irresponsible. The laws not only protected those who used their property well, they made possible the organization and division of goods throughout the empire, which sustained both its institutions and those living under them. Brown documents extensively how grandiose divestments of wealth like the one by Paulinus of Nola, which were championed by Christians in the Roman Empire's confident fourth century, became suspect and problematic as confidence in the empire waned. Following the sack of Rome by the Visigoths in 410, massive divest-

---

25. Peter Brown, *Through the Eye of a Needle: Wealth, the Fall of Rome, and the Making of Christianity in the West, 350–550 AD* (Princeton: Princeton University Press, 2012), 167–72. See also 347–52.

26. Brown, *Eye of a Needle*, 303–21.

27. Brown, *Eye of a Needle*, 359–65.

ments of wealth were no longer understood as a sign of heroic virtue but were seen as a sign of temperamental and irresponsible immaturity, as Roman and Christian responses to the divestment by Melania the Younger and her spouse, Pinianus, show.[28]

Even patristic theologians such as Basil and John Chrysostom, who have a much less positive view of property, argue that property is materially useful for sustaining society. They concern themselves less with macro-level questions about responsibility to society and its structures. When they emphasize the material benefits of property, they focus rather on stewardship and its usefulness for distributing the goods of the earth. Chrysostom does not advocate the abolishment of property nor its complete renunciation, but only its renunciation as a power of exclusive and personal use. He seems to presume its legitimacy: "This is why God has allowed you to have more . . . for you to distribute to those in need. . . . For you have obtained more than others have, and you have received it, not to spend it for yourself, but to become a good steward for others as well."[29] The rich person is as much a steward as the deacon who dispenses alms for the church. Both must take care to use their goods not as though they were their own but "for the maintenance of the poor . . . to 'give them their meat in due season' [Ps. 145:15]."[30]

Basil's position is almost indistinguishable from Chrysostom's. The rich ought to "imitate the earth; bring forth fruit as it does. . . . The earth brings forth fruits not for its own pleasure but for your service."[31] The rich have received their wealth as stewards, to bring forth good fruits for the sustenance of all and not for their exclusive use or privilege. The true mark of those who hold their wealth properly is thus a genuine rejoicing when they distribute alms, "as those who relinquish what is not really theirs, instead of becoming downcast like those who are stripped of their own."[32] In his shorter rules, Basil makes this point explicitly: "The Lord's command does not teach that we have to reject and flee possessions as though they were bad, but that we should administer them. And the ones who are condemned are condemned not because they possess things, but because they make a bad use of what they possess. Therefore, a detached attitude towards and a sound respect for the

---

28. Brown, *Eye of a Needle*, 208–300 and 365–80.
29. *St. John Chrysostom on Wealth and Poverty*, trans. Catharine P. Roth (Crestwood, NY: St. Vladimir's Seminary Press, 1984), 50.
30. Chrysostom, *Homilies on the Gospel of Matthew*, in Rhee, *Wealth and Poverty in Early Christianity*, 96.
31. Basil, "I Will Tear Down My Barns," sec. 3 (p. 62).
32. Basil, "To the Rich (Homily)," in Schroeder, *On Social Justice*, sec. 3 (pp. 46–47).

earthly goods and a wise administration of them according to the command of the Lord are of great help in obtaining many things."[33] Basil considers that in the giving of alms and distribution of property it is not merely the divestiture that matters, though certainly this is spiritually beneficial to the giver. Rather, the distribution of property to the poor should be done effectively: the rich should distribute their alms through those who know best how to distribute, whom to distribute to, and already have the structures in place for the care and maintenance of the poor.[34] Not only the church but also the growing Christian hospitals and poorhouses, such as Basil's Basiliad, offered efficient and effective means by which to perform the acts of stewardship and facilitate the proper and just administration of one's property.

The three church fathers known as the Cappadocians—Basil, his brother Gregory of Nyssa, and their friend Gregory of Nazianzus—were born into wealth and remained wealthy throughout their lives, and yet each is noted for his critical perspective on the questions of wealth and property.[35] In a discussion of the Cappadocians, Justo González points out that among their enemies, "who sought every opportunity to attack them," and the rich in their churches, none leveled accusations of hypocrisy against the Cappadocians regarding their critiques of wealth and property, even though they benefited from their families' wealth throughout their lives.[36] González concludes that despite what might appear to be inconsistency in their position to modern eyes, it is more likely that modern readers who see this inconsistency are misreading the Cappadocians. As Basil's injunction that the distribution of alms should be in the hands of the expert shows, they were not concerned with "a dogmatic and legalistic selling of all possessions to give to the poor" but rather with "the relief of suffering." According to González, that "goal can best be served, not by one magnanimous act of giving all away, but by the much more difficult practice of making all available to respond to whatever needs might arise."[37] It seems clear that the Cappadocians thought some would be called to complete renunciation, but González's

---

33. Basil, *The Shorter Rules*, Question 92, in Rhee, *Wealth and Poverty in Early Christianity*, 69.

34. González, *Faith and Wealth*, 179 and 183–84.

35. Thomas A. Kopecek, "The Social Class of the Cappadocian Fathers," *Church History* 42, no. 4 (1973): 453–66. Kopecek argues that the Cappadocians were most likely of the *curial* class. See his comments on Nazianzus's retirement on his extensive familial estates at 454–55. Gregory of Nyssa, Basil's brother, writes in a letter that their mother had such extensive estates that she had to pay taxes to three provincial governors. See 461.

36. González, *Faith and Wealth*, 183–84.

37. González, *Faith and Wealth*, 184.

claims suggest that for them, the retention of property with the intention of effective distribution was also seen as a legitimate path. González's portrait of Cappadocian thought in this regard anticipates a significant part of the scholastic tradition on the legitimacy and morality of wealth and property.[38]

Beyond merely restraining evildoers, supporting the structures of political society, and acting as a conduit for the proper administration of material goods, property regimes were also understood by almost all of the patristic authors as offering opportunities for the practice of virtue and trading worldly treasure for heavenly treasure through alms and gifts to the church. Holding one's goods as the property of others to be properly stewarded and administered not only satisfies the demands of justice but also fosters virtues, among rich and poor, that will serve one well in this life and the next. Right next to his exhortations to hold one's goods justly and for the sake of others, Basil discusses the benefits of such possession, "the reward of benevolence and faithful stewardship" for the rich and, for the poor, the honor of "patient endurance in their struggles."[39] Almsgiving is a spiritual practice that constitutes the pinnacle of piety, a point reiterated in a sharp way by Leo the Great, who writes that compared to mercy (exemplified in works of charity), it is as if there were no other virtues and, compared to avarice, no other offenses.[40]

Chrysostom emphasizes the cultivation of virtue at more length than Basil and, despite the renown of his passages on justice, much more extensively than his discussion of the principle of stewardship. Noting that no one can take their goods with them when they die, Chrysostom continually emphasizes that in the giving of alms one receives virtues that remain with one eternally. One cannot truly claim one's external possessions: "Only those things are our own which we have sent before us to the other world. . . . Only the virtues of the soul are properly our own, as almsgiving and charity."[41] Despite the apparently less radical nature of such an emphasis on virtue, Brown notes that it is precisely this language that caused so much discomfort for the imperial courts at Constantinople (for Chrysostom) and Milan (for Ambrose) and turned the court against the former.[42]

---

38. Though it is outside the scope of this study, the concerns about the efficient distribution of alms are later shared by the scholastics. Tierney, *Medieval Poor Law*, 44–67.

39. Basil, "I Will Tear Down My Barns," sec. 7 (p. 69).

40. Leo the Great, Sermon 10 (November 444), in Rhee, *Wealth and Poverty in Early Christianity*, 143.

41. Chrysostom, *Homilies on the First Letter to Timothy*, in Rhee, *Wealth and Poverty in Early Christianity*, 99.

42. Brown, *Eye of a Needle*, 142.

Brown helps to identify yet another aspect of this language that introduced relatively new practices regarding property in the Christian churches. When Chrysostom discusses sending things before us to the other world, he is not merely using a rhetorical trope to encourage giving on the part of his congregation. The idea of a "treasury in heaven" receives more and more theological emphasis throughout the third and fourth centuries, and bishops such as Ambrose and Augustine make it a centerpiece in their discussions of wealth. Whereas in the predominantly pagan circles of the Roman Empire almsgiving and benefactions were typically thought of as appropriate primarily for the upper echelon, the superrich, in Christian churches the practices of almsgiving were democratized, so to speak. The idea that alms, charitable giving, and benefactions to the churches are loans to God that receive exorbitant returns means that even small gifts, when given by the poor, are of inestimable value to the giver.[43] As Brown notes, the return on such "loans," compounded by untold heavenly multiples, levels the differences between what might be considered large and small gifts on the basis of this world's standards.[44]

The heavenly treasury could be interpreted in different but equally beneficial ways. For Chrysostom, it appears that this treasury in heaven is constituted in part in this life by the reward of virtue. For Leo the Great, this treasury is framed in terms of good works that overshadow one's sins.[45] For Clement of Alexandria, the treasury consists of the prayers of the holy ones whose friendship one wins through almsgiving—widows, orphans, monks, and nuns—which are efficacious for both one's salvation and earthly needs.[46] In all cases, however, the spiritual exchange is founded in an act of sharing one's goods with those in need, whether directly or through the institutions of the church.

Nonetheless, even among the patristic authors, the material and spiritual usefulness of property casts a long shadow of avarice and luxury that always threatens those who possess wealth. Each of the patristic authors just discussed holds this position in one way or another. In various sermons and reflections on the Psalms, Augustine establishes the limits of the usefulness of property: "It is enough that riches do not ruin [the wealthy]; it is enough that they do them no harm, for they can do them no good."[47] Property can only provide for

---

43. See Gary Anderson, *Charity: The Place of the Poor in the Biblical Tradition* (New Haven: Yale University Press, 2013), for more on the development of this idea.

44. Brown, *Eye of a Needle*, 85–87.

45. Leo the Great, Sermon 10, 143.

46. Clement of Alexandria, *The Rich Man's Salvation*, trans. G. W. Butterworth (Cambridge, MA: Harvard University Press, 1960), secs. 33–35 (pp. 339–45).

47. Augustine, *Enarrationes in psalmos* 85.3, in Dyson, *The Pilgrim City*, 120.

an individual's spiritual welfare in its divestment: "Every reduction in earthly gifts allows an increase in heavenly ones, provided of course that the former are reduced through love for the latter."[48] Those who have little are exhorted to "seek what is enough, and want no more. Anything else is a weight rather than a help, a burden rather than an honor."[49]

Basil, too, sees in property a hazardous burden on the soul. Whether miserly or profligate, wealth threatens the well-being of the rich. For the miser, "what would cause others to rejoice causes the greedy person to waste away.... [He] is pricked to the heart by the wealth that slips through his fingers."[50] And for the one who spends freely, "some device has been concocted by the devil, suggesting innumerable spending opportunities to the wealthy, so that they pursue unnecessary and worthless things as if they were indispensable."[51] For Basil, the hold of wealth over one's heart threatens to make the property owner a murderer: "For whoever has the ability to remedy the suffering of others, but chooses rather to withhold aid out of selfish motives, may properly be judged the equivalent of a murderer."[52] Similarly, for Chrysostom, excessive attachment to property equates to theft and the illicit deprivation of others.[53] The luxurious or excessive use of goods, especially when conjoined with a parsimonious attitude toward almsgiving and charity, is enough to warrant condemnation for the property holder.[54]

If all of these views demonstrate the relationship between property and sin through the potential misuse of one's property, a minority strand in the tradition takes this a step further by identifying an act of sin at the very roots of the institution of property. In the West, Ambrose is the foremost exponent of this view, which he presents in his *On the Duties of the Clergy*. This text derives its title and inspiration from Cicero's *On Duties*. Ambrose self-consciously positions it as an update of Cicero's text for a Christian society. His position

48. Augustine, Sermon 335C, in *Augustine: Political Writings*, sec. 5 (p. 54).

49. Augustine, Sermon 85.4–7, in Dyson, *The Pilgrim City*, 121.

50. Basil, "I Will Tear Down My Barns," sec. 1 (p. 61). Basil's division reflects what David Cloutier suggests is lost to contemporary moral vocabulary: a division between the vice of avarice, characteristic of the miserly, and the vice of luxury, characteristic of the profligate, in *The Vice of Luxury: Economic Excess in a Consumer Age* (Washington, DC: Georgetown University Press, 2015), 35–43.

51. Basil, "To the Rich," sec. 2 (p. 44).

52. Basil, "In a Time of Famine and Drought (Homily)," in Schroeder, *On Social Justice*, sec. 7 (p. 85).

53. Chrysostom, Second Sermon on Lazarus, in *St. John Chrysostom on Wealth and Poverty*, 49.

54. Chrysostom, Second Sermon on Lazarus, 50.

Property in Gratian and His Patristic Sources

on property is, however, quite consciously a departure and contradiction of the Stoic philosopher's position. In contrast to the preponderance of Stoic thought, especially as captured in Seneca's Letter 90, Cicero holds that there is nothing questionable or morally dubious with the occupation of common things that then results in the establishment of private property. In some passages, he even seems to associate the institution of property with the establishment of law in general, which for Cicero separates peaceful life in society from a violent state of nature.[55] There is nothing wrong with the institution of property, and, indeed, one of the government's primary concerns ought to be to protect and defend the private property of its citizens.[56] Far from being morally ambiguous, for Cicero the institution of property is a step toward civilization and a step away from the warring and barbarism that characterized precivilized life. *On Duties* thus offers a defense of the first acquisition of an unowned object, which can be attained in any number of legitimate ways: "by long occupation (as when men moved into some empty property in the past), or by victory (when they acquired it in war), or by law, by settlement, by agreement or by lot."[57] Overall, Cicero's position has more in common with Roman law than with either Stoic or Christian thought, and represents a third major body of thought on the question of property in antiquity.[58]

Ambrose draws on a separate strand of Stoic thought to critique Cicero and develop his own understanding of property. Influenced by the idea of the Golden Age theorized by Stoics like Seneca, who endorse the idea that the division of the world in some way constituted all or part of the fall from a primordial grace,[59] Ambrose writes:

---

55. Garnsey, *Thinking about Property*, 112.
56. Garnsey, *Thinking about Property*, 114.
57. Cicero, *De officiis* 1.21–22, in Garnsey, *Thinking about Property*, 114.
58. All three influence medieval scholastic thought, with Roman law having the greatest influence over the scholastic civil lawyers (the "civilians"). On Cicero and Roman law, including where Cicero goes further than Roman law in positing the occupation of land, see Lauren Benton and Benjamin Straumann, "Acquiring Empire by Law: From Roman Doctrine to Early Modern European Practice," *Law and History Review* 28, no. 1 (2010): 13.
59. Thus, in Seneca's Golden Age, "the boundaries of nature lay open to all, for men's indiscriminate use, before avarice and luxury had broken the bonds that held mortals together." Seneca, Letter 90, cited in Garnsey, *Thinking about Property*, 124. The idea was prevalent in ancient Roman thought more generally, as the poetry of Vergil can attest: "No ploughman tilled the soil, nor was it right / To portion off the boundaries of property. / Men shared their gain, and earth more freely gave / Her riches to her sons who sought them not." From *Georgics* 1.125–128, also cited in Seneca's Letter 90.

CHAPTER ONE

> The next expression of justice, [Cicero and others] thought, is that a person who holds common, that is to say public, property, should regard it as public, and a person who holds private property should regard it as private. This is not even in line with nature, for nature generously supplies everything for everyone in common. God ordained everything to be produced to provide food for everyone in common; his plan was that the earth would be, as it were, the common possession of us all. Nature produced common rights, then; it is illicit appropriation [*usurpatio*] that has established private rights.[60]

In this passage, three of the principles examined in this chapter come together. It is the dominion of God, understood through a theological interpretation of nature, that grounds common dominion. Ambrose goes on to note that God created the world for the sustenance of all—the theological and moral principle that I address in the next section. For Ambrose, like Augustine, this quite clearly entails that property or private rights are established not by God but by humans. In contrast to Augustine, however, Ambrose glosses the establishment of property with a decidedly negative valence.[61] The establishment of property constituted at least in part a fall from grace and an act of hubris brought on by avarice. It is not licit appropriation but rather usurpation that first brings the institution of property into the world.[62] Humans improperly divided up a nature "so luxuriant a source of common wealth, so teeming with life" that it was capable, and indeed would still be capable, of sustaining all of humanity.[63]

Ambrose's understanding of property is apparently also held by Gratian's source Pseudo-Clement. This, then, brings us back to where we began with

---

60. Ambrose, *On the Duties of the Clergy* 1.132, in Garnsey, *Thinking about Property*, 126.

61. Peter Brown notes how their different contexts partially ground the differences between the two thinkers, with Ambrose preaching at a time of Roman confidence and Augustine at a time of crisis. See his discussion of Ambrose in *Eye of a Needle*, 120–35, which is set under "Part II: An Age of Affluence," and contrast that with his discussion of Augustine's later context under "Part III: An Age of Crisis," 291–307.

62. The word *usurpatio* does not straightforwardly connote "illicit appropriation," as Garnsey translates it. A. J. Carlyle translates the word as "habit" in Carlyle, *A History of Medieval Political Thought in the West*, 6 vols. (New York: Barnes & Noble, 1950), 1:136. Garnsey argues that Ambrose is explicitly distancing himself from Cicero here and, further, that Ambrose uses *usurpatio* elsewhere in its negative sense. Garnsey's translation seems preferable, as Carlyle notes that in a commentary on Ps. 68, Ambrose writes that "it was avarice which produced the rights of property." Carlyle, 1:137.

63. Brown, *Eye of a Needle*, 132.

C. 12 q. 1 c. 2. In Case 12, regarding ownership by clerics, Gratian cites Pseudo-Clement's exhortation to all Christians, but especially his fellow clerics, to hold things in common in order to serve God uprightly and "imitate the life of the apostles and of their disciples." The precise meaning and normative implications of the apostolic community as recorded in Acts, especially the holding of all things in common, would become a highly contentious issue in the Michaelist controversies of the fourteenth century.[64] It can be taken for granted that Pseudo-Clement thinks that in the apostolic community no one held property, including the apostles. This is confirmed by his text in C. 12 q. 1 c. 2, where Pseudo-Clement explains why all things were common in the apostolic community: the apostles were imitating the perfect mode of human life, and it is only "through iniquity" that things are held as proper to someone or some group. Pseudo-Clement further cites Plato as a philosophical authority to support his claim about the imperfection of property. The main focus for the canonists, however, is not on the nature of the common life in the apostolic community or in Plato's ideal republic but on the apparent and troubling connection of property to sin that the supposed authority of Pope Clement explicitly identifies.

If it is through iniquity that one calls one thing his and another hers, then in what way are any claims to property legitimate or, at least, not sinful? Even Ambrose, dour on property as he is, does not think the holding of property in the present is sinful. The common life is an ideal for the church but not something to be actively pursued at this stage of the church's pilgrimage. One might claim that only the first act of appropriation was sinful; subsequent acts of appropriation and private possession would then not be sinful. But the shift from sinful to not-sinful demands some explanation. What made the first act of appropriation and private possession sinful that is missing from some or all subsequent acts of appropriation and possession? The question occupies the few scholars who endorse this idea of the origins of property in iniquity. Gratian's patristic sources tend not to address or entertain the idea that property was instituted in sin, the

---

64. The Michaelist controversies refer to the disputes between Michael Cesena, at one time the minister-general of the Franciscan order, William of Ockham, and Francisco Bonagratia, on the one hand, and Pope John XXII on the other, about whether Christ or the apostles ever possessed anything individually or in common. Malcolm David Lambert offers an excellent summary of this dispute and its distinction from the prior Franciscan controversy involving the "Spirituals" and the primary polemicist in that dispute, Peter Olivi. See Malcolm David Lambert, *Franciscan Poverty: The Doctrine of Absolute Poverty of Christ and the Apostles in the Franciscan Order, 1210–1323* (St. Bonaventure, NY: St. Bonaventure University Press, 1998), 133–269.

exception of course being Ambrose. The medieval canonists do not have the liberty of not addressing the question of the origins of property in sin, since this authoritative text for canon law appears to make exactly that claim.[65]

Here we should note how one of the primary effects of an approach to property that emphasizes its usefulness is to implicitly reaffirm the conventionality of property. That is, the thrust of all of the endorsements regarding the usefulness and cautions regarding the hazards of property is to suggest that property is something conducive but not basic to the ends of human life. Of course, this is most evident in Ambrose, where property is something clearly unnatural, an institution founded on avarice and violence. Even for Ambrose, however, the natural life of common possession remains what Brown calls a "deep, humane dream" and not a real reform program in the church.[66] Property can be tolerated and, for Ambrose, presents the possibility of building up the bonds of solidarity necessary for a true Christian society through the constant giving and distributing of alms. For those scholars with a decidedly less negative view of property, even its usefulness is always framed in terms of how it is conducive to the more basic ends of the institution of common dominion and human life. In other words, property does not possess its own logic or its own ends; it is at best a tool of society that serves for the distribution of what is meant for all and that, if used well, can build up the possessor in virtue through wise and judicious divestment.

What is more implicit in patristic discourse becomes explicit in medieval discourse: property is a product of human political society pursuing a set of basic individual and societal ends in a particular set of circumstances. Some circumstances are similar then as now: the context of general scarcity and some general tendencies, one might be tempted to say shortcomings, in human nature. The overriding force of C. 12 q. 1 c. 2 in the canonistic tradition is that in addition to confirming the conventionality of property alongside D. 8 c. 1, it also highlights one of the relevant conditions or circumstances that frames this convention: the state of sin characteristic of postlapsarian humanity.

This interpretation of the relationship between property and sin raises its own set of questions. What is the purpose of property? What parameters and guidelines should determine the shape and structure of the institution of property, and how should different possibilities be judged against one another? As

---

65. This might in part explain the absence of any explicit discussion of sin and property in Aquinas, whose reflections on property do not take the form of a gloss or commentary on the *Decretum*.

66. Brown, *Eye of a Needle*, 132.

Property in Gratian and His Patristic Sources

Gratian's patristic sources discuss at length, the institution of property is useful for a variety of political, social, and moral ends, but it also entails serious political, social, and moral hazards. Presumably, different property regimes will be more or less conducive to the attainment of certain ends and the minimization of certain moral hazards. This will inevitably raise a host of questions when comparing actual institutions of property and the trade-offs and decisions that must be made in adopting any one of them. Some property regimes will be more conducive to certain ends as well as more susceptible to certain hazards. We will see in later chapters the tension between property and sin play out in a tension between the attainment of certain ends at the expense of instituting certain deficiencies in the establishment of property. No particular property convention can be selected on the basis of a general theory, then, since the actual selection of property institutions demands a knowledge of the concrete mores and circumstances of the society making the decision.

The whole discussion of the usefulness and hazards of property thus goes beyond a mere justification of the institution and caution for individuals against certain pitfalls in that institution. It provides a set of considerations for implementing specific property regimes, though admittedly this is not a central theme in patristic reflections on wealth and property. The more immediate point is that the conventionality of property, raised in the context of its usefulness and potential sinfulness, pushes scholars to think beyond just the legitimate mechanisms by which an institution might derogate from natural law and to the logic of the natural law itself. Even when an institution of property is taken for granted (and thus the legitimacy of the institution is not called into question), scholars must still explicate the logic of common dominion and the more basic ends of human individual and social life in order to discover what property is useful for in the first place. For Gratian and his sources, the central principle that emerges in understanding the logic of the natural law of common dominion is the theological and moral principle that the earth and all its goods are for the sustenance of all. This is a principle I have had occasion to discuss already, but in the next section I show how it is a centerpiece of reflection for Gratian's sources.

Sustenance for All and the Tension between the Common and the Private

The central concepts in working out the meaning and implications of common dominion are the principle that the earth and all its creatures are for the sustenance of each and all alike and the tension between common possession and private acquisition, or, simply, between the common and the private.[67] Gratian first introduces the idea of common dominion incidentally in a list of examples of what constitutes the natural law. In D. 1 c. 6, Gratian cites Isidore to provide one way of dividing and conceptualizing law: "Law is either natural, civil, or [the law] of nations." This division of law is central to the scholastic discussion of the institution of property, but it is the examples of natural law that Gratian provides in D. 1 c. 7 that illustrate some key challenges regarding the question of common dominion for the canonists, including the tension between the common and the private in questions of property.

In D. 1 c. 7, Gratian provides a clear connection between the natural law and common dominion, as well as a working definition of common dominion. Quoting Isidore, he writes, "Natural law is common to all nations because it is held everywhere through natural instinct, not because of any enactment. For example: the union of men and women, the bearing and rearing of children, the common possession of all things and the one liberty of all, the acquisition of things that are taken from the heavens, earth, or sea, as well as the return of a thing deposited or of money entrusted. . . . This, and anything similar, is never held to be unjust but is held to be natural and equitable." Though Isidore provides a working definition of common dominion—the common possession of all things—as well as a core principle of high scholastic thought ("the one liberty of all"), his examples of the content of natural law also involve some confusing juxtapositions. For Isidore, the natural law consists of both "the common possession of all things" *and* "the acquisition of things that are taken from the heavens, earth, or sea." Further, the return of deposits or money held in trust presupposes private possession that is not obviously compatible with "the common possession of all things." Note also that to the extent that Gratian identifies the natural law with what is given in Scripture (D. 1 d.a.c. 1), the commandments against theft and covetousness confirm Isidore's position that the return of another's goods is part of the natural law, a point noted not just among the canonists but also among key civilians such as Azo and Accursius.[68] These issues occupy theologians and canonists at least as late as Francisco Suárez, who develops one of the more formidable explanations of how

---

67. Daniel Finn sees this same divine intention as the central conviction of patristic reflection. See *Christian Economic Ethics*, 88–89.

68. Rudolf Weigand, *Die Naturrechtslehre der Legisten und Dekretisten von Irnerius bis Accursius und von Gratian Bis Johannes Teutonicus* (Munich: Max Hueber, 1967), pp. 96–97. Weigand transcribes civilian and canonist texts arranged in numbered paragraphs and interspersed with his commentary. Unless I indicate with "p.," I am referring to the paragraph number (transcribed text) in Weigand. All translations are my own.

common dominion and prohibitions of theft can both be a part of the natural law.[69] Though evidently Gratian floats several tensions in this distinction, it is that between common possession and acquisition that is most relevant to understanding scholastic approaches to property.

This issue, in fact, underlies each of Gratian's four canons on property, and is related to each of the theological and moral principles that we find in Gratian's sources. The principle of God's dominion over all things suggests an apparent contradiction in the acquisition of things by humans, whether from air, land, or water. This is even more so given the corresponding principle that God intends the earth and all its creatures to be for the sustenance of all humans. Under the dominion of God, all things are made available for the sustenance of all. This is the kernel of all the various ways of rendering the natural law of common dominion: the common possession of all things; that all things are common to all; or that all things become common in times of necessity (a medieval understanding that I discuss in the next chapter). In different ways—through the scriptural grant of dominion to humans in common or an interpretation of the ends of the earth and its nonhuman creatures according to the light of reason—both patristic and scholastic thinkers see the principle that the goods of the earth are for the sustenance of each and every human alike as following from the theological principle of God's dominion and as grounding the logic of the natural law of common dominion. This idea emerges in different ways in all of Gratian's patristic sources, which underscores its importance.

According to Basil, the rich ought to imitate the earth, which "does not nurture fruit for its own enjoyment, but for your benefit."[70] For this Greek father, such fruits cannot be thought of as one's own. Here Basil strikes a tone as apparently radical as that of Saint John Chrysostom elsewhere.[71] For both Chrysostom and Basil, the rich seize and hoard their wealth from what is intended to be a common store.[72] God "left the earth free to all alike. How come

---

69. Francisco Suárez, *A Treatise on Laws and God the Lawgiver*, in *Selections from Three Works*, ed. Thomas Pink, trans. Gwladys L. Williams et al. (Indianapolis: Liberty Fund, 2015), 2.14.14–17 (esp. 17) (pp. 315–18). Brian Tierney discusses Suárez's position in *Liberty and Law: Studies on the Idea of Permissive Natural Law, 1100–1800* (Washington, DC: Catholic University of America Press, 2014), 205–8.

70. Basil, "I Will Tear Down My Barns," sec. 3 (p. 62).

71. Chrysostom, *Homilies on the First Letter to Timothy*, 99.

72. Though we might be inclined to dismiss the economic arguments of Basil and Chrysostom, their thought might not be so deficient for the economy of the late Roman Empire, where wealth was largely contained in land and the fruits of the land, often pro-

CHAPTER ONE

then, if it is common, you have acres and acres of land, while your neighbor has not a portion of it?"[73] Humans may not treat things in any absolute sense as their own, no matter the reason they happened to appropriate prior to and more than others. In generating fabulous amounts of wealth, the rich person is like the one who takes "the first seat in a theater, then bar[s] everyone else from attending, so that one person alone enjoys what is offered for the benefit of all in common—this is what the rich do. They seize common goods before others have the opportunity, then claim them as their own by right of preemption."[74] Indeed, for Basil, taking more than one needs is at the origin of the creation of rich and poor.[75] On this, Chrysostom draws the connection explicitly between Psalm 24:1 (23:1), God's dominion, and common dominion: "Is not this an evil, that you alone should have the Lord's property, that you alone should enjoy what is common? Is not 'the earth God's, and the fullness thereof'? Thus, if our possessions belong to one common Lord, they belong also to our fellow servants."[76]

Similar views on the purpose of the material world being open to and for the sustenance of all are also widely present among the Latin fathers. We have already seen how Augustine alludes to such an idea in his *Tractates on the Gospel of John*, saying that the "poor and the rich God made of one clay

---

duced by slaves. As Brown notes, contrary to a modern society where power depends on one's possession of wealth (perhaps acquired through one's ingenuity, resourcefulness, and productivity), in the late Roman Empire wealth depended on power (and the quite separate set of skills and habits on which the acquisition of power depends). Unlike the modern economy, where the creation of wealth seems to some extent to benefit others, most in the Roman Empire "failed even to begin to share in the moderate amount of economic growth" that the rich enjoyed. Add to this the crushing burden of taxation that fell almost entirely on the classes below the rich (as Brown notes, the rich often were also the tax collectors), and we might be inclined to give these patristic commentators the benefit of the doubt with respect to their economic claims. For a brief examination of the social-economic system of the Roman Empire at this time, see Brown, *Eye of a Needle*, 5–16, and his sources.

73. Chrysostom, *Homilies on the First Letter to Timothy*, 101.
74. Basil, "I Will Tear Down My Barns," sec. 7 (p. 69).
75. Again, any accusations of economic naïveté here are complicated by the analysis of preeminent economists like Adam Smith: "Wherever there is great property, there is great inequality. For one very rich man, there must be at least five hundred poor, and the affluence of the rich supposes the indigence of the many." *An Inquiry into the Nature and Causes of the Wealth of Nations*, ed. R. H. Campbell and A. S. Skinner, 2 vols. (Oxford: Oxford University Press, 1976), 709–10.
76. Chrysostom, *Homilies on the First Letter to Timothy*, 101. Rhee, *Wealth and Poverty in Early Christianity*, compiles sources from both the Greek and Latin churches that demonstrate the prevalence of this view.

and he supports the poor and the rich by the same earth." Among Gratian's sources, Augustine emphasizes this aspect of the patristic moral framework the least. His mentor and predecessor, Ambrose, though, emphasizes this point as strongly as Basil or Chrysostom. Ambrose, in fact, draws on Basil and sources in Stoic philosophy to develop an account of common possession and the principle that the earth is for the sustenance of all.[77] In particular, Ambrose draws from the Stoic idea of the "Golden Age" to historicize the Greek father's theological and moral discussion of common dominion. Likewise, at the foundation of Ambrose's account is the idea of common dominion. "Earth at its beginning was for all in common, it was meant for rich and poor alike." Again, Ambrose's argument resembles Basil's and draws on something like a theology of creation as he makes his point: "Nature knows nothing of the rich; all are poor when she brings them forth. Clothing and gold and silver, food and drink and covering—we are born without them all."[78] And, as with Basil and Chrysostom, Ambrose condemns the accumulation of wealth as a problem in itself: "The world was created for all in general, yet a handful of the rich endeavor to make it their own preserve."[79] Though Ambrose is typically given more credit for his administrative abilities than his creative thought, the association of the theological principle that the earth is meant for the sustenance of each and all alike with the Stoic's historical conception of the Golden Age foregrounds a connection between the institution of property and original sin that becomes an important topic in scholastic reflections on property.

The theological, moral, and historical idea of common dominion centers around the theological and moral principle that the earth and all its good things are for the sustenance of all. And yet, Gratian or his sources do not widely discuss our need to use the things of the earth in order to draw sustenance from it. The issue would become central to later discussions of common dominion and property, reaching a fever pitch in the Michaelist controversy and then being steadily unpacked by scholars afterward. At least for now, we need not get bogged down in the intricate distinctions between *usus facti* and *usus iuris* and whether one could consume something that is destroyed in its consumption without own-

---

77. Ambrose's use of Basil's homilies is well established. Brown notes an example in *Eye of a Needle*, 141. He cites Lellia Cracco Ruggini, *Economia e società nell' "Italia annonaria": Rapporti fra agricoltura e commercio dal IV al VI secolo d. C.*, 2nd ed. (Bari, Italy: Edipuglia, 1995), 14–16, for more textual analysis on Ambrose's use of Basil's homilies.

78. Ambrose, *On Naboth*, in Rhee, *Wealth and Poverty in Early Christianity*, 106.

79. Ambrose, *On Naboth*, 107.

ing it.[80] Gratian, his sources, and those who follow immediately after him presuppose the institution of property in their discussions—the nature of use in the state of prelapsarian common dominion was not an issue that demanded disputation until the Franciscans claimed to reinstate the prelapsarian condition in their way of life. Presupposing the institution of property, however, does not erase the tension that exists between common possession and private acquisition. Since the logic of the natural law of common dominion is grounded in the theological and moral principle that the earth is for the sustenance of each and all alike, the acquisition of things from the common store for private and exclusive use raises critical questions about the legitimacy and limits of acquisition.

This brings us to the central question in scholastic theories of property, one that cannot be emphasized enough in all its plural manifestations and one that I return to several times throughout this and the following chapters. That is, we can see better that the challenge of a theory of property is not merely in showing how the conventional may derogate from, specify, or add to the natural, but how it can preserve the logic of the natural in those various movements. If the earth is for each and all alike and, so, according to natural law, is the common possession of all, how does one justify removing something from this store of common goods? As I have alluded to already, in some ways this challenge is already provoked by the question of making *use* of common goods, especially those that are consumed in use. However, the question is only sharpened when one proposes to acquire something not merely for use but also for exclusive possession. If all things are possessed in common, we could see (glossing some finer details) how one could make use of, say, an apple for one's sustenance without offending the institution of common possession, since other apples are available for the sustenance of others.[81] On the other hand, it is more difficult to see how one could claim anything like the bundle of rights long associated with property—rights to exclusivity, development, and transfer—over anything beyond what one intended to consume in use. Even here, whatever of this bundle of rights that may appear to be exercised over a good that one intends to consume in use is exercised *de facto* and not *de iure*.[82] In other words, although in a state of common dominion no one claims

80. See note 64 above on the Michaelist disputes. Lambert's account discusses this central and disputed distinction.

81. The argument here anticipates Locke's discussion of common dominion and possession in his *Second Treatise*. See John Locke, *The Second Treatise of Government*, in *John Locke: Political Writings*, ed. David Wootton (Indianapolis: Hackett, 2003), chap. 5.

82. Thus, immediately a divergence with Locke appears, who saw in the labor and use of unowned goods the foundations of a natural right to property.

an exclusive right over an apple, when an individual consumes an apple, there is just no other way of construing the matter than that she has, in some sense, made an exclusive use of the apple in using it up. This, at least, is the case of the Michaelist Franciscans and their supporters, which contrasts primarily with Locke's theoretical forebears, the civil lawyers, including Pope John XXII. More broadly, this Michaelist view becomes accepted by those who take up and continue the canonistic view of property, as can be seen in the Dominican Domingo de Soto's defense of the Franciscans in the sixteenth century.[83] Beyond the very specific question of simple use, the question regarding the transition from common to private we might call the question of origin: How does private possession legitimately originate in a state of common dominion?[84] Even for those like Ambrose who hold that property originated in sin, some account of origination must be offered in which a legitimate institution of property can emerge from sinful possession.

While a key part of scholastic theories of property addresses the question of origin, the tension between the common and the private raises equally significant questions for understanding contemporary institutions of property. Up to today, certain spaces are still regarded as both *de facto* and *de iure* common—the atmosphere, the seafloor, the deep ocean, asteroids and other space objects—and the governance of such common spaces, including questions about private profit from and pollution of those spaces, remains a difficult and contentious question.[85] For the scholastics, who assume the legitimacy of property, questions also emerge about the legitimate scope and nature of private possession given the apparent normative logic of common dominion. How much (morally and legally) may one privately possess of what

---

83. Domingo de Soto, *De justitia et jure (De la justicia y del derecho)*, lib. 4: *De dominio rerum et de justitia commutativa*, trans. Marcelino González Ordoñez and Venancio Diego Carro, OP, Colección Clasicos Políticos (Madrid: Instituto de estudios políticos, 1968), 282–83. See also John Kilcullen, "The Origin of Property: Ockham, Grotius, Pufendorf, and Some Others," in *A Translation of Ockham's Work of Ninety Days*, vol. 2 (Lewiston, NY: Edwin Mellen Press, 2001), 893–94: "Vazquez explicitly follows de Soto, who follows Vitoria and was followed in turn by Molina and Lessius. All of these writers . . . decide that Ockham [the Michaelist] was right." Kilcullen follows this with a detailed summary of Soto's position.

84. In addition to Kilcullen's more focused discussion of the medieval and early modern periods, Peter Garnsey offers a broad summary of the approaches to this question in *Thinking about Property: From Antiquity to the Age of Revolution* (New York: Cambridge University Press, 2007), chaps. 5–6.

85. The mention of asteroids might seem like something from a science fiction novel, but William P. George discusses the prospects of asteroid mining in *Mining Morality: Prospecting for Ethics in a Wounded World* (New York: Rowman & Littlefield, 2019), chap. 7.

is naturally common? And in what ways is an individual permitted to possess things privately? If possession entails some bundle of rights covering administration, development, and use, are all of these modes of possession to be understood as private, so that one may do as one pleases with one's own with respect to the administration, development, and use of one's goods? Further, what obligations attach to an individual's private possessions? If an individual possesses a legitimate amount, are there any remaining moral or legal obligations toward the community, toward her neighbor, or toward the poor, in light of the more basic and natural orientation of one's possessions toward the sustenance of all?

I have now entered more directly into the normative questions that the natural law of common dominion raises for the institution of property. The Middle Ages generates different responses to the normative scope and force of the natural law of common dominion, but in general, as I discuss in what follows, the scholastics understand that the natural law of common dominion exerts at least some normative force over the institution and activity of private possession. Indeed, the normative questions that emerge from the tension between the common and the private tie directly to the tension that I examine next between property and theft. My discussion in this section also anticipates the patristic and medieval principle associated with this tension: that property should primarily be understood as a power (or, in contemporary language, a right) of *distribution*, but not of exclusive use.

The Power of Distribution and the Tension between Property and Theft

The prior principles, and especially that the earth is for the sustenance of all, push toward more normative questions regarding the conditions of legitimate possession (morally and legally) in the present. I have already discussed certain commonalities among Gratian and his sources, such as the presupposition of the legitimacy of at least some institutions of property. I have mentioned, too, differences among them, such as whether the initial act of appropriation was presupposed to be legitimate, as in most of the sources we have examined, or whether it was explicitly understood to be an act of sin, as in Ambrose and possibly in Pseudo-Clement. For most scholars, however, the conditions under which property can be held legitimately in the present constitute a more directly relevant line of inquiry than speculations about the nature of the initial act of appropriation, especially when, whatever happened at the beginning, at least some kinds of property institutions are now generally assumed to be licit. If there are disagreements regarding the initial act of appropriation, should we expect also disagreements about the normative conditions for holding property morally and legitimately in the present? Disagreement here on general principles would demand adjudication in a way that speculative disagreements about the origins of property would not, since such disagreements could introduce crippling ambiguity into the laws and moral teachings of the church regarding such an everyday occurrence as the private possession of some property.

With respect to general principles, however, Gratian's sources are unanimous not just about the legitimacy of property but also about certain limits and conditions regarding what can be considered licit or just possession. The key consideration here is the use an individual makes of his property, specifically how much he uses for superfluous or luxurious ends and how much he shares with those unable to meet their more basic needs. In most of Gratian's sources, the line between property and theft is, as it were, a line between sharing and hoarding. They consistently assume that an individual's property first goes to satisfying his needs, but beyond his needs the use and consumption of his property should take into account the needs of others.

In contemporary language, Gratian and his sources disavowed the idea that private possession conferred on the proprietor the exclusive use of all that she possessed, at least morally. We have already seen Basil, in a homily partially translated and incorporated in D. 47 c. 8, castigate those in his congregation who would hide behind such a claim to exclusivity as an excuse not to make their property common for the use of those in need. Later in this homily and also incorporated into D. 47 c. 8, Basil explicitly identifies the superfluous or luxurious use of one's property with theft: "Let no one call his own what is common, what more than satisfies need was also violently obtained."[86] When the canonists later refer to D. 47 c. 8, it is often this specific passage that they have in mind, perhaps because it is the passage that appears most to call into question the legitimacy of private property.

A bit of history on this passage is relevant to uncovering the kernel of the tradition hidden beneath its sharp but poorly constructed rhetoric. The Latin itself is a bit difficult.[87] Though Gratian attributes this passage to Ambrose, an

---

86. *Proprium nemo dicat, quod est commune, plus quam sufficeret sumptum et violenter obetentum est.* Gratian, *Corpus Iuris Canonici*, 171. The text offers *etiam* (also) as another possibility for *et* (primarily "and," but also "also"). I translate this passage using *etiam*, as it seems to tighten the logic of Rufinus's translation of Basil's dictum. Otherwise, there seems to be no reason to connect "what more than satisfies need" with "what was violently obtained."

87. It could also be translated: "Let no one call his own what is common, what more

attribution transmitted through authorities such as Thomas Aquinas into the thirteenth century,[88] this is in fact a translation of one of Basil's homilies by the fourth-century Latin scholar Rufinus of Aquileia. And, as Rudolf Weigand notes, the translation might best be called a "free," certainly not a literal, translation of Basil's homily.[89] The passage rendered directly from the original Greek into English reads much more like a condemnation of luxurious consumption in the face of dire destitution than a vituperative critique of those possessing privately more than they strictly need: "And you, are you not greedy? Are you not a robber? The things you received in trust as a stewardship, have you not appropriated them for yourself? . . . The bread you are holding back is for the hungry, the clothes you keep put away are for the naked, the shoes that are rotting away with disuse are for those who have none, the silver you keep buried in the earth is for the needy. You are thus guilty of injustice toward as many as you might have aided, and did not."[90] The argument Basil makes is still very demanding, but it is also more nuanced. Rufinus's translation, by contrast, seems to call into question the legitimacy of the institution itself.

Recall the discussion from the previous section about the issue of use in the state of common dominion: no one possessed anything, but all could make use of everything to meet their needs. Rufinus's translation suggests that possession beyond this minimal level is theft and, indeed, in some way an act of maleficence. While C. 12 q. 1 c. 2 could perhaps be seen as suggesting a similar argument, it is the contemporary force of D. 47 c. 8 that makes it so challenging. C. 12 q. 1 c. 2 is historical and ambiguous: at some point, related in some way to iniquity, someone said, "this is mine," and division among humans in the form of property began. D. 47 c. 8 has none of this historical sense and is far less ambiguous and more condemning in its language: let no one today call what he has that he does not need his property, as doing so can be considered an act of violence against others. This is presumably one of the reasons the canonists gloss and reinterpret this passage so extensively with respect to the question of property. The passage is ripe for comment, especially given the

---

than satisfies need *and* was violently obtained." If my rendering seems to overaccentuate the accusation in Basil's original homily, this translation seems to weaken it so much by emphasizing not superfluity alone but only the conjunction of superfluity and violent acquisition so that it seems to lack any real connection to Basil's condemnation of luxurious use.

88. The translations of Aquinas are mine, though I check them against the English translation of the Fathers of the English Dominican Province. Thomas Aquinas, *Summa Theologiae [1265–1274]* (Scotts Valley, CA: NovAntiqua, 2010), II-II, 66.2 ad 3.

89. Weigand, *Die Naturrechtslehre*, p. 308.

90. Basil, "I Will Tear Down My Barns," sec. 7 (pp. 69–70).

way it contrasts with what are evidently the presuppositions of the legitimacy of ownership beyond what one strictly needs.

The kernel of the tradition that the more faithful rendering of Basil reveals is the principle that, morally speaking, property is a power of distribution.[91] I touched on this principle earlier when I noted how patristic theologians thought that one of the things property was good for was the administration and distribution of the goods of the earth. Gratian's sources, though, devote more explicit attention to the question of misuse and hoarding than to explicating the principle of distribution itself. In a different homily addressed to the rich, Basil describes the proper attitude of Christians toward their wealth: "they have received wealth as a stewardship, and not for their own enjoyment; thus, when they are parted from it, they rejoice as those who relinquish what is not really theirs."[92] Chrysostom echoes these points in several places. In one of his better-known passages he writes: "wealth is not a possession; it is not property, it is a loan for use. . . . Property, in fact, is but a word; we are all owners but of other people's possessions."[93] And, in another place, he draws explicitly on the motif of stewardship: "You too are stewards of your own possessions, no less than he who dispenses the alms of the church. Just as he has no right to squander at random and at hazard the things given by you for the poor, since they were given for the maintenance of the poor, so you may not squander your own. . . . Everything belongs to God. . . . For this end, he left these things in your hand, in order to 'give them their meat in due season.'"[94]

These two passages are particularly illuminating, as Chrysostom connects the three previous principles with his exhortation to proper use and critique of misuse of property. The dominion of God, God's intention that the earth be given for the sustenance of all, and the subsequent relativizing of property all inform the way Chrysostom and Gratian's other sources interpret the general principle governing the proper use and misuse of wealth, the power of property as a power of distribution. Elsewhere, Chrysostom makes the practical implications of this point even more explicit: "if [the rich man] spends more on himself than his need requires, he will pay the harshest penalty hereafter."[95]

---

91. Avila describes this moral principle in its more explicitly theological dimensions in *Ownership*, 144–46.

92. Basil, "To the Rich (Homily)," sec. 3 (pp. 46–47). See also the passage from *The Shorter Rules*, Question 92, on this same point above (note 33 above).

93. Chrysostom, *Homilies on the First Letter to Timothy*, 99.

94. Chrysostom, *Homilies on the Gospel of Matthew*, in Rhee, *Wealth and Poverty in Early Christianity*, 96.

95. *St. John Chrysostom on Wealth and Poverty*, 49.

CHAPTER ONE

Depending on the controversy he was addressing, Augustine is more or less lenient but always consistent with this principle.[96] Recall his letter to Macedonius, in which he argues that possessions "certainly do not belong to someone else if they are held lawfully; but lawfully implies justly, and justly implies well. If so, then everything that is possessed wrongly belongs to someone else; but if someone uses possessions wrongly, he possesses them wrongly."[97] The letter is not clear on what is entailed in "using wrongly," though it is rhetorically placed on the level of theft. And Augustine is not explicit in connecting this misuse to hoarding and not sharing with the needy, at least here. Nonetheless, in connection with other passages from Augustine's corpus, the hoarding and luxurious use of wealth would certainly have fallen under the misuse of property. Augustine writes that "God is commanding [the rich] not to give away their own property, but His; and those who do give alms to the poor should not suppose that they are doing so with what belongs to themselves."[98]

As for how much of what is God's should go to the poor, Augustine is noticeably more lenient in his exhortations than Basil and Chrysostom. In a gloss on 1 Timothy 6:18, he writes, "[Paul] said, 'Let them communicate,' not 'let them give everything away.' Let them keep for themselves as much as is sufficient for them; let them keep more than is sufficient: let us give a certain portion of it."[99] The standard is still set, so to speak, at what is sufficient, but the line is not drawn too strictly. One gets the sense that for Augustine, the Christian ought to aspire to a sparse and detached use of her property, but she can have a clear conscience if she is only approaching this by giving away some of her property that is beyond what she needs for sufficiency and subsistence. Indeed, as I noted above, Justo González's analysis of the Cappadocian fathers suggests that Basil (and both Gregorys) likely do not hold to a rigorous understanding of sufficiency either, as Gregory of Nazianzus retired to a family estate and Basil and Gregory of Nyssa in part lived off of the wealth of their family.[100]

This is an important point to properly interpret Gratian and his sources on this principle and the tension between property and theft: agreement on a general principle still leaves room for different interpretations of the correct application of that principle in different situations. This is especially complex

96. Sierra Bravo, *Doctrina social y económica*, 311.
97. Augustine, Letter 153, 87.
98. Augustine, Sermon 50.2–7, in Dyson, *The Pilgrim City*, 122.
99. Augustine, Sermon 85.4–7, in Dyson, *The Pilgrim City*, 120.
100. See note 35 above.

when it comes to defining metrics like subsistence and sufficiency, a point I return to later. For now, it is enough to know that among the sources I examine in this chapter, none would argue that things can only be possessed up to the level of bare subsistence—the nourishment, shelter, and clothing that would just be needed to keep an individual alive, which might only entail food and water a few times a week and a doorway to sleep in. For Christians in the twenty-first century, what might appear more rigorous and radical is the idea, nascent in patristic thought, that property is "a right of distribution" and not "a right of personal use," let alone a right "of unlimited use."[101] This position, while allowing for the accumulation of wealth, also makes the distribution of one's wealth primarily a matter of justice, of achieving right order between individuals, and only secondarily a matter of charity and mercy.[102]

As we have seen, some of these bishops and theologians, like Basil, touch on this idea explicitly, but most often this principle must be inferred from patristic discourse condemning the hoarding and luxurious use of wealth and exhorting the wealthy to see themselves as only stewards and distributors of the goods of the earth to the poor. This principle, however, is systematized and developed throughout the medieval period, so that by the fifteenth century the canonist Juan de Torquemada outlined the various levels of need and the obligations that fall upon the individual with property at each of those levels. According to Torquemada, "one owed one's superfluity to those who stood in want of resources to maintain their status or vocation; one owed what maintained one's status or vocation to help those who stood in need of physical necessities; one owed one's physical necessities to save those in extreme necessity or in peril of death."[103] The twelfth- and thirteenth-century canonists focus on obligations toward those "in extreme necessity or in peril of death," but the whole logical trajectory of this principle leads to Torquemada's more elaborate and expansive application of this principle. We will see, further, how this more elaborate formulation is already anticipated in the thirteenth century with Aquinas's argument that, with respect to use, one's possessions should always be thought of as common.

Of course, the questions raised here apply just as much to the one with resources as to the one in need, as Torquemada's distinctions illustrate. Is an indi-

101. Carlyle, *History of Medieval Political Thought*, 1:138, 142.
102. Rubianes, *El dominio privado*, 37.
103. Scott G. Swanson, "The Medieval Foundations of John Locke's Theory of Natural Rights: Rights of Subsistence and the Principle of Extreme Necessity," *History of Political Thought* 18, no. 3 (1997): 409.

vidual obligated to help his neighbor maintain his station in life, as Torquemada indicates? If an individual can just barely survive, is she not considered to be in a state of extreme necessity? More generally, how can need and different levels of need be defined in a way that can establish action-guiding moral principles?

This question is already pressing in a strictly moral context, but as the canonists reflect on this principle in a legal context, the question becomes pressing in a different way. Gratian's patristics sources did not think in evidently legal terms when discussing the theological and moral principles of property. Basil offers an ad hoc exhortation to the rich in his congregation: a drought had caused widespread crop failures in Cappadocia, where he preached, and many were truly starving. Basil was less concerned with a systematic or legal understanding of wealth and property than with moving his church's rich to alleviate what suffering they could. The bishops Ambrose and Chrysostom appeared to exercise real political power with their moral exhortations against the extravagant use of wealth, with dramatically different outcomes.[104]

We might recall Augustine's comment about the purpose of civil laws with respect to property as a point where patristic reflections on wealth and property touch the question of law and legal institutions. If, as Augustine suggests, the goal of property law is to restrict and minimize the ill effects of the misuses of property, to what extent should hoarding in the face of dereliction fall under the purview of the law? The question is apropos here as well in light of the comparison of such hoarding to theft. Still, Augustine does not seem to have imagined legal mechanisms to enforce the obligations of those with property nor to protect those who, in desperate need, take from the surplus of others. Among Gratian's sources, then, there seems to be nothing like an institutional or legal response to the problem of hoarding and luxurious use of property in the face of neighbors' need. To what extent can such a vague general principle as the obligation to share one's surplus be enforced legally? If the line between making one's own common and hoarding one's own is the line between property and theft, presumably the question of law can be legitimately raised. And if it is determined that such an act can be legally enforced, what institutions would enforce it?

These questions can be applied both to the one obligated and to the one in need. Gratian's patristic sources say very little about what would become a mainstay of scholastic thought: the morality and legality of taking from another when one is in need. That is, the scholastics ask, and so might we, what does this constellation of principles have to say about how to handle a

---

104. See note 42 above.

case when a person suffering extreme need simply takes of the resources of a rich person without his permission? The principles certainly seem to suggest that such an act is morally licit, but how can this be accounted for in law? We have run into a problem that cannot be answered without addressing some of the theoretical tensions of the previous sections. This is perhaps a reason why Gratian's sources never entered into a discussion of this question in the same depth as the scholastics. Evidently, the taking of what one needs for sustenance would seem licit under the natural law, but it would also seem to run afoul of otherwise reasonable laws against theft.

The tension between the natural and the conventional, and the normative force of the natural, are evidently at issue here. At its most radical, someone might ask whether laws against theft are tolerable at all, given that by nature all things are common to all.[105] The basic legitimacy of derogation from, specification of, or addition to the natural must be established before answering such a question. In more sophisticated terms, someone might also ask whether any law can contravene the basic principle that the earth and its creatures are for the sustenance of each and all alike, as a blanket and strictly enforced law against theft, even in cases of extreme necessity, might. On the other hand, a general law sanctioning acts of taking in times of necessity would present a host of practical challenges, not the least of which is prescribing a general account of what constitutes extreme need and determining whether a person was suffering it or not at the time. To resolve this set of questions and tensions, the scholastics develop the idea and language of subjective rights, at first implicitly. By the fourteenth century, however, they explicitly begin to theorize about natural and positive rights. Though scholars such as Brian Tierney have already extensively documented this development of the idea of subjective rights and its relation to extreme necessity, I discuss in more detail in later chapters how the idea of the right of subsistence shapes scholastic and more generally Christian conceptions of property.

Finally, turning back to the property owner, there is a question at the end of this line of inquiry that is central to contemporary discussions of property. Legal scholars today understand property as a bundle of rights that the owner of such property may choose to exercise or not.[106] These include the right of alienation, meaning to sell or in some other way relinquish one's proprietary

---

105. This issue is addressed by the canonists. See, e.g., Alanus's rejection of the radical position in Weigand, *Die Naturrechtslehre*, 537 (p. 318).

106. Anthony Honoré, *Making Law Bind: Essays Legal and Philosophical* (Oxford: Clarendon, 1987), 165–79.

right over that property; the right of exclusivity, that is, the power of preventing others from making use of or participating in the use of one's property; and, among others, the right of using as one wishes, which is fairly self-explanatory. How does the patristic and medieval principle that property is a power of distribution fit within or qualify the contemporary bundle of property rights?

The way in which we answer this question has implications today for the way the legislature and the courts handle questions of taxation and redistribution, the limits of expropriation, and the ways different cases of theft are prosecuted. It may, indeed, affect the discrete rights we think ought to be included in the bundle of rights associated with property. It may also, however, merely change the way we interpret certain rights. Thus, for example, the right of exclusivity can be interpreted in different moral and legal terms, and these different interpretations can entail different legal consequences. On some interpretations, one's property is an extension of oneself, and the right of exclusivity has the same strength as rights to bodily integrity. On such terms, it is taxation, not hoarding, that is the equivalent of theft.[107] This is a point that I return to in later chapters, but it is worth noting again as I make this transition that these four moral and theological principles will constitute the background from which the scholastics interpret property and its legal implications. However, even at this point, one can gain some insight into a different applied question. The task of Christian theologians and philosophers, that is, remains very similar to the task the scholastics faced: to formulate some lens, consisting of some set of moral and theological principles, through which to analyze and interpret the bundle of rights that constitutes property in contemporary law and the legal implications of that bundle of rights.

Conclusion

The four texts I have examined in this chapter and the concomitant questions they raise directly structure and influence scholastic understandings of property. Though Gratian evidently leaves open some theoretical difficulties about the question of property, the canonists who follow him produce a flurry of commentaries and glosses that begin to resolve and explain some of these difficulties and that would influence and shape canonistic and theological discourse over the next several centuries. By the time Gratian's text was supplanted as the primary source of canonistic commentary by the *Decretals* or *Liber extra* of Gregory IX (1234), two of the most influential and important

107. Robert Nozick, *Anarchy, State, and Utopia* (New York: Basic Books, 2013), 171–72.

scholastic approaches to property had been produced by two canonists from Bologna, Rufinus and Huguccio. In the next two chapters, I will explore how the scholastics respond to and resolve many of the questions I raise in this chapter, drawing on, systematizing, and adding to the four principles and central texts that animated patristic discourse. Their efforts span the broadly theoretical problems of the normative relationship between nature and convention, which is the focus of the next chapter, as well as some of the practical and directly moral implications for medieval society, which, along with an application of their thought to contemporary society, is the focus of chapter 3.

These principles and tensions offer an important background to scholastic discussions of property—the roots, as it were, of an emerging tradition—but it would be misleading to say that the scholastics made each tension and principle I draw out of the *Decretum* central or explicit in their own discussions. It might better be said that some, such as the tension between the natural and the conventional, were explicit in scholastic discourse, and others, such as the principle that the earth is for the sustenance of each and all alike, are presupposed and then expressed in a different way, such as in the recognition that one suffering from extreme necessity may legitimately take from the surplus of another. What become the central moral principles in scholastic reflection and the focal points of the next two chapters—equity, equality, subsistence, and liberty—find their theological and theoretical grounding in the principles I highlight in this chapter. These principles will remain touchstones for understanding and explaining scholastic thought. The tensions, though not always clearly acknowledged by the scholastics, manifest the conceptual forces pushing the scholastics to resolve theoretical problems or elaborate on the received tradition—to develop more systematic approaches to property.

Further, with the exception of the very earliest, the commentaries on the *Decretum* were not written in isolation from surrounding canonistic, civilian, and theological discourse. However much the texts of the *Decretum* influence the approaches to property that I examine in the next three chapters, they are not the sole source of influence. The canonists who comment on the *Decretum* are influenced by independent reading of Scripture, by patristic texts not referenced in the *Decretum*, by other commentaries and glosses, by the newly rediscovered codes of Roman law (Justinian's *Institutes* and the *Digest*), and by the work of theologians such as Hugh of St. Victor and Peter Lombard. I will occasionally reference some of these other sources, though my analysis of scholastic thought would not change significantly were I to make each one the focus of its own examination. It is enough to note that there is a broad intellectual ferment at this point in medieval Europe.

CHAPTER ONE

Finally, the principles and tensions I highlight in this chapter are not as systematically separated and organized as I treat them. As I have tried to note along the way, each principle and tension does not appear only in the text of the *Decretum* under which I discuss it. They are related to one another, and multiple tensions and principles are present in each of the texts I discuss. My presentation already entails, in other words, some anticipation of how the scholastics read these texts as well as my own constructive interests in the retrieval of the question of property. This is but one interpretation of how to connect the dots, so to speak, of the *Decretum* and Gratian's sources on property, but I believe that my organization will prove informative and my interpretation defensible in the following chapters.

TWO

A Natural Law Framework for Property

THE PROBLEMS THAT GRATIAN'S *Decretum* leaves unresolved suggest that the place to start thinking through a theory of property is in the relationship of common dominion to property, a topic that has already gained some salience in contemporary political philosophy.[1] To do so, I turn to a close reading of three central scholastic thinkers, each of whom offers a distinct answer to how a convention of property can be legitimate if it appears to derogate from the natural law of common dominion, which is the natural law articulated by Gratian's sources that all things are common to all.[2] Rufinus and Huguccio are twelfth-century canonists whose thinking on property in their respective *Summae* gives rise to two distinct, canonistic approaches. There are many other canonists, and in the thirteenth century some more illustrious than Rufinus, at least, but Rudolf Weigand has demonstrated that for the most part their thinking on property are variations on what Rufinus and Huguccio set forth in the twelfth century.[3] Though Aquinas is a thirteenth-century theologian whose approach to property closely resembles Huguccio's,

---

1. Michael Otsuka, *Libertarianism without Inequality* (Oxford: Clarendon, 2003); Mathias Risse, *On Global Justice* (Princeton: Princeton University Press, 2012).

2. This chapter nuances the brief discussion of these very figures in Peter Garnsey, *Thinking about Property: From Antiquity to the Age of Revolution* (New York: Cambridge University Press, 2007), 131–33.

3. Rudolf Weigand, *Die Naturrechtslehre der Legisten und Dekretisten von Irnerius bis Accursius und von Gratian bis Johannes Teutonicus* (Munich: Max Hueber, 1967), 2.B, esp. pp. 316–22 and 327–34. As an example of the power of the two models inaugurated by Rufinus and Huguccio, see each represented in a discussion of property in the sixteenth century in Domingo de Soto, *De justitia et jure (De la justicia y del derecho)*, lib. 4: *De dominio rerum et de justitia commutativa*, trans. Marcelino González Ordoñez and Venancio Diego Carro, OP, Colección Clasicos Políticos (Madrid: Instituto de estudios políticos, 1968), esp. 299.

CHAPTER TWO

he is even more systematic and his distinctive language and ideas are, more than the other two and indeed most other scholastic thinkers, transmitted widely, continuously, and up to today.

Though the details of their approaches differ, across these three scholastics one can identify two theoretical pillars of the scholastic systematization of Christian thinking on property. Before any other question, the scholastics recognized that they needed some account of how a convention of property can be legitimate if it appears to derogate from the natural law. If all things are by nature common, how can any person or group claim some object exclusively as their own? Without a coherent answer to this question, property itself loses its fundamental legitimacy, and any other theoretical or moral consideration is irrelevant. In response to this question, these three scholastics each offers an account that, though differing in their respective details, rests on two fundamental pillars. The first is that property is a convention that humans institute in response to certain exigencies of human nature. The conventionality of property, so central to patristic thinking, also forms the foundational conviction of scholastic thinking on property.

From this, though, follows the second pillar of the scholastic approach to property, one not systematically investigated in patristic thought. Though as a convention it is not of the natural law, the legitimacy of property depends on the fact that it does not contravene and ideally ought to be structured according to the moral principles enshrined in the natural law of common dominion. Said more generally, Rufinus, Huguccio, and Aquinas think that human law can (in the case of Rufinus) derogate from or (in the case of Huguccio and Aquinas) specify the natural law only so long as it does so within the normative framework established by the natural law. These two insights are the theoretical foundations of the scholastic approach to property, which emerge as they attempt to answer basic questions regarding the legitimacy of private property.

This chapter is limited to a formal consideration of these two theoretical principles. I begin with Rufinus, the earliest and least nuanced response to the question of the legitimacy of property. I then turn to Huguccio, who chronologically comes between Rufinus and Aquinas but also presents a theory of property more nuanced than Rufinus and whose theory points toward the eventual systematization that Aquinas offers. The last section, then, shows how Aquinas develops his own theory of property through his theories of law and justice. Readings of Aquinas on property tend to emphasize either its natural qualities or its conventionality, while my account demonstrates how Aquinas systematically preserves both by drawing on the *ius gentium*. Throughout, I show how the theories in this chapter faithfully preserve the principles pres-

A Natural Law Framework for Property

ent in patristic thought, even as they extend and develop that thought in light of specifically juridical questions. The next chapter builds on this chapter's formal analysis and takes up the substantive discussion of what it means for the moral principles of the natural law of common dominion—equality, equity, sufficiency, and liberty—to norm property regimes.

Rufinus and Permissive Natural Law

In his *Summa Decretorum* (ca. 1159), Rufinus is one of the earliest canonists to comment on Gratian's *Decretum* and thus one of the first to try to resolve some of the challenges it presents, among which is the relationship between nature and convention.[4] Rufinus extensively addresses the tension between these two by utilizing an ancient tradition of permissive natural law to deal with some of the challenges the *Decretum* presents. In so doing, he presents a theory of natural law that offers a powerful lens of legitimation and evaluation for social and political institutions. It relies on the idea that certain natural laws, like common dominion, are what he calls "demonstrations." Human conventions, such as property, though not permitted to derogate from the commands and prohibitions of the natural law, are permitted to derogate from its demonstrations. Rufinus's recovery of permissive natural law, and specifically his use of demonstrations, becomes central to later scholastic interpretation of troublesome institutions like property and servitude. It is thus important to show that, as with Huguccio and Aquinas, this approach maintains both the conventionality of property and the normativity of common dominion. Though Rufinus's approach makes the conventionality of property evident, it is more difficult to see how the natural law of common dominion, as a demonstration of the natural law, remains normative for property conventions. The key to the normativity of demonstrations turns on understanding the moral principles enshrined in each one, and Rufinus's corresponding claim that even conventions that derogate from the natural law must be intelligible in terms of those moral principles.

Rufinus first appeals to permissive natural law when he discusses two troubling areas where derogation from the natural law has occurred: "in one liberty of all and in common possession."[5] What he has in mind are slavery and

---

4. Rufinus, *Summa Decretorum*, ed. Heinrich Singer (Paderborn, Germany: Scientia-Verl. Aalen, 1963). Translations of Rufinus and Huguccio are my own.

5. Rufinus, *Summa Decretorum*, 7.

private property, established in antiquity and carried through, in one form or another, all the way up to the second half of the twelfth century. Here, Rufinus takes up and advances an equally ancient tradition that saw the institutions of civil society—especially slavery, property, and coercive government—as in some way consequences of or made necessary by a primordial fall from grace.[6] Because they seem to frustrate the liberty and equality of all humans that the Stoics emphasized and that became central to Christian political thought, these institutions could only be tolerated as concessions deviating from ideals made unattainable by human sin.

For Rufinus, however, the "concessions" to slavery (or the more common institution in the Middle Ages, servitude) and property raise a significant, systematic question. Granted that they can be justified in terms of useful deviations from unattainable ideals, how can they be justified precisely as contradictions of or deviations from the natural law? That is, the derogation from the natural law raises a theoretical question about the meaning and significance of that law. If the institutions of slavery and private property can emerge and, what is more, appear to be (from the vantage point of the scholastics) legitimate institutions in spite of the natural laws of one freedom and common possession, then what exactly is the significance of the natural law? Is it normative for human actions and human social life? If so, one is cast back to explain how the social institutions that diverge from it are not merely *useful* but also *licit*.

Rufinus responds to these questions by drawing on a long tradition of permissive natural law and dividing the natural law into distinct, constituent parts. He then applies this distinction of laws to some of the problems that the *Decretum* leaves unresolved. Rufinus draws on the Roman lawyer Modestinus, for whom the force of law is to command, to prohibit, to permit, and to punish.[7] Rufinus identifies these different forces with conceptually distinct kinds of law—commands, prohibitions, and demonstrations—with different rationales and different normative implications. This division allows him to explain how and from which natural laws human laws may diverge while also

---

6. The question of "one liberty," servitude, and slavery lies outside the scope of this project, though without a doubt it is one of the more troubling aspects of scholastic thought that the canonists and theologians could legitimate the institution of slavery, as Rufinus does in his comments on D. 1 c. 1 (p. 7). For more on these questions, see Orlando Patterson, *Freedom*, vol. 1, *Freedom in the Making of Western Culture* (New York: Basic Books, 1991), 347–401.

7. See Charles Henry Monro and William Warwick Buckland, eds. and trans., *The Digest of Justinian*, vol. 1, 2 vols. (Cambridge: Cambridge University Press, 1904), 1.3.7 (p. 20).

preserving natural law as a normative framework for moral and political life, even for conventions like slavery and property that seem not simply to diverge but to outright contravene the natural law.

It is first important to see how commands and prohibitions fit within Rufinus's more general account of natural law. Along with the preponderance of the canonist tradition, Rufinus primarily understands the natural law not as a set of commands and prohibitions but as "a kind of natural propulsion" that inclines the human to do good and avoid what is evil.[8] When defined as a natural faculty, it is difficult to understand how one can even speak of the "commands and prohibitions" of natural law. Still, even if the idea of natural law as a faculty or power is primary, the canonists use the term in a plurality of ways.[9] Sometimes they speak of it in terms of general moral principles—the kinds of principles, like the principle of nonmaleficence, that approximate the inclinations or tendencies of a well-functioning natural moral faculty—and the commands and prohibitions that closely approximate these general moral principles. So, for Rufinus, the natural law "commands what is beneficial, as in 'Love the Lord your God'; it prohibits what does harm, as in, 'Do not kill.'"[10] Though found in the Decalogue, these are principles, Rufinus suggests, that each person can in theory ascertain from the natural law.

After the Fall, however, the moral faculty of humanity was impaired, though not extinguished. On its own it was now insufficient to prompt consistent and constant recognition of what was entailed in doing good and avoiding evil. God's first step in rectifying human conduct was to specify general principles of upright conduct in the commands and prohibitions of the Decalogue, which the canonists and theologians tend to identify with precepts of natural law. Beyond this partial and external reestablishment of the natural law in the Decalogue, the gospel completes the reestablishment of the natural law, in that it shows the internal dispositions and not merely the external actions that conform to that law. In human history, then, the Mosaic law and the gospel, with respect to the natural law, are a correction, guide, and revivification of that primeval moral faculty. And the correction and instruction of that faculty occur in part through the explicit restatement of those general principles

---

8. Both Brian Tierney and Jean Porter affirm this understanding of the primary sense of the natural law in scholastic canon law. Brian Tierney, *The Idea of Natural Rights: Studies on Natural Rights, Natural Law, and Church Law, 1150–1625* (Grand Rapids: Eerdmans, 2001), 62–65; Jean Porter, *Natural and Divine Law: Reclaiming the Tradition for Christian Ethics* (Grand Rapids: Eerdmans, 1999), 88–90.

9. Tierney, *Idea of Natural Rights*, 60–62.

10. Rufinus, *Summa Decretorum*, 6.

and the closely related commands and prohibitions that a well-functioning natural moral faculty ought to consistently and everywhere arrive at through its ordinary exercise.

The general principles, commands, and prohibitions of natural law still leave space for the exercise and operations of human reason to specify and extend them. Rufinus indicates as much when he notes how human law relates to the general principles of natural law. So, for example, while the union of man and woman is of the natural law, societies develop customs and laws of marriage that give structure, decorum, and a necessary public expression to this general framework.[11] The necessary specification of this general natural law leaves a certain space for human freedom, or a sphere of permissiveness that attaches not just to the demonstrations of natural law but to its commands and prohibitions. The sphere of permissiveness with respect to the commands and prohibitions is limited, though, to this specification and extension of those principles, and never to divergence from them.

Whereas the commands and prohibitions of the natural law admit of no derogation, the demonstrations do. The force of demonstrations is distinct from the force of commands and prohibitions. As Rufinus says, the natural law *commands* what is beneficial, *prohibits* what does harm, and "*demonstrates* what is fitting, as in 'Let all things be held in common' or 'Let there be one freedom for all,' etc."[12] Or, later, by the *demonstrationes* of natural law, "nature does not forbid or prescribe but shows to be good."[13] The language is certainly indicative of an important distinction: to command and prohibit signal binaries, admit only of obedience or disobedience, and as such lack any quality of permissiveness. To *demonstrate* and *show*, however, indicate space for discernment, evaluation, and choice. A demonstration can be normative to the extent that it is reasonable and suitable to the one who receives the demonstration, but for whatever reason it may still admit of some other legitimate course(s) of action, even apparent disregard or contravention.

We can illuminate this contrast further with two examples—capital punishment and servitude—that show the differences between how the commands/prohibitions and demonstrations of natural law relate to human laws. When a civil law appears to contradict a prohibition or command of natural law, the scholastics in general reinterpret one or both to show how the laws do not in

---

11. Rufinus, *Summa Decretorum*, 7.
12. Rufinus, *Summa Decretorum*, 6 (emphasis added).
13. Rufinus, *Summa Decretorum*, 7.

fact conflict. On capital punishment, Rufinus largely restates Gratian's extensive interpretation, in C. 23 q. 5, of the prohibition against killing: "Briefly, it is said that no one may kill another, except the one who has the power of the sword. The one who has the power of the sword, however, can kill another, if he knows that person to be guilty [and] punishes that person according to the laws of punishment."[14] Gratian argues that capital punishment is legitimate as the killing is ultimately attributed to public authority, since it is not prohibited "to deliver the guilty to death by the authority of law."[15] Though such punishment is prohibited to private individuals, as the institution with the responsibility for public safety, public authority can authorize individuals to either execute capital punishment for certain grave crimes or to kill enemy soldiers in war. As such, properly authorized, one does not "sin [in killing] a person on account of one's office."[16] The key here, for Gratian and Rufinus, is that in neither case does the human law diverge from the natural law *properly interpreted*. Rather, once the prohibition has been explained and interpreted, the canonist can show that civil laws authorizing capital punishment or enlisting soldiers to fight and kill enemy combatants only appear to contradict the prohibition against killing and thus can be in accordance with the commands and prohibitions of the natural law.

Even regarding demonstrations, Rufinus suggests that there are limits to the manner and extent to which civil laws may diverge from the natural law. Deviations from the demonstrations of natural law are permitted so long as the civil laws "which seem opposed to natural law, ultimately refer back to that very law."[17] Rufinus demonstrates this point with an analysis of slavery.[18] On Rufinus's account, the institution of slavery was established so "that obstinate rebels against rightful authority should, when subjugated and captured in war, be enslaved perpetually." The practice is legitimate not because of the benefits or advantage it gives to the rightful authority but to accomplish a moral purpose:

---

14. Rufinus, *Summa Decretorum*, 408.
15. Gratian, *Corpus Iuris Canonici: Pars Prior: Decretum Magistri Gratiani*, ed. Aemliius Friedberg (Graz, Austria: Akademische Druck-U. Verlagsanstalt, 1959), C. 23 q. 5 d.a.c. 7.
16. Gratian, *Corpus Iuris Canonici*, C. 23 q. 5 c. 8.
17. Rufinus, *Summa Decretorum*, 7.
18. For more on the medieval treatment and legitimation of institutions of servitude, see Marc Bloch, *Slavery and Serfdom in the Middle Ages: Selected Essays* (Berkeley: University of California Press, 1975), which was later qualified and defended in Pierre Bonnaissie, *From Slavery to Feudalism in South-Western Europe*, trans. Jean Birrell (Cambridge: Cambridge University Press, 1991).

"That those whose moral indiscipline made them savage, arrogant, and destructive, should become tame, humble, and innocuous through the discipline imposed on slaves... in accordance with the natural law arrogance and malice are abhorrent, innocence and humility to be preferred. By this channel, then, the streams of human decency flow back to the sea of natural law."[19] Though one might be willing to grant that the enslavement of prisoners in a just war is preferable to capital punishment, which is part of the background to Rufinus's argument and made explicit in other scholastic sources, the substance of this argument warrants critical analysis.[20] A critique is especially relevant given that similar rhetoric has been used to justify the contemporary United States prison system, which historically and still today can mirror and reinforce with the coercive power of law the racism present in US society and culture.[21]

To understand the significance of Rufinus's argument, we first must address some of the inconsistencies or silences in his discussion of slavery. If the inculcation of humility and decency is the aim of the institution of slavery, then why must it be perpetual? Of course, it need not be, but Rufinus might suggest that since the perpetual nature of this institution does not impede the cultivation of virtues preferred by the natural law, it is a permissible but not a necessary or even necessarily desirable feature. The problem is that this solution seems to evacuate Rufinus's earlier statement that the demonstration of natural law, "Let there be one freedom for all," shows what is good. That is, while the natural law might certainly enshrine the virtue of humility as a human good, it also seems to offer a principle of freedom that *is* violated by the perpetual nature of slavery. Though Rufinus might suggest that due to their lawlessness, certain peoples, "like the Acephali, without a ruler, committing every conceivable crime without punishment," cannot enjoy the freedom that natural law demonstrates to be good, by the logic of his own argument Rufinus could argue for the legitimacy of the institution of slavery while also critiquing its perpetuity. Once the virtues of natural law have been inculcated, the freedom

---

19. Rufinus, *Summa Decretorum*, 7.

20. An early authority that prompts this reflection is Justinian's *Institutes*, which claims that "both captivities and servitudes, which are contrary to natural law, are stirred up by and follow wars." See Weigand, *Die Naturrechtslehre*, 100 (p. 66). See also the explicit affirmation of this position in the *Summa "Sicut vetus testamentum,"* in Weigand, 456 (p. 271).

21. Michelle Alexander, *The New Jim Crow: Mass Incarceration in the Age of Colorblindness* (New York: New Press, 2012). The relationship between racism and mass incarceration, though, has been nuanced and set in relation to other aspects of the criminal justice system. See Anthony B. Bradley, *Ending Overcriminalization and Mass Incarceration: Hope from Civil Society* (Cambridge: Cambridge University Press, 2018).

that the natural law indicates can be enjoyed by participation in an ordered and law-governed society.

Rufinus does not make this critique, however, and there seem to be two ways of interpreting his silence. First, the freedom that the natural law shows to be good truly is a pure permission, something neutral that society can or cannot pursue without detriment to its character or the flourishing of those within it. As I suggest below, the language of *demonstration* as opposed to *permission* suggests, however, that this freedom is not a neutral institution. Rather, the language of demonstration suggests something closer to what the scholastics might have understood as a "counsel," something desirable and to be pursued in favorable circumstances. Alternatively, one could suggest that Rufinus could also remain consistent if the one freedom of the natural law points to the more weighty, spiritual freedom of the gospel. That is, spiritual freedom from sin and death is indicated externally by the natural demonstration of one freedom (and the absence of any natural institution of slavery), but, following an argument like Paul's in Colossians 3:22–25, the conditions of slavery would not impair this spiritual freedom.[22] But even in this case, Rufinus's language suggests that outer freedom is a good that society should pursue, at least in circumstances when it is conducive to what Rufinus might consider the weightier matters of the natural law. Nonetheless, it is possible to conceive, on Rufinus's terms, of the outer freedom as a simple permission, conducive to the recognition and attainment of the freedom of the gospel but lacking any real moral or normative force beyond its expedience or convenience. This is not a view that Christians ought to defend today, especially in the wake of the documented atrocities of slavery and the insights of liberation theology on the integral connection between the material and spiritual fulfillment of the gospel, but from Rufinus's perspective one can at least construct an argument in which the canonist is consistent and his idea of the demonstrations of natural law can be coherently understood.[23] For Rufinus, the institution of slavery can

---

22. Patterson suggests that such a "dualist" approach to the question of freedom, most influentially held by Augustine, is not faithful to Paul's "highly sophisticated [holism] with respect to the human body and its relation to the spiritual." Patterson's remarks suggest that if indeed Rufinus held such a view, it might follow Augustine's interpretation of Paul and not other, perhaps better interpretations. See Patterson, *Freedom*, 1:379.

23. This discussion might be an example of what Jean Porter calls the disturbing and yet potentially fruitful aspects of scholastic social analysis and the natural law. "Disturbing, because despite the radical implications of their analysis, the scholastics defend social practices that appear to us to be problematic or clearly unacceptable. Potentially fruitful, nonetheless, because the scholastic analysis of social institutions contains the seeds of its own revision

be understood as legitimate with reference to the fallen condition of humanity and the imperatives of the natural law. It is not an ideal expression of human relations but, given appropriate circumstances and conditions, it "refers back to the natural law" by aiming at the goods of human life in circumstances in which the pursuit of those goods is difficult or impeded by sin.

The question that this discussion raises is whether the things indicated in demonstrations, like one freedom, are simply neutral or are legitimate goods that ought to be taken into account in the structuring of societal institutions. In other words, we have come back to the fundamental question of Rufinus's approach: *Are the demonstrations themselves normative for the institutions that deviate from them?* We can begin to answer this by situating Rufinus's account within the broader conversation of permissive natural law, which goes back as far as Stoic philosophy. Like the present question, the Stoics themselves disagreed about whether things that were neither strictly virtuous nor vicious, what they called *adiaphora*, were simply neutral or existed along a continuum between virtue and vice. The idea and question were picked up by the church fathers, especially Augustine, and in the twelfth century began to be systematically integrated with the prevailing conception of natural law, first by Hugh of St. Victor and Ivo of Chartres, and then by Gratian and the Decretists.[24]

A cursory glance into the development of this tradition provides good reasons to think that Rufinus held the demonstrations of natural law to be normative. In the process of systematizing permissive natural law, it was divided into a number of intermediate categories. The terms for these categories— "*demonstratio, permissio, fas, libertas, perplexitas, tolerantia, licitum*"— designate different statuses of permission.[25] For example, the canonists understood the permission to divorce given in the Mosaic law as *tolerantia*, a concession, something undesirable but allowed by law to prevent worse effects, such as adultery or murder.[26] The language of demonstration, on the other hand, had been associated at least since Hugh of St. Victor with "what God approved of and loved."[27] The canonist Alanus explicitly divided permissive natural law into "counsels, permissions, exhortations, and dissuasions." John

---

while at the same time offering a nuanced and powerful vision of human society as seen from the perspective of Christian theology." See *Natural and Divine Law*, 246–47.

24. The first three chapters of Brian Tierney, *Liberty and Law: Studies on the Idea of Permissive Natural Law, 1100–1800* (Washington, DC: Catholic University of America Press, 2014), provide this history in detail.

25. Tierney, *Liberty and Law*, 22.

26. Tierney, *Liberty and Law*, 21.

27. Tierney, *Liberty and Law*, 10.

of Rochelle followed suit, associating *demonstratio* with the idea of a counsel, which Rufinus's contemporary and fellow instructor at Bologna, Rolandus, referred to as "not obligatory but most excellent."[28] Though the language used by twelfth- and thirteenth-century canonists and theologians can be imprecise, so that sometimes "demonstration" means something like counsel and other times simply permission, Rufinus's definition of *demonstratio* as something "which nature does not command or prohibit but shows to be good" suggests that he has something more akin to "counsel" in mind when he introduces the concept, at least with respect to one liberty and common dominion.[29]

This linguistic analysis can be strengthened by reconstructing a theoretical account of the normativity of demonstrations through a more general examination of Rufinus's theory of natural law. We can start by posing a few relevant questions. On Rufinus's account, what exactly makes commands and prohibitions inviolable in comparison to demonstrations? Or, how does one determine whether any given natural law is a command/prohibition or a demonstration? Rufinus does not provide much guidance on this question, in part because most of his comments here aim at legitimating long-standing practices within his society and not providing a theoretical treatise on permissive natural law. He does, however, indicate the substance of natural law: "natural law follows the essential nature of things, showing only that one thing is in its nature just and another unjust."[30] Rufinus makes this point to explain the need for human law in the first place: in addition to knowing what is essentially just, an orderly and peaceable political society demands its own set of laws, mores, and customs. The other point that emerges here, though, is that the commands and prohibitions either are themselves general principles of justice or are so closely tied to them that they can almost be substituted for the general principle. The conceptual distance between the principle of justice and the command or prohibition, in other words, is so small that the latter takes on the normative and logical characteristics of a general principle of justice. The prohibition against killing is an exemplum of the general principle

---

28. Tierney, *Liberty and Law*, 27 (Alanus); 61 (John of Rochelle); 16 (Rolandus).

29. The Decretists hold no clear or unanimous position on whether *demonstratio* refers to something like a permission or a counsel. The *Summa Lipsiensis* and Ricardus Anglicus, for example, both clearly refer to demonstrations and common dominion as permissions. See Weigand, *Die Naturrechtslehre*, 541 (p. 320) and his discussion on 322. At the least, the canonists who follow Rufinus seem to have few pressing concerns with the normativity of the demonstrations of natural law, except to emphasize that positive law does not err, nor is it null and void simply because it departs from the demonstrations.

30. Rufinus, *Summa Decretorum*, 7.

against nonmaleficence that the scholastics hold as a quintessential principle of justice. Any kind of killing that could properly be interpreted as violating this prohibition would be a violation of the principle of nonmaleficence and an act of injustice, without qualification. It is precisely due to this close connection to justice that these two constitutive parts of the natural law cannot tolerate deviance.

If the commands and prohibitions capture in general terms what is essentially just or unjust, what is the relationship between what is just and the demonstrations of natural law? Rufinus is silent on the question, but the practical distinctions he draws between commands and prohibitions, on the one hand, and demonstrations on the other, make it possible to infer the connection between justice and the demonstrations of natural law. If such laws allow for derogation, then what is demonstrated cannot be essentially just, lest his theory sanction what is essentially unjust. The various categories of permissive natural law demonstrate various connections between these laws and what is just. Some demonstrations are simply neutral, bearing no intrinsic connection to what is just, as for instance, "to seek a prize" (or not).[31] Properly speaking, this is an area of free choice, designated as such by the natural law itself. Other demonstrations manifest precepts of morality other than justice. The concession of divorce deviates from the ideal of indissoluble marriage, which demonstrates the host of moral virtues, such as temperance and fortitude, necessary to preserve such a marriage. According to the scholastics, the demonstration admits of derogation in order to avoid the transgression of the graver precepts of justice and charity.

At least some parts of permissive natural law, though, like one liberty and common dominion, also seem to indicate or instantiate principles of justice, which nonetheless can find expression in different institutions or, perhaps, necessitate different institutions on account of the sinful condition of humanity. So, for example, for the scholastics, no one's freedom may be taken away arbitrarily or for the sake of pursuing some societal good. The institution of slavery is most often justified as a licit response to the crime of initiating an unjust war.[32] As such, individual freedom appears to be a principle of justice in

---

31. An example offered by Gratian in *Corpus Iuris Canonici*, D. 3 d.p.c. 3, and followed by Huguccio in his *Summa Decretorum: Tom. I: Distinctiones I–XX*, ed. Oldřich Přerovský (Vatican City: Biblioteca Apostolica Vaticana, 2006), 70.

32. Another understanding of the beginning of the institution stems back at least as far as Ambrose, who saw in Noah's condemnation of his son Ham in Gen. 9 the origins of slavery in drunkenness. In the twelfth century the scholastics understand it primarily as an institution that is a consequence of just war and conducive to reducing violence in the

A Natural Law Framework for Property

that it can only be legitimately infringed upon as a consequence or punishment for some action that the individual herself (or in the case of an unjust war, an authority representing her) undertakes.

The key question for this section is whether common dominion is one of these latter demonstrations. Within the broad canonistic discussion, common dominion is often discussed with reference to several principles of justice, first and most often, natural equity. Johannes Teutonicus writes in the Ordinary Gloss to the *Decretum*, "The third mode [of understanding natural law] is an instinct of nature coming forth from reason and the law coming forth from such nature [i.e., reason] is called natural equity, and according to this natural law all things are said to be common." This is a position affirmed by, among others, the canonists Alanus, Stephanus, and Simon Bisgnano.[33] Alternative approaches, as in the account of Aquinas below, connect the natural law of common dominion with natural equality, another principle closely connected to justice. Though the canonists generally affirm that common dominion is a demonstration or permission of natural law, they also consistently connect that demonstration with principles of justice. Though Rufinus never explicates such a connection, one way to construe Rufinus's account in line with the prevailing canonistic thought is that common dominion embodies and enshrines principles (natural equity and equality) that must in some way be preserved or fostered in any institution that deviates from it. Common dominion manifests principles of justice that, though admitting of other institutions for achieving those principles, nonetheless is normative for those institutions by providing a set of principles or ends that they must in some way aim toward.

While this more substantive and robust form of normativity must be inferred from Rufinus's account and is not ubiquitously held among the canonists, Rufinus's presentation at least establishes a minimal account of the normativity of common dominion. That is, for Rufinus common dominion is what we might call the morally presumptive or ordinary form of human life. Since this demonstration shows what is good and is not a simple, neutral permission of the law, any deviation from it needs some justification: of what was good about the morally presumptive form, of why it is not expedient or convenient to pursue that form, and of why some alternative form of human life is both expedient *and* moral to pursue. And this more minimal account

---

resolution of such wars by avoiding the slaughter of captured enemy soldiers. See note 20 above. For Ambrose's position, see Weigand, *Die Naturrechtslehre*, 440 (p. 261).

33. For Johannes Teutonicus, see Weigand, *Die Naturrechtslehre*, 435 (p. 255). See also the texts in Weigand, pp. 339–43.

will still push theorists back to the principles of natural law to justify and legitimate alternative forms of life, even if those principles are not privileged or intrinsically expressed in the ordinary institution itself. In either case, Rufinus's account preserves the natural law of common dominion as normative for later conceptions of property. In the more substantive case, it is an institution that embodies or enshrines the principles of equality and equity in an exemplary way and, as such, establishes these principles as grounds and ends of institutions that deviate from it as circumstances (like sin) necessitate. In the more minimal account, it is simply the norm of human use of the material world, necessitating justifications for institutions that deviate from it even if those justifications only reference the natural law more generally and not the natural law of common dominion itself.

The logic of permissive natural law might be rephrased in this way: civil laws that seem to institute something contrary to the demonstrations of natural law may be tolerated so long as they accomplish, even if imperfectly or in a less than desirable mode, what is good according to the natural law. Rufinus clearly sees this primarily as a way of legitimating the institutions of his own civil society. As a lens for legitimation, that is, as a tool for showing how conventions are rooted in the normative and preconventional aspects of human nature, this approach to natural law offers a powerful way of grasping and reconstructing the logic of institutions whose origins and purposes are often overshadowed by the challenges they present. Still, the framework that Rufinus presents is not without critical purchase. Indeed, once the logic of the institution is understood, windows for more nuanced and penetrating critiques present themselves, as for example the critique of the perpetuity of slavery. What appears at first glance as a simple process of legitimization shows itself, in an engagement with and extension of Rufinus's presentation, as a complex tool of legitimation, evaluation, and critique, and, thus, a promising lens through which to analyze the institution of property.

Evidently, this approach is not without its weaknesses. It requires a significant amount of conceptual effort to make sense of how the demonstrations both admit of derogation and remain normative for the institutions that depart from them. It also leaves further questions about distinguishing between commands and prohibitions, on the one hand, and demonstrations, on the other, as well as the usefulness of the whole idea of demonstrations outside of interpreting apparently problematic political and social conventions. Nonetheless, Rufinus's presentation exemplifies how the natural law might provide criteria for legitimizing conventions that, in Huguccio's language, are permitted by or, in Aquinas's language, build on or specify the natural law. As such, Rufinus

A Natural Law Framework for Property

provides a compelling touchstone for thinking about the normative criteria the natural law provides for the establishment of political institutions as well as the scope of freedom for constructing different and diverse political institutions on the basis of such criteria.

Huguccio and the Social-Ethical Solution

Twenty years after Rufinus wrote, circa 1180, Huguccio's approach raises an inverse set of questions to Rufinus's. In his *Summa Decretorum*, it is clear that the natural law of common dominion has normative force. Rather than a historical or ideal state, Huguccio interprets common dominion as an ethical mandate to share one's surplus and the theological framework for all ownership. In the first part of this section, I examine Huguccio's interpretations of the natural law of common dominion first as an ethical mandate and second as a theological framework within which all property relations exist. Each of these interpretations offers important contributions to the development of scholastic thought: each relativizes the importance of a historical or idealized state of common possession and foregrounds the normative significance of common dominion. The second interpretation also establishes a cogent framework to understand the normative force of the natural law of common dominion for the convention of property.

While Huguccio's approach clearly shows that property relations are normed by the natural law, elsewhere he states that "by natural law some things are mine and some things are yours," which evidently casts doubt on the conventional status of property.[34] In the second part of this section, I interpret Huguccio's statements on the natural law and property in light of linguistic conventions and other passages in his *Summa*. Rather than defending natural appropriation, as the above passage might suggest, Huguccio establishes the corollary of Rufinus's claim that common dominion as common possession is a demonstration of the natural law. If common possession is not commanded but only counseled, then property must be allowed. Nonetheless, what is permitted by natural law is not private appropriation but the establishment of property regimes, meaning that while the institution of property by law or custom is a permission of natural law, any specific instances of ownership are necessarily conventions dependent on those laws or customs. As with Rufinus, a careful reading of Huguccio shows that he holds the two central tenets of a

---

34. Huguccio, *Summa Decretorum*, 35–36.

natural law theory of property, though his formulations offer a simplicity and coherence that both exceed Rufinus's earlier approach and anticipate Aquinas's own treatment of the topic.

Huguccio first defines the meaning of common dominion in the following way: "the common possession of all things [*communis omnium possessio*]," which he glosses as "the sharing of all things [*communicatio omnium*] that we possess in a time of necessity."[35] He grounds this interpretation in the idea of natural law as "reason or a judgement of reason," which tracks closely with Rufinus's language of "natural propulsion." To demonstrate the rationale of his ethical mandate, Huguccio cites the Golden Rule, drawn from Matthew 7:12 and cited by Gratian as the first and primary sense of the natural law, and the command to "love your neighbor," from Leviticus 19:18 and Matthew 19:19. The Golden Rule, as both a judgment of reason and a precept of Scripture, commands that in all things one do to others as one would wish others to do to oneself. This gives content to the precept "love your neighbor": "that is, support him in necessities just as you would wish to be supported." In this way, Huguccio argues, the natural law of common dominion is not a perpetual command to hold all things in common but is rather an ethical dictate that emerges through reasoned reflection, "by which we approve of retaining nothing for ourselves beyond what is necessary and distributing the remainder to our neighbors in a time of necessity."[36] In his first approach to the question, Huguccio arrives at his formulation of the natural law of common dominion without any reference to a historical or ideal *state* of common possession, but rather solely with reference to the reasonableness of the Golden Rule and the moral exigency of human need.

By offering arguments for this mandate distinct from the idea of common dominion as a state in which all things are common for the use of all, Huguccio offers an interpretation of the texts and problems Gratian presents that, unlike Rufinus, places the normative and ethical implications of common dominion at the forefront. If Rufinus's approach can be interpreted so that the demonstration of common dominion is nothing more than a simple permission or what happened to be the primitive state of humanity, then one need not derive any normative conclusions. Huguccio, instead, reverses the logic: the meaning of common dominion is, first, normative, and, indeed, neither depends on nor forces one to draw any conclusions about the primitive state of humanity and the significance of a historical or ideal state of common dominion as common possession.

---

35. Huguccio, *Summa Decretorum*, 35.
36. Huguccio, *Summa Decretorum*, 35.

It is paramount that Huguccio offers an ethical interpretation that not only makes the historical state itself of secondary concern but also does not depend on that earlier state. From the earliest commentaries on the *Decretum*, some Decretists had openly doubted whether there ever was a time in which all things were common to all. The *Summa Parisiensis* argues that C. 12 q. 1 c. 2, which noted how the apostolic community held all things in common and how Plato argued for this in his ideal republic, only shows "on what grounds, where, and how all things might be common to all by natural law," and not that at one time all things *were* common to all.[37] The *Summa 'Queritur'* and *Laurentius* both argue that "neither naturally nor legally can something be possessed by many in common [and] unbroken." As Weigand notes, these interpretations doubt the plausibility of common dominion "on fundamental considerations."[38] The *Summa 'Antiquitate et Tempore'* puts it most bluntly: common property is not "preserved by natural law or by custom, but indeed in no manner at all, as many things are private." Weigand sums up this position with the logical conclusion: "thus there is no common to all common property."[39] These positions all suggest the fragility of an ethical interpretation of common dominion based solely on the idea of it as a primitive (or even ideal) condition.

As the previous analysis of Rufinus's position shows, on a strict reading of permissive natural law one need not see any ethical implications for the present from a lost or unattainable state of common dominion. The force of the ideal will be eroded only further if its historical and present plausibility is called into doubt. By securing his ethical interpretation of common dominion directly on the words of the gospel and the Golden Rule, Huguccio insulates it from the uncertain or disputed normativity of common dominion as a state of common possession.[40] Huguccio's approach to the problem of property and common dominion, then, must always be interpreted within what appears to be a strong desire to capture and preserve the normative force of the natural law alongside a weaker but equally palpable skepticism about whether common possession is historical or a political ideal and, even if it were some kind of ideal, whether that would provide much guidance for canon law and the church with respect to the morality of property and ownership.

37. Weigand, *Die Naturrechtslehre*, 531 (p. 315).
38. Weigand, *Die Naturrechtslehre*, 530 (p. 314).
39. Weigand, *Die Naturrechtslehre*, 531 (p. 315).
40. Brian Tierney, *Medieval Poor Law: A Sketch of Canonical Theory and Its Application in England* (Berkeley: University of California Press, 1959), 31–32, and Tierney, *Idea of Natural Rights*, 72, 138–39.

Huguccio provides a second ground for the natural law of common dominion as an ethical mandate by developing a theological account of common dominion. Here, again, Huguccio draws on the idea of natural law as a judgment of reason to develop an account of what Catholic social thought today calls the common (or universal) destination of material goods. In his comments on D. 8 c. 1, Huguccio restates that the ethical mandate is a proposition of "reason or sensuality, that is, of [the natural] order or an instinct of nature." He then says this ethical position can also be grounded in the divine Scriptures. For this argument, Huguccio points to the same scriptural text Augustine cites in his *Tractates*, "The Earth is the Lord's [Ps. 24:1 (23:1)], etc.," which Gratian quotes in D. 8 c. 1. Huguccio shows how a reasonable interpretation of nature can provide a hermeneutical key to interpreting and confirming the scriptural text without relying on a simple appeal to the authority of the scriptural proof text. Huguccio's exegesis not only reaffirms the scriptural claim of the dominion of God over all things but also argues for another key principle of the Christian tradition, that the things of the earth are given for the sustenance of all: "For since I see that there is one author of all things and one Earth common to all and one sky common to all and one sun and one moon and one world common to all, it is enough that a judgment of reason and an instinct of nature dictate to me that also all the rest ought to be common to all."[41] With this reasoning, Huguccio explicitly develops a second ground for his ethical interpretation of the natural law of common dominion in the prior commonness of all things.

The form of Huguccio's argument is distinctive to his own context and style, but even in this brief passage it is apparent that his approach resembles the method characteristic of the patristic theologians. From Psalm 24:1 (23:1) and Augustine's text in D. 8 c. 1, Huguccio arrives at a very similar mode of argument as Augustine and Basil regarding the dominion of God. And utilizing his own distinctive approach to a theology of creation, he also demonstrates an argument for the principle that the earth is for the sustenance of each and all alike. As Basil draws on the doctrine of *creatio ex nihilo*, and Augustine on the *telos* of the material world, Huguccio reasons that since one can see that things that cannot be divided are appropriately understood to be held in common, as the sun (or sunlight) and sky (or atmosphere), so too one's exercise of reason or natural instincts shows that, by the same logic, prior to division, all the other things of the earth ought also to be understood as common to all. In his argument, Huguccio is not appealing to a historical time prior to the

---

41. Huguccio, *Summa Decretorum*, 125–26.

division of "all the rest" of the things of the earth but is appealing to a basic fact about things that can be divided, which is that, in considering the way things that cannot be divided are held in common, they too ought first to be considered as common and only secondly as divided in whatever way human laws have divided them.

Huguccio's theological argument has surprising resonances with other prominent interpretations of the exigencies of the human relationship to the material world. In Roman law, for instance, some things were withdrawn "from the possibility of private ownership," such as "the rivers themselves, all running water, the air, the sea, and the sea-shore," and declared "common to all people," a conviction that was carried through to the scholastic period.[42] And this classification had legal implications: each person was "entitled to a reasonable quantum of light," restricting the height one could build without acquiring legal permission from one's neighbor.[43] Today, international law speaks of certain things as the "common heritage of humanity" in treaties dealing with the moon and the deep seabed.[44] There is a movement to recognize Antarctica as a part of this common heritage as well.[45] From Basil to Huguccio, this Christian tradition interprets the prior commonness of all things as a scriptural, doctrinal, and reasonable claim. As far as its reasonableness goes, it at least does seem to converge with some other prominent traditions, suggesting a cogent interpretation of nature that prompts one to ascertain the common destination of material goods.

As Weigand shows, this approach also represents a significant canonistic trajectory reflecting on the ownership of God in light of Psalm 24:1 (23:1). Earlier texts, including texts skeptical of the historical state of common dominion like the *Summa Parisiensis*, argue in comments on D. 8 c. 1 that "God is the property owner of things and we are only usufructuaries."[46] The *Summa Monacensis* extends this reasoning in a comment on D. 1 c. 7: "God alone is the Lord and owner of all things and we are only usufructuaries. . . . Our relationship to our 'property' is according to this [view] like the slave to his

---

42. Peter Birks, "The Roman Law Concept of Dominium and the Idea of Absolute Ownership," *Acta Juridica* 1 (1985): 9.

43. Birks, "The Roman Law Concept," 17.

44. Gennady M. Danilenko, "The Concept of the 'Common Heritage of Mankind' in International Law," *Annals of Air and Space Law* 13 (1988): 247–66.

45. Francesco Francioni and Tullio Scovazzi, eds., *International Law for Antarctica* (Milan: Guiffrè Editore, 1987).

46. The following three positions are from Weigand, *Die Naturrechtslehre*, 546–548 (pp. 323–25).

'money.'" Gandulphus, the first to take up this position in the Bologna school, where Rufinus had earlier taught and Huguccio would soon teach, comments on D. 8 c. 1: "'The Earth is the Lord's and the fullness thereof.' The judgment of reason dictates this to be so. For since there is one author of all things, who created one earth and one heaven, just as these had a common author [and were] rightly [common] to all, so the remaining things should have been held in common." On this reading, common dominion is and remains the theological (and logical) background to all property ownership. It is without much if any historical significance, but retains an ongoing and perpetual theological and normative significance.

In the broad context of Huguccio's thought, the practical conclusion of this argument seems to be best interpreted that all things "ought to be (treated as) common to all," since he prioritizes the ethical interpretation of common dominion and also clearly articulates the legitimacy of private property. Seen in this light, Huguccio provides another early church principle: that property is a power of distribution and not a power of personal use. Huguccio's ethical mandate to make one's own property common in a time of necessity captures almost verbatim the ethical dictums of the patristic theologians cited in chapter 1, summing up the early church's moral and theological principles in his interpretation of the natural law of common dominion. As Rudolf Weigand states, Huguccio's solution "corresponds to the spirit and letter of the ... fathers as well as the entire early Christian teaching on property."[47] With respect to external things, their prior commonness establishes normative limits on the acquisition, possession, and use of private property without abrogating it.

What then can we say about Huguccio's understanding of common dominion? Huguccio provides an account of common dominion as a sort of framework for human social life. As his comments on D. 8 c. 1 and the positions of the other canonists make clear, the dominion of God, and God's grant of dominion to all in common, is not abrogated by the institution of human property. Rather, it sets the framework and conditions for all institutions of property. And if the dominion of God is not abrogated, neither is common dominion as a judgment of reason that from one author of all things one can see that all things ought to be (treated as) common. Common dominion, in other words, continues to be the basic theological and logical datum of the human relationship to the material world. Whatever else, understood in this way, it is not a mere permission or neutral state that stands alongside property as an equal. It is the theological and, as we have seen, moral background and

47. Weigand, *Die Naturrechtslehre*, p. 330.

frame for institutions of property, not as a historical ideal to be re-created but as a perduring judgment of reason about the purpose, meaning, and significance of creation.

Though this interpretation hints at the status of property as a convention, Huguccio writes in his discussion of D. 1 c. 7 that "also by the natural law something is mine and something is yours." This raises the question of whether Huguccio in fact holds the conventionality of property. How can this statement be understood as anything but a recognition of some sort of natural right of appropriation? Indeed, so far I have only affirmed in Huguccio the subordinate place of all institutions of property with respect to common dominion as a perduring judgment of reason. Though subordinate, a natural right of appropriation might still be found, even if it were limited by the more basic moral exigencies of the natural law of common dominion (an approach Locke takes, for example). The appropriate interpretation of Huguccio here depends on an adequate analysis of his discussion of common dominion and property as permissions of natural law.

There are two interpretive keys in this section. First, immediately after announcing in D. 1 c. 7 that "by the natural law something is mine and something is yours," Huguccio expands that this is by permission, "because the divine law never prescribes everything to be common or some things to be private, but permits everything to be common and some things to be private." Huguccio establishes property as a permission not by derogation but as a corollary to the status of common possession as a demonstration or a permission, which offers a simpler and more coherent basis for property than Rufinus's.

Second, the phrase "something is mine and something is yours" functions as a metonymy in canonistic discourse, standing in for something like "property laws." Huguccio makes the claim in D. 1 c. 7 with explicit reference to D. 8 c. 1: "nor does this oppose what is said in D. 8," where both Gratian and Augustine claim that it is only by human law that one says, "this is mine" and "that another's." For both Gratian and Augustine, the phrases "this is mine" and "that is yours" are substantively interchangeable with the distinctive conventions ("the laws of emperors and kings") that govern the distribution of property—common, corporate, and private—within a political society.[48] On this usage, to say that "by the enacted law, this is mine and that another's," as

---

48. Gratian cites Augustine in *Corpus Iuris Canonici*, D. 8 c. 1, as stating: "It is by the laws of kings that possessions are possessed." And, of course, it is by "the laws of kings" that some things remain common, some things are held corporately, and some things are held privately.

Gratian does in D. 8 c. 1, is consistent with saying that "by the enacted law, society establishes its property regime." What appears to be a straightforward endorsement of a natural right of appropriation is complicated by the linguistic significance of the phrase that Huguccio employs. Huguccio might be using it to endorse a natural right of appropriation, but he might also simply be using (in a manner consistent with Gratian and Augustine) metonymy in which the most significant implication of the convention of property (specific instances of ownership) represents the convention itself.

When we turn back to Huguccio's comments on D. 8 c. 1, it becomes evident that he employs the phrase "something is mine and something is yours" and associated phrases ("something is private") metonymically and not in a substantively different manner than Gratian and Augustine. Commenting on Augustine's text in D. 8 c. 1, Huguccio repeats that by "divine law" (following Augustine's terminology) "it is permitted that some things be held and possessed." He then immediately expands on this point: "nonetheless, it is not shown by [divine law] in what manner something is to be possessed individually, as it certainly is by human law, as by purchase, by donation ... and other such modes. And it is permitted in divine law that the issue of these things be discussed, nevertheless not as fully as [it is] in human law. And therefore according to divine law everything is said to be common and nothing to be possessed individually."[49] By the natural law, one can establish conventions of property, but when it comes to the actual act of possession, one can only do so after and on the basis of the establishment of human or civil laws of property. There is no private possession and no natural right of appropriation under natural law. Huguccio reiterates this point throughout D. 8 c. 1. He notes a contrary point from C. 23 q. 7 c. 1, "where it says that some things are possessed by divine law." There, Huguccio argues, divine law is not used in the sense of "natural law" but rather "is received in a different manner, namely as canon law that is included under human law."[50] He again glosses Psalm 24:1 (23:1) ("The Earth is the Lord's and the fullness thereof"), this time more specifically than we saw above, going into detail about the specific extent of God's dominion: "By 'Earth' is understood villas and estates and possessions of this sort, by 'fullness' whatever is contained on the Earth. And if all these things are the Lord's, then nothing is anyone else's."[51] Finally, Huguccio later explicitly identifies the phrase "this is mine, that is yours" with human law. Glossing Augustine's words

49. Huguccio, *Summa Decretorum*, 125.
50. Huguccio, *Summa Decretorum*, 126.
51. Huguccio, *Summa Decretorum*, 126.

"therefore by human law," Huguccio writes, "for by that law it is said: this is mine, that is yours."[52] What Huguccio means, then, when he states in D. 1 c. 7 that "thus by natural law something is common and something is private," is that natural law permits the establishment of property laws in which some things remain common and some things may be possessed privately. The permission of natural law is not, then, for individual appropriation but for the creation of property conventions in the first place.[53]

The implications of Huguccio's approach go far beyond simply reaffirming the conventionality of property in his own distinctive way. Huguccio has effectively removed the pall of sin and suspicion from the idea of property. Rufinus could only characterize property as a deviation. In a comment on D. 8 c. 1 of the *Decretum*, Rufinus in fact explicitly calls the establishment of property a sin (closely echoing Ambrose and Ambrose's influences among the Stoic philosophers).[54] Huguccio, by distancing himself from Rufinus's formulation and insisting that if common possession is a demonstration then property must also be an explicit permission of the natural law, establishes an argument for the legitimacy of property that does not require derogating from the natural law nor rescuing property from its origins in sin. Indeed, he explicitly contrasts his position with Rufinus's position in D. 8 c. 1. After noting that it is by human law that one says "this is mine, that is yours," Huguccio quotes Augustine again: "*cum ius humanum sit ius* [since human law is in fact law]. Therefore [one says this is mine, that is yours] *not* through iniquity."[55]

By stating the corollary to the idea that common possession is a demonstration of natural law, Huguccio has introduced into the scholastic discussion a way of making sense of the apparently condemnatory statements of Gratian and the early church with respect to property. The evident presupposition that property was in some way not natural but also legitimate, widely held within the patristic tradition, has received theoretical formulation in Huguccio in a way that does not undermine but rather strengthens the normative force of the natural law of common dominion. Aquinas continues in the line of Huguccio's thought, adding clarity to the relationship between the natural law of common dominion and the convention of property and utilizing an approach that, though it does not make use of permissive natural law, comes close to

---

52. Huguccio, *Summa Decretorum*, 127.
53. This is a point echoed by Alanus explicitly. See Weigand, *Die Naturrechtslehre*, 564 (p. 332).
54. Rufinus, *Summa Decretorum*, 21.
55. Huguccio, *Summa Decretorum*, 127.

CHAPTER TWO

replicating Huguccio's conclusions while further distancing the convention of property from any necessary or intrinsic connection with sin.

Aquinas and the Synthetic Approach

When it comes to Aquinas, we are faced with similar challenges to understanding his theory of property. Though Aquinas does not explicitly utilize the same texts as the canonists,[56] the questions and approaches to property that Aquinas inherits and that his interlocutors discuss are largely a reflection of the trajectories initiated in Rufinus, Huguccio, and the other Decretists and adopted and developed in central and influential theological treatises that precede Aquinas.[57] In contrast to the previous two thinkers, though, Aquinas's theory seems to call into question *both* the conventionality of property and the normativity of common dominion. Aquinas's treatment of property is complex enough to deal with in two parts. In the first part, I address the question of the conventionality of property, and in the second I address the question of the normativity of common dominion.

Aquinas and the Conventionality of Property

Aquinas's approach to property, including whether he holds that property is something natural or conventional, cannot be understood except through a prior and adequate understanding of his approach to law. This section begins with an analysis of Aquinas's conception of natural law, human law, and what he calls the conclusions and determinations of the natural law, each of which concerns the question of common dominion and property. After establishing the relationship of the conclusions and determinations to natural law and hu-

---

56. By Aquinas's time, the *Decretum* had been superseded by the *Decretals* of Gregory IX (1234) as the standard canonistic text. Nonetheless, the approaches to property and related laws in the twelfth and thirteenth centuries were largely recirculated—with more distinctions and subtlety—up to the fourteenth and fifteenth centuries. See Tierney, *Medieval Poor Law*, chap. 6. Aquinas's contemporaries in both theology and canon law would thus be working with a very similar set of concerns and trajectories.

57. William of Auxerre, a secular theologian and author of the *Summa Aurea* (ca. 1220), restates Rufinus's position on permissive natural law and emphasizes the normativity of demonstrations as commands that oblige conditionally. John of Rochelle, the likely author of the treatise on law in the *Summa Halensis*, takes up Huguccio's line of thought. Tierney, *Liberty and Law*, chap. 3 (esp. 51–69).

man law, I turn to Aquinas's discussion of property in several questions of the treatise on justice. In one question (*ST* II-II 57.3), Aquinas argues that property is a product of human reason, but so closely follows upon the general principles of the natural law that it needs no human agreement to be instituted.[58] Shortly thereafter (II-II 66.2 ad 1), however, Aquinas explicitly remarks that property is a product of human agreement, appearing to contradict his earlier claims.

This tension can be resolved by suggesting that Aquinas discusses property at different levels of generality in each question, levels that correlate to the different kinds of law Aquinas develops in the treatise on law: property as, in one sense, a conclusion and, in another sense, a determination of the natural law. In this section, I show how both senses refer to property as a convention, which puts Aquinas within this natural law approach and in close relation to Huguccio's theory. This interpretation resists overemphasizing either the naturalness or the conventionality of property in Aquinas and provides a natural law theory of property that converges with Elinor Ostrom's arguments regarding the proper plurality of resource governance regimes.

In its primary sense, for Aquinas the natural law consists of those principles that are general, immutable, and in accord with reason as it pertains to action (i.e., practical reason). The principles approximate "all those things to which the human has a natural inclination, [that] reason naturally apprehends as good."[59] Reason can apprehend the world under a variety of aspects: "being," "truth," and "goodness." And the "good" is the aspect upon which the natural law is grounded, since the natural law pertains to the governance of the acts of the human and "every agent acts for an end under the aspect of good." If every agent seeks what he or she grasps as good, the first precept of the law (the first general principle) is that "good is to be done and pursued and evil is to be avoided." All the precepts of the natural law are in a formal way founded upon this most general principle, but nonetheless, the natural law does not contain just this one but multiple precepts, such as, for example, the precept that Aquinas elsewhere provides that "one should do no harm to another."[60] The multiplicity of principles comes from the multiplicity of ways humans can possess inclinations to the good, including inclinations that humans share with all other beings (e.g., to preserve ourselves), with all other animals (e.g., to reproduce and raise offspring), and only with other humans (e.g., to know the

---

58. Thomas Aquinas, *Summa Theologiae [1265–1274]* (Scotts Valley, CA: NovAntiqua, 2010). Hereafter cited as *ST*.
59. The following discussion of natural law is taken from *ST* I-II 94.2.
60. *ST* I-II 95.2.

truth about God and live peaceably in society). The key here is that the general principles of the natural law approximate these manifold natural inclinations and so are in principle self-evident and require little if any reasoning to arrive at. They also form the starting points for the exercise of practical reason and the choice of human action.

Human reason proceeds beyond these starting points for action as it moves from general to particular considerations and forms what Aquinas calls conclusions of the natural law. In much the same way that reason draws conclusions in speculative matters from the first principles of metaphysics, it also draws conclusions from the general principles of the natural law in matters pertaining to human action. Many of these conclusions are themselves also a part of the natural law (what Aquinas calls its "secondary precepts"), though some require more reasoning than others to arrive at, and some are given explicit expression in human law, though none require this expression to obtain their force.[61] Other conclusions, as I discuss below, are a part of the *ius gentium*, the law of nations, and are distinct from conclusions that are a part of the natural law.

This theory of natural law is both distinct from and similar to Rufinus's and Huguccio's. The idea of adding something to the natural law is evidently distinctive from Rufinus's and Huguccio's theories of the natural law. Aquinas never explicitly discusses permissions of natural law, and Rufinus and Huguccio never suppose that the natural law is changed through addition. Consider, however, two examples of Aquinas's additions to the natural law: the return of goods held in trust (I-II 94.4) and "one must not kill" (I-II 95.2). Both are treated as parts of the natural law. While Rufinus discusses these as part of the commands and prohibitions of the natural law and Aquinas discusses them as conclusions, in both it is at least implicit that these commands

---

61. The easiest way to understand the conclusions of the natural law is to look at Aquinas's discussion of the moral precepts of the Old or Mosaic law and, more specifically, the Decalogue in *ST* I-II 100.1 and 100.3. In I-II 100.1, Aquinas argues that all the moral precepts are a part of the natural law, though some can be known with a minimum of reflection (e.g., "Thou shalt not kill") while others require the reflection of the wise person (e.g., "honor an aged person"). In I-II 100.3, Aquinas specifies that the precepts of the Decalogue are *exempla* of the former, "which with but a little reflection can be perceived at once from the first general principles." In the same article, Aquinas then notes that those moral precepts that require the insight of the wise relate to the precepts of the Decalogue as "conclusions to principles." Thus, the natural law admits of degrees of perspicacity, where the general principles are self-evidently known to all, intermediate principles like the Decalogue are known almost immediately as flowing of necessity from those general principles, and more specific or detailed principles are known only through the instruction of the wise.

and prohibitions are the product of reflection on the general principles of the natural law itself. Aquinas here seems simply to be giving expression to what was implicit in Rufinus's account: that the general principles that seem to be arrived at almost or in actuality by simple inclination yield commands and prohibitions that are closely but not perfectly identified with them and demand the exercise of reason to determine their implications in the present context. Though Aquinas calls them "additions" to the natural law, at least some seem to follow by necessity upon its general principles—without prohibitions against killing and theft, justice and the general principle of nonmaleficence could not be upheld.[62]

In I-II 95, Aquinas turns from the natural law to consider human law. Human law is a body of law distinct from the natural law but nonetheless necessarily related to it. Though human law is not a product of natural inclination or natural reason but of human agreement or the decision of a lawgiver, the laws given by humans may never contravene the general principles and almost never contravene the conclusions of the natural law. And the human law relates to the natural law, Aquinas says, in two distinct ways.[63] The first is to give positive effect to its conclusions. Recall that the conclusions of the natural law have moral force even when they are not expressed in human law. Thus, the conclusion "that 'one must not kill,'" derived from the general principle of nonmaleficence, does not need to find expression in human law to obtain as a prohibition for individuals. Nonetheless, human law *does* give expression to the conclusions of the natural law. Aquinas writes that human laws that derive from the natural law by giving expression to its conclusions have their force primarily from the natural law. Some of the conclusions that find expression in human law Aquinas groups together as a distinctive subset of human laws, the *ius gentium*, which are those things "without which humans could not live together" (I-II 95.4).

The second mode of derivation is the determination of the form of certain general principles or conclusions. Aquinas likens this mode of derivation to an art, where "general forms are determined according to specific details." Thus, the craftsperson must make the general form of a house—walls, a roof, doors, windows, rooms—into a particular house—with this many walls, this style roof—by specifying or determining that general form. Likewise, it is a conclusion of the law that "the one who sins is to be punished, but that he is to be punished in

---

62. On the integral relationship of general principles to the fulfillment of justice, see *ST* II-II 79.1.

63. This and the following are taken from *ST* I-II 95.2.

such a way, this is a determination of the natural law" (I-II 95.2). And such determinations receive their force only from the human law, since in many cases the natural law admits of a variety of possible determinations, given the diverse circumstances and aspirations of different societies. As with those human laws that give expression to the conclusions of the natural law, Aquinas also groups the determinations as a subset of human laws, the civil law, "according to which each state might determine what is suitable to itself" (I-II 95.4).

We need recourse to the conclusions and distinctions of law to see how Aquinas's discussion of property in the treatise on justice is consistent. In II-II 57.3 Aquinas claims that property is a part of the *ius gentium* and requires no human agreement to be instituted, but in II-II 66.2 he explicitly states that property is a product of human agreement. The distinction between the conclusions of natural law (and the corresponding *ius gentium*) and the determinations of natural law (and the civil law) is the key to interpreting Aquinas on the question of property. The prior analysis of the treatise on law shows that a single concept, for example, punishment of evildoers, can fall under the law in different ways. It can, on the one hand, be a conclusion of the natural law that the one who does evil should be punished. It can, on the other hand, be a determination of the natural law that the evildoer is punished in this way for that crime. The key to understanding how Aquinas is consistent on property, and how for him property is ultimately a convention, is to see how he utilizes the idea of property in different ways with respect to different categories of law.

To see how this all applies to property, one must turn to II-II 57.3, where Aquinas compares the "natural right" (*ius naturale*) with the "right of nations" (*ius gentium*). The "right," the rendering of equality due between two parties (II-II 57.1), is the object of justice, and thus the consideration of right opens Aquinas's treatise on justice. The right can be spoken of in different ways: as that which is natural (natural right) or as that which is agreed upon by two parties or a group of people (positive right). And, further, that equality or right that is natural can be thought of in two ways: as something that absolutely considered is just according to nature (as the rearing of children by their parents) or as something that is just relative to some other considerations. Natural right is an equality due according to what inheres in the nature of things; the right or law of nations according to the exercise of human reason that follows upon the apprehension of what is just according to nature and formulates conclusions regarding the right relative to some other considerations.

Earlier in the treatise on law (I-II 95.4), Aquinas identifies the *ius gentium* as those conclusions that all peoples recognize as vital for the sustaining of human social life. Some conclusions, those that have to do with things that are just, absolutely considered (such as "thou shalt not kill"), are, properly speaking, part of the natural law. Those, however, that have to do with things that are just relative to other considerations, like what would be vital to living peaceably together in society, are a part of the *ius gentium*. Importantly, Aquinas states in *ST* I-II 95.4 that the conclusions that have to do with the *ius gentium* are best considered a part of the human law. Its contents are, properly speaking, human laws, since they do not follow of necessity from the natural law (as "thou shalt not kill" follows of necessity and with little reflection from the general principle "do not harm another"), but only through the operation of human reason regarding what is vital for human society.[64]

Aquinas uses the example of the division of property in II-II 57.3 to explain his reasoning, stating that such a division is, properly considered, a part of the *ius gentium*. For Aquinas, nothing in a field itself (for example) suggests that it ought to belong to one person or group as opposed to some other person or group. The division of property thus fails to attain the status of natural right, since there is nothing in the nature of material things themselves such that their division would bring about some kind of equality (as, say, the education of children by their parents would bring about some kind of equality between what is owed by progenitors and what is due to progeny). On the other hand, anticipating his comments in II-II 66.2, Aquinas writes that when a field is considered relative "to the advantage of it being cultivated and the peaceful use of the field . . . it holds a certain commensuration to be the property of one and not of another."[65] The division of property, considered relative to goods advantageous to human social life, can bring about some kind of equality between parties, as each person or group knows which field or other external goods are their responsibility and are available for their generally unimpeded use, and each ought to benefit from such a division relative to a state of no division.

With respect to the *ius gentium*, then, Aquinas speaks of the division of goods only in the most general terms. The issue in question is whether it is useful that humans divide responsibility and powers of administration and use. Aquinas responds that it is indeed useful, without going into very many details regarding the manner and form of division. That Aquinas believes things could be held in common is without doubt, as he defends a variety of schemes of

---

64. Francisco de Vitoria likewise disavows that the *ius gentium* follows by necessity upon the natural law, "because if it followed by necessity from natural law, indeed it would be the natural law." See Francisco de Vitoria, *Comentarios a la Secunda Secundae de Santo Tomas*, ed. Beltran de Heredia, vol. 3 (Salamanca, Spain, 1932), ad q. 57.3.4.

65. *ST* II-II 57.3.

common possession in his defense of mendicant poverty.[66] Aquinas's example, then, ought not to be thought of as pertaining specifically to private property (though Aquinas indeed justifies and defends private possession later), but as pertaining simply to the idea that resources are best managed and society best served when *someone* has responsibility for them and *everyone* knows who has responsibility for what. What pertains to the *ius gentium* with respect to property and, consequently, what is also a conclusion of the natural law, is a principle of stewardship, which indicates that the material order ought to be subject to human stewardship and governance through customs and statutes properly responsive to diverse societies and environments.

In his thoughts regarding the usefulness of the governance of the material order, Aquinas is in accord with the preponderance of contemporary political and economic thought. The generality of his solution, however, is in some ways in remarkable agreement with the argument put forth by Elinor Ostrom against the dominant stream in political and economic theory as recently as the early twenty-first century. At least up until Ostrom's work, economists and political theorists had largely fallen into one of two camps with respect to common resource problems. All thought common resources needed to be subject to some sort of property regime, but most further argued for either state and state-level regulatory schemes *or* the privatization of resources. Different problems, according to mainstream academic theory, were all to be resolved through one solution, either the state or the market. Ostrom's field-advancing insight was to suggest, based on extensive empirical evidence, that a wide variety of state, local, and private schemas could be constructed to resolve what the field refers to as "common pool resource problems."[67] The schemas can be so diverse because they reflect the historical and political circumstances and cultural mores and needs of those who develop and participate in the governance. The insight that the material order is best subject to some scheme of governance is the less remarkable feature of Aquinas's theory than the theoretical insight, corroborated in contemporary scholarship by Ostrom's now widely accepted empirical analysis, that this can only be a general conclusion requiring adaptation and determination in response to the details of any set of material goods and those who will make use of them.[68]

---

66. Thomas Aquinas, *Summa contra Gentiles, Book 3: Providence Part II*, trans. Vernon J. Bourke (Notre Dame: University of Notre Dame Press, 1975), chap. 135 (pp. 182–90).

67. Elinor Ostrom, *Governing the Commons: The Evolution of Institutions for Collective Action* (Cambridge: Cambridge University Press, 1990), chap. 1.

68. The same point is made by Jeremy Waldron, *The Right to Private Property* (Oxford: Clarendon, 1988), chap. 2. On page 38, Waldron cites Marx affirming a similar thought:

Second, this approach to Aquinas's thought brings it close to Huguccio's approach to the question of natural law and property. Just as Huguccio holds that the establishment of property conventions (and not a natural right of appropriation) is a permission of natural law, Aquinas argues that the governance of the material order through property conventions is a conclusion of natural law. The difference between the language of permission and conclusion need not be overdrawn. For Huguccio, property is a permission precisely as a judgment of reason. He seems to think that the judgment of reason dictates that in the fallen state, the external order ought to be subject to a mixture of common and private possession. One might say that the effect of Aquinas's argument is to carry forward Huguccio's apparent openness to property as something at root legitimate and not iniquitous. Instead of describing property laws as a permission of natural law, Aquinas describes them as a product of reasoned reflection on the general principles of the natural law and what would make for a flourishing life in human society. However, Aquinas describes the actual possession of things privately in the very language of permissive natural law that the canonists had used to discuss private property: with respect to the power of administering and distributing property, "it is licit [or, permitted] for the human to possess privately."[69] Some of the theologians of the Second Scholastic period would extend this line of thought to claim that property need not be a consequence of sin.[70] With respect to sin, rather than deny its connection to property, Aquinas is merely silent on the issue.

The conventionality of property in Aquinas becomes apparent when he moves from property as a principle of stewardship, part of the *ius gentium* that is established through human reason, to property in a determinate form, part of civil or positive right that is established by human agreement or common consent (II-II 66.2 ad 1). As a principle of stewardship, property is a conclusion of the natural law; as a concrete property regime, property is a determination of the natural law. Recall that Aquinas treats one idea under these two different

---

"That there can be no such thing as production, nor, consequently, society, where property does not exist in any form, is a tautology.... But it becomes ridiculous when from that one jumps at once to a definite form, e.g. private property."

69. *ST* II-II 66.2. The Latin *licitum* can also mean "lawful," as in the Fathers of the English Dominican Province translation.

70. Vitoria, *Comentarios a la Secunda Secundae*, 3:ad q. 62.2.20; Francisco Suárez, "On the Work of Six Days: Book 5, on the State That Wayfarers Would Have Had in This World If the First Parents Did Not Sin: Chapter 7, What Kind of Corporeal or Political Life Men Would Have Professed in the State of Innocence," trans. Matthew T. Gaetano, *Journal of Markets and Morality* 15, no. 2 (2012): 560.

aspects of natural law when he discusses the punishment of evildoers. That, in general, evildoers ought to be punished is a conclusion of natural law, but the manner of punishment for which evil deeds is a determination of natural law (that is, a civil or human law), instituted by the lawgiver in a way that is "just, possible to nature, according to the customs of the country, [and] adapted to time and place."[71] In a similar way, Aquinas has already established that the governance of things through some sort of division is reasonable for the flourishing of human society and, so, a conclusion of the natural law and part of the *ius gentium*. But the actual division of things according to a particular set of laws is a determination of the lawgiver(s), who will ideally formulate such a set of laws in accordance with appropriate standards of positive law. Any actual division of property is a determination of the natural law and, properly considered, belongs to the civil law and the category of human convention.[72]

These claims can be corroborated by a close analysis of the logic of each article. In II-II 57.3, Aquinas specifically asks whether there is anything in *an external object* (in this case, a field) that dictates that it be the possession of one and not another, while in II-II 66.2, he asks whether humans possess *a legitimate power* to possess something privately. The object of inquiry in each question is distinct. In the first question, the object is the external object, which is only seen fit to be possessed through the operation of human reason, considering the act of possession not in relation to the object itself but in relation to the goods attainable through possession. In the second question, the object is the power of an individual to possess privately, which is only granted through the institution of positive laws of property. The actual power to possess, and any concrete division of property, is only brought about through human convention. On this point, Aquinas's thought once again closely approximates Huguccio's. After affirming that property is a permission (Huguccio) or conclusion (Aquinas) of the natural law, each then further affirms that actual property laws, divisions of property, and personal possessions are only the product of law or custom and thus are constituted by human convention. Though their language is distinctive, the logic and method are strikingly similar.

Placing Aquinas's approach to property within the framework of his treatise on law guards against tendencies to overemphasize its naturalness as a conclusion of the natural law or its conventionality as a determination of the natural law. On the one hand, a careful analysis of the logic of property as a conclusion guards against any tendency to read in Aquinas any sort of natural right to prop-

---

71. *ST* I-II 95.3.
72. *ST* II-II 66.2 ad 1.

erty, as Drostan MacLaren does in his otherwise informative analysis of Aquinas on property. Despite noting the apparent plurality of forms of property, he appears to read *ius* in II-II 57.3 as a subjective power and not an object of justice.[73] This leads him to claim that private property is a natural right, but Thomas does not at all seem to be implying that property as a part of the *ius gentium* entails any specific natural moral power on the part of humans. Property is indeed a right, but it is one granted by civil authority and not intrinsic to human nature.

On the other hand, this approach adds theoretical clarity to claims that private property has "only conventional justification of a historical and empirical nature."[74] As a determination, any scheme of property has only the force of a human law and does not derive its force from the natural law. Nonetheless, it would be a mistake to emphasize the conventionality of property without recognizing Aquinas's argument that the principle of stewardship, of dividing responsibility and use of material goods, is a product of natural reason that derives its force from the natural law. Indeed, to the extent that Aquinas imagines that legitimate property regimes will include a place for private possession (which seems plausible given that this is the example he uses in II-II 57.3 to discuss property as a conclusion of the natural law), then private property as a principle of just division might also derive its force from the natural law, even if any particular instance derives its force from the human law. My analysis largely corroborates what has already been written on Aquinas and property, though it guards against misreading Aquinas on the naturalness of property or overemphasizing its conventionality.

Aquinas and the Normativity of Common Dominion

Aquinas's conviction regarding the normativity of common dominion is stronger than Rufinus's and more systematic than Huguccio's. Though Aquinas makes statements that seem to suggest that common dominion is just the primitive state of humanity—neither a rational nor ideal state—when he discusses the shift from a state of common possession to the state of propertied relations, it is evident that for him the rational and moral understanding of common dominion shapes legitimate property regimes. In this same discussion Aquinas also presents a more systematic and clearer understanding than

---

73. Drostan MacLaren, *Private Property and the Natural Law: A Paper Read to the Aquinas Society of London on March 10, 1948* (Oxford: Blackfriars, 1948), 7–8, 15.

74. Anthony Parel, "Aquinas' Theory of Property," in *Theories of Property: Aristotle to the Present*, ed. Thomas Flanagan (Waterloo, ON: Wilfrid Laurier University Press, 1979), 96.

CHAPTER TWO

Huguccio of just what is normative about the state of common dominion and how it ought to shape property institutions. In the end, the implications of Huguccio's and Aquinas's thought once again fall along similar lines, though Aquinas extends and strengthens Huguccio's formulations. For Huguccio, the normative implications of common dominion mean that in property regimes all things ought to be common in times of necessity. For Aquinas, they mean that in property regimes the use of one's property as such ought to be treated as common, so that one is ready to dispose of one's property for the need or good of another, in a time of necessity or not.

Of course, times of necessity create an especially urgent circumstance for the exercise of this obligation, and here again, Aquinas extends Huguccio's thought. While Huguccio frames the morality of property in the state of common dominion solely in terms of the obligation that obtains on the one with property, Aquinas does so in terms of both the one with property and the one in necessity. The property holder has the same obligation as in Huguccio's approach, but in Aquinas's approach the individual in need also explicitly possesses the moral power of taking what she needs from the property holder's excess, with or without the latter's knowledge or consent (II-II 66.7).[75] The ambiguous statements of Aquinas on common dominion notwithstanding, he provides a clear and articulate affirmation of the normativity of the natural law of common dominion.

Aquinas discusses common dominion in two different ways, which accounts in part for the apparent ambiguity regarding its normativity in his thought. First, Aquinas discusses common dominion as simply a primitive state prior to the division of goods. He does not think the natural law can be changed except by addition, namely, through the addition of conclusions to the natural law that were discussed above. In I-II 94.5, however, Aquinas raises the objection that if "the common possession of all things and one liberty are of the natural law," as Isidore claims, then the natural law must be changeable. In this case, by enacting human laws of private possession and servitude, humans have changed the natural law in the sense of discarding common possession and one liberty.

Aquinas refutes this objection by claiming that some things are of the natural law since nature inclines humans toward them, but other things are of

---

75. Aquinas's discussion is preceded by the canonists, who also formulate a sort of right of taking, though whether the poor possessed such a licit power of taking was not held ubiquitously among them. See Tierney, *Medieval Poor Law*, 37–39. On "right" in Aquinas on this point, see Porter, *Natural and Divine Law*, 274.

the natural law "since nature did not introduce the contrary." In the latter category, Aquinas groups human nudity, common dominion, and one liberty. Since nature does not incline the human toward nudity, it is no deviation from the natural law for human ingenuity to invent clothing, but rather an addition to the natural law through the exercise of human reason (for all the reasons humans find clothing useful and necessary). Likewise, since nature does not incline the human toward common possession, it is no deviation from the natural law for human ingenuity to invent property, once again as an addition to the natural law in the form of a conclusion. The language here does not seem to indicate that there is much to the state of common possession, especially in its comparison to a sort of primitive human nudity.[76] It is not enough to say, though, that Aquinas has ruled out any normativity for common dominion. Rather, he sometimes refers to it simply to indicate what is a merely primitive and, to that extent, nonnormative institution that admits of the addition of laws that are contrary to it.

The second way that Aquinas discusses common dominion is, to use Huguccio's terminology, as a judgment of reason. We can distinguish between these different uses because, in the primitive sense of the term, Aquinas discusses common dominion as *common possession*, whereas he uses the phrase *natural dominion* when discussing it in the second sense. In II-II 66.1, Aquinas asks whether it is natural to humans to possess things. The earth and all the good things of the earth are intended for the use and sustenance of the human. In this respect, it is natural for humans to possess external things, by which Aquinas means humans making use of external things through the application of reason and will. It is in the freedom to use all the things of the earth for her own advantage that Aquinas writes that the human has "natural dominion over external things," a dominion that each and all alike exercise over all nonhuman creatures (living and nonliving) of the earth. Much as Huguccio and the early church tradition do, Aquinas fits this judgment within an overarching theological account. Citing Psalm 24:1 (23:1), Aquinas notes that dominion belongs

---

76. This is probably the place where Aquinas comes closest to associating the division of property with human sin to the extent that he compares it to the initiative to invent clothing, which is associated with sin in Scripture (though neither the invention nor clothing are sinful in themselves). The Franciscan Bonaventure, Aquinas's contemporary, does associate nudity and evangelical perfection, since in the state of perfection humans would have appropriated nothing, even clothing, to themselves and, even in the lapsed state, are born and die naked. Saint Bonaventure, *Disputed Questions on Evangelical Perfection,* trans. Thomas Resit, OFM Conv., and Robert J. Karris, OFM (St. Bonaventure, NY: St. Bonaventure University, 2008), 70.

CHAPTER TWO

to God with respect to both the natures and the use of things, but that in the latter God "by his providence has ordained certain things for the sustenance of the human body."[77] Aquinas corroborates this point with the Genesis account, where he links his philosophical and theological anthropologies by defining the image of God in the human, on which account God gives the human dominion over the earth and its creatures, as human reason.

Question 66.1 is the crucial article for understanding Aquinas's account of common dominion. Though the language is of possession, by "possession" Aquinas means the ability of humans to take up and use material goods. By affirming that possession of external things is natural to the human, Aquinas is affirming that each and every human can rightfully make use of the things of the earth. Though Aquinas uses the term "natural" dominion instead of "common" dominion, the effect is the same, as what he outlines is the dominion each human exercises on account of her nature. The language of natural dominion further emphasizes two crucial points for understanding scholastic accounts of common dominion in general. First, though Aquinas references the scriptural and ostensibly historical account of God's donation of dominion to the first humans in Genesis, his argument is much more substantially based on a philosophical and theological interpretation of the human in the world. That he emphasizes his anthropology more than any historical donation can be seen in his direct linking of the *imago Dei*, on which the historical donation is predicated, with the exercise of reason in humans. Much as plants make use of nonliving things for growth and sustenance, and animals make use of nonliving things, plants, and other animals for their sustenance, so humans, as the animals that participate in reason and are thus capable of ordering and governing the material world, may make use of nonliving things, plants, and all the other animals for their sustenance (and in a providential capacity, for the good of other creatures).[78] The second thing to note is that the warrants for natural dominion—the capacities for reason and free will—are also the fundamental bases of natural equality in scholastic thought. Although he does not make this explicit, Aquinas's account of common dominion is therefore predicated on closely connected philosophical and theological accounts of equality.

When we turn to II-II 66.2, the significance of this account of natural dominion as a common power to make use of the things of the earth becomes

---

77. *ST* II-II 66.1 ad 1.

78. Aquinas does not emphasize the providential nature of humans over the material order as much as he emphasizes its instrumental value to the sustenance of the human, but he still makes this point in several different places. See Thomas Aquinas, *Summa contra Gentiles, Book 2: Creation*, trans. James F. Anderson (Notre Dame: University of Notre Dame Press, 1975), 45.4 (p. 137) and *ST* I 96.1 ad 2.

A Natural Law Framework for Property

apparent. In this question, Aquinas asks whether it is permitted to anyone to possess something as his own. Aquinas responds by distinguishing three ways in which humans possess external things. The first two involve the administration and distribution of external things. With respect to these two modes of possession, Aquinas writes that it is permitted to individuals to possess some things as their own, since it is conducive to the proper care of many goods, the orderliness of society based on a sort of division of labor, and the peace of society when each person knows what belongs to her and what belongs to another. This trio of reasons should be read as a more specific justification of the reasonableness of property and its status as a conclusion of the natural law and part of the *ius gentium* in II-II 57.3. The third mode of possession, the use of external things, does not permit of private possession. For, with respect to the use of external goods, "one should hold them as common, so that she might readily share them with others in their needs."[79] At this point, the normativity of the state of common dominion, in which each person was uninhibited from exercising his natural dominion, that is, from using all of the things of the earth, is apparent. Though the division of property might serve some useful ends, it is always conditioned by that more basic imperative that the earth and all its goods serve for the sustenance of each and all alike, an imperative both grounded and realized in the exercise of natural dominion. Each property holder is charged with holding her property in a manner that recognizes and respects this more basic imperative precisely by treating her property as though it were common and available for use by others in order to satisfy their needs. The act of property-holding is bound to the logic and ends of the natural law of common dominion.[80]

---

79. This passage more literally reads "one should hold them as common, as, namely, regarding the ease with which one would share them [to provide for] the needs of others" (*ut scilicet de facili aliquis ea communicet in necessitates aliorum*). I flag this because although it reads more clearly and succinctly as I have translated it in the body, Aquinas is talking about a *disposition* that leads to certain kinds of actions. For Aquinas, the focus is on how justice as a virtue conditions the way an individual relates to external goods. Nonetheless, as these pertain to matters of equivalence between individuals, they admit of public expression in the laws of society. The issue for Aquinas is not that laws ought to somehow enforce that individuals use their things with the disposition of treating them as though they were common. Rather, the issue is that laws ought to take into account that justice between individuals demands such a disposition and be shaped to realize that equivalence to the extent possible and protect against egregious violations of the actions that ought to result from that disposition.

80. Duchrow and Hinkelammert make the same point, though they do not recognize that property is treated under both the *ius gentium* and positive law. My analysis here only strengthens their argument that property ought to serve the power of use. See Ulrich

CHAPTER TWO

Themes from early church discourse, as in Huguccio, figure centrally in Aquinas's reasoning. By now it should be apparent that the linchpin of theological reflection on the question of property is the affirmation that all things are under the dominion of God. This is the point Aquinas begins with in 66.1, where he notes in the first objection that it is not natural for humans to possess external things since "The Earth is the Lord's," etc. It is proper for humans to make use of external things, Aquinas argues, since God "has ordered certain things to the sustenance of the human body" (66.1 ad 1). As the early church and other medieval thinkers do, Aquinas deploys a theology of creation to interpret and explain the relevant scriptural texts (Ps. 24:1 [23:1] and Gen. 1) and to explain both the dominion of God and the common dominion God grants to humanity. The latter is specifically explained with reference to the principle that was so central to early church reflection: that the earth and all that is on it are for the sustenance of each and every human alike. Aquinas resolves the tension between the natural and the conventional not through permissive law but through the idea of additions to the natural law through the exercise of reason. His approach not only establishes the conventionality of property but also, as with much prior Christian thought, grounds that conventionality in the usefulness of property for ameliorating certain precarities of bodily and social life.

Aquinas develops these claims in a systematic fashion across 66.1–2, beginning with the dominion of God, proceeding through the divine intention for the material world to be for the sustenance of all, the legitimacy of the convention of property in light of its usefulness for serving more basic or natural ends, and concluding, almost explicitly, in the idea that property is a power of distribution and not a power of personal use. The very last words of Aquinas in *ST* II-II 66.2 ad 3 are an interpretation of that difficult passage from D. 47 c. 8, "let no one call his own what is common." To this, Aquinas notes that Ambrose means let no one call anything his own "with respect to use."[81] This is why, Aquinas argues, Ambrose adds: "what more than suffices for need is violently obtained."

At this point, we can see how, despite being innovative in many ways, Aquinas is also firmly grounded in the same set of moral and theological principles

---

Duchrow and Franz J. Hinkelammert, *Property for People, Not for Profit: Alternatives for the Global Tyranny of Capital* (London: Zed Books, 2004), 164.

81. Aquinas is presumably getting this passage from the *Decretum*, where the words of Basil, translated by Rufinus of Aquileia, are wrongly ascribed to Ambrose.

A Natural Law Framework for Property

that have shaped Christian reflection on property since the days of the early church. Like Rufinus and Huguccio, Aquinas attempts to work out the challenges that those principles present through a systematic application of his concept of natural law and a careful development of the multiple senses in which the language of common dominion can be used. As with the canonists, he is firmly committed to the conventionality of property laws and instances of ownership as a product of human reason, both as a general principle and as a product of human agreement in its concrete forms. And, as with the canonists, Aquinas develops a clear case for the way that common dominion, as a claim that each individual possesses natural dominion, establishes the limits and, in some way, the logic of the development of institutions of property. The earth is given to all for the sustenance of all, and no human convention can contravene the natural and moral power each has to make use of the things of the earth for his sustenance in a time of need.

Each individual has a duty to use her property not just to support her neighbor in times of extreme necessity but also in the general satisfaction of her neighbor's needs. When something becomes private, the manner of use formally changes from common to private, but the just individual is always disposed toward her property as though it were for common use. Among the other ends property serves (such as peace in society), property can also be seen to serve the very end of common use. Since, according to Aquinas, things are often better managed and distributed when they fall under the responsibility of some person or group, the goods of the earth that remain in principle available for the use of all are more readily and peacefully procured.[82] As with the approach of the early church to property, Aquinas then can provide a positive interpretation of the usefulness of property for attaining more basic and natural ends. Aquinas, though, directly connects a primary use of the institution of property, improving the administration and distribution of the things of the earth, with a primary end of the institution of common dominion, the common use of the things of the earth, in a way that the early church did less systematically, when it made the connection at all. It is in this way that in Aquinas common dominion can not only limit the institution of property but also establish the core of its logic.

---

82. It must be emphasized that this is not an isolated appeal in Aquinas to any economic value of property, but an appeal to the economic value of property (i.e., as conducive to efficiency, productivity, etc.) in service to the political values of property (i.e., common use for each one's advantage).

CHAPTER TWO

Conclusion

Each of these scholars, central to scholastic canon law and theology, maintains that property is a human convention, created through human customs and statutes. The three scholars present a twofold trajectory. On the one hand, the conventional status of property is complicated in the development from Rufinus to Huguccio to Aquinas. In Rufinus, property is a convention that simply derogates from a demonstration of natural law. Huguccio resolves the challenge of property without appealing to the idea of derogation by recognizing that one implication of the permissive status of common dominion is that property, too, must in some way be permitted under natural law. Without compromising on the conventional status of property, Huguccio argues that the division of property in and through human custom and law must also be a permission, and not a derogation, of natural law. Aquinas comes to a similar conclusion, but without appealing to the language of permission. The ordering and governance of the things of the world are a conclusion that human reason arrives at when considering external things in relation to human social and political life. Property has gone from being a derogation, to a permission, to a product of reasoned reflection.

The conventional status of property in the scholastic trajectory does not leave the structure of property regimes completely up to the community or lawgiver. Rufinus, Huguccio, and Aquinas each show how any convention, custom, or statute is limited by more basic moral considerations. Some of these are basic principles, like the Golden Rule and the command to love one's neighbor. But each of these scholars also provides a way of understanding the moral structure of property in terms of the moral structure of the natural law of common dominion, establishing a direct normative relationship between the two, in which principles of equity, equality, sufficiency, and liberty play a central role in establishing the moral and legal legitimacy of diverse property regimes.

THREE

The Principles of Property

Having laid out the formal framework for the scholastic approach to common dominion and property, I turn in this chapter to a substantive discussion of their relationship and the moral principles that inform that relationship. The scholastics understand common dominion and property in terms of the political nature of the human and the moral principles of the natural law: equity, equality, a right of subsistence, and liberty. These principles have a wide application in scholastic political thought, which, together with their multiplicity, resists the reduction of political morality to a single foundational principle. Further, the principles function differently in different contexts and with respect to different spheres of life: marriage, crime and punishment, war, authority, and common resources and property regimes.

This chapter does not investigate the meaning of these principles as such; it investigates the principles as the moral infrastructure of human social and political life with respect to the nonhuman material world. They are a lens through which to understand what is morally significant about common dominion, and they simultaneously gain substance and shape through an investigation of common dominion and property. Importantly, as the principles are operative in the framework of common dominion, they are also operative in structuring the property relations that exist within that framework (as we would expect, given the normativity of common dominion for property laws). However, the manner in which these principles apply differs between the general framework of common dominion and specific property regimes. There is no single expression of these principles in the relationship between humans and the material world, which is precisely what enables the legal division of things that are common. The key point here is twofold. First, property regimes are indeed an expression of the political will and aspirations of

CHAPTER THREE

a community, as property is a convention that can be established in diverse legitimate ways. However, despite property's conventionality, the previous chapter demonstrated that for the scholastics it has its own intrinsic logic that precludes arbitrary and unjust property laws: it is instituted for the sake of the preservation of justice in societal relations and the pursuit of legitimate societal ends. The fundamental claim a scholastic approach to property makes is that property regimes are an expression of the political nature of the human, mediated through the development of custom and lawmaking institutions and always subject to the natural law of common dominion.

The intrinsic logic of the relationship between humans and the material world is one of the most significant claims of a natural law approach for theories of property. One of Locke's primary concerns in establishing a natural right of acquisition was to insulate property holders from the arbitrary or unjust will of the lawgiver. His opponent, Robert Filmer, held that all property was the personal property of the "patriarch," given initially by God to Adam and passed down through successive patriarch-monarchs.[1] According to such a view, all property is a loan received from the Crown, which would evidently undermine individuals' freedom with respect to their property (and, thus, with respect to their lives in general), given the power political authority would then possess over each person's property. Against this, Locke, along with other contemporaneous scholars and political figures, defends the idea of common dominion—that individual property originated not in the monarch's personal stock but in what everyone owned in common.

This much Locke and the scholastics have in common. Locke diverges from the scholastics (and many of his contemporaries) in part as a response to Filmer's objection that if everyone owned everything, one would have to secure the agreement of *everyone* before taking *anything* (a situation that would make the emergence of any property regime nearly impossible). Locke responds to this criticism by working out his labor-mixing theory of property, which posits that unowned goods are appropriated as property through the exercise of one's labor.[2] Instead of suggesting that political society is natural to the human, through which a division of goods could take place by some mechanism of consent within a given society and *not* the consent of the whole world

---

1. Robert Filmer, *Patriarcha; or, The Natural Power of Kings*, 2nd ed. (London, 1685), 2.4.5 (p. 43).
2. Jeremy Waldron discusses the background to Locke's argument in Filmer's *Patriarcha* in both *The Right to Private Property* (Oxford: Clarendon, 1988), 148–57, and "Disproportionate and Unequal Possession," in *God, Locke, and Equality: Christian Foundations of Locke's Political Thought* (Cambridge: Cambridge University Press, 2002), 153–55.

The Principles of Property

(as Filmer mockingly charged), Locke posits that appropriation is natural to the human.

Locke's method doubly assures the political insulation of property. It is not the property holders who receive their property from the state; it is, rather, the state that receives its property from the original holders. Political authority may do nothing with property that has not already explicitly received the consent of the property holders. Taken in its strongest form, a Lockean approach might hold that *each* property holder must consent before a general taxation of property holders can be morally acceptable.[3] There is no stronger safeguarding of property than the moat that a strong conception of self-ownership builds. The scholastic approach, as described in this chapter, cannot claim to establish such strict boundaries around individual property. However, it is precisely these overridingly strict boundaries that many contemporary political philosophers and theologians see as frustrating the pursuit of justice in society, because such strict boundaries make a social life in which principles of equity, equality, sufficiency, and even liberty struggle to find expression. If the idea that property is a personal loan from the patriarch-monarch forms one extreme conception of property, the idea that property is completely untouchable except by its holder's consent forms the other.[4]

The scholastic and natural law approach avoids both extremes. According to this approach, property is established in accordance with a set of principles natural to human social life—a set of principles crystallized in the natural law of common dominion that all things are common to all. Property is distributed by convention: if customary, then by the community, if according to law, then by political authority. And a society establishes a property regime precisely because it is useful for pursuing desirable ends. This is evidently more conducive to the taking of individual property by political authority for the satisfaction of legitimate political ends, since one's property is received from a common store

---

3. This is a libertarian interpretation of Locke's understanding of property and self-ownership. Nozick is one of the more prominent defenders of this view. See Robert Nozick, *Anarchy, State, and Utopia* (New York: Basic Books, 2013), 172. Locke's own views (chaps. 9 and 11 of the *Second Treatise* are central) are sufficiently ambiguous as to continue to engender a vigorous debate. Edward Andrew summarizes this debate in "Possessive Individualism and Locke's Doctrine on Taxation," *Good Society* 21, no. 1 (2012): 151–68, https://tinyurl.com/342su4kf.

4. John Dunn is particularly scathing in his assessment of the latter position as an interpretation of Locke in "Consent in the Political Theory of John Locke," in *Political Obligation in Its Historical Context: Essays in Political Theory* (Cambridge: Cambridge University Press, 1980), 43.

through distributive mechanisms precisely for the pursuit and achievement of certain ends. Exactly what constitutes legitimate ends can only be determined concretely within the context of any given society, but the scholastic approach insists that such ends be commensurate with the preservation or pursuit of those moral principles that structure the relationships between humans and between humans and the material world. The ends pursued by political society through property, in other words, must be pursued justly and in accordance with the natural law of common dominion. The individual's property remains accountable for the pursuit of goals established by political society as part of its rationale for dividing property in the first place. And in this view, individual property *is* immune (at least morally) from any taking that cannot be defended in light of principles of justice as well as these concrete political or societal ends.

This chapter articulates these latter claims in detail, providing a substantive account of how the principles of equity, equality, sufficiency, and liberty might shape property institutions in such a way as to still admit of a plurality of legitimate arrangements for the pursuit of plural legitimate ends. Each of these principles makes concrete demands on the structures of society. Nonetheless, each also can be expressed in a variety of ways in a multiplicity of contexts: no single instantiation completely determines the expression of any one of these principles. It is precisely in this range of applicability that space opens for the legitimacy of diverse forms of property regimes within the overarching framework of common dominion.

As I examine the scholastic understanding of the principles that inform both common dominion and different regimes of property, I also concretely demonstrate the fundamental claim of this manuscript: at its root, in scholastic thought, property is a political convention that gives partial expression to the political nature of humans, specifically as it is manifested through their relationship with and ordering of the world. It is instituted to protect and further the ends that basic moral principles set for humans in their relationship to each other and the material world. Property, then, is intelligible not primarily in light of a set of basic economic considerations (efficiency, productivity, development) but primarily in light of the principles that form the heart of this chapter.

On Common Dominion and Common Possession

What, exactly, do I mean by dominion, and how does that relate to property or ownership? Evidently, Huguccio's conception of common dominion as a theological framework that all things ought to be treated as common to all differs from Rufinus's conception of common dominion as a state of common possession, but there is a further distinction regarding the powers associated with "dominion" itself. By the time of the scholastics, dominion had acquired a twofold sense from its origins as absolute ownership in Roman law: one of mastery (especially political) and the other of ownership.[5] Each meaning is associated with a variety of different powers.[6] Political mastery is associated with powers of directing, ordering, and commanding. In Aquinas, from whom I take my own account of the meaning of dominion, this applied to mastery generally, including the mastery one exercises over oneself.[7] Though one could distinguish it from the dominion that pertains to ownership by calling it political dominion, to capture its much more general sense, I call it directive dominion.

The powers of directive dominion all pertain to the realm of politics and social life, as they are the powers that ordinarily belong to legal and political authorities, but they also pertain to individuals, as the individual exercises these powers over his own faculties and body by directing each part to the good of the whole individual.[8] In fact, dominion as a power of self-direction is, one might say, the primary referent of the whole notion of directive dominion. In his discussion of reason, will, and action, Aquinas makes frequent analogies between self-dominion and political rule.[9] Likewise, in the part of *De regno* attributable to Aquinas, he univocally compares self-dominion and

---

5. The change may be related in fact to the scriptural sense of dominion as a power of ruling. Patristic theologians interpret the grant of dominion as conferring powers of governance, not owning, the earth and its creatures. Morwenna Ludlow, "Power and Dominion: Patristic Interpretations of Genesis 1," in *Ecological Hermeneutics: Biblical, Historical, and Theological Perspectives*, ed. David G. Horrell et al. (New York: T&T Clark, 2010). This is followed by Aquinas in *Summa Theologiae* I 96 (Scotts Valley, CA: NovAntiqua, 2010).

6. Not every scholar sees the development of a distinction of powers, as, e.g., Janet Coleman treats *dominium* all as relating to the notion of ownership in Roman law, even in Aquinas. The distinction is most obvious, though, in the work of theologians like Aquinas, as I discuss in this section. Janet Coleman, "Property and Poverty," in *The Cambridge History of Medieval Political Thought, c. 350–c. 1450*, ed. J. H. Burns (New York: Cambridge University Press, 1988).

7. See, for example, Thomas Aquinas, *ST* I-II 1.1, 9.2 ad 3, and 12.1.

8. For more detailed accounts of the role of reason and will in an individual's dominion over his acts, see Stephen L. Brock, *Action and Conduct: Thomas Aquinas and the Theory of Action* (Edinburgh: T&T Clark, 1998), and Jean Porter, *Justice as a Virtue: A Thomistic Perspective* (Grand Rapids: Eerdmans, 2016). I make no claim that Porter and Brock would agree with my insistence that this is the primary referent for other modes of directive dominion, at least in Aquinas.

9. *ST* I 81.3 ad 2; I 82.4; I-II 9.1, 9.2 ad 3; I-II 12.1.

political rule as two forms of "ruling force."[10] It is from powers of self-direction that powers over material things and the powers of political dominion are understood. What is meant by common dominion is not primarily common ownership, or even common possession, but rather common powers of self-direction. The natural law of common dominion, then, means first and foremost that the things of the earth are available for each person to exercise his proper powers to direct himself in part through making use of, directing, and ordering the world around him.[11] Property is not merely about private possession and unequal wealth, it is about how powers of self-direction are either limited or protected by restricting access to material resources, a claim that is at the center of this chapter.

Dominion of ownership, unlike directive dominion, is not commonly, if ever, referred to in an unqualified way as *dominium* in scholastic and medieval thought. Aquinas himself does not use *dominium* to refer to ownership at all, and prefers instead the language of *possessio proprium*, to possess as one's own (*ST* II-II 66.2). For my own purposes, I refer to this sort of dominion as proprietary dominion. Proprietary dominion refers to a set of powers characteristic of private ownership. These powers of private or exclusive use, development, and transfer are paradigmatic of private property. Though any one of these powers can be curtailed by law, and other powers can be granted that also are a part of the bundle of rights characteristic of private property, these are the foremost powers associated with proprietary dominion.

What does all of this have to do with the discussion of common dominion and property? Primarily, it cautions us against equating common dominion with common ownership, as occasionally occurs in contemporary evaluations of the idea of common dominion.[12] Besides this limit, however, the distinction between directive and proprietary dominion also fills in some of the substance

---

10. R. W. Dyson, *Aquinas: Political Writings* (New York: Cambridge University Press, 2002), 7. On what can be attributed to Aquinas, see p. xix.

11. In his dispute with John XXII, Ockham argues that it is *this* political dominion that Adam and Eve had in the state of innocence and *not*, as John XXII seems to argue, proprietary dominion: "the *dominium* of all temporal things given to our first parents was a power of reasonably ruling and directing temporal things without their violent resistance." See William Ockham, *A Translation of William of Ockham's Work of Ninety Days (Early 1330s)*, trans. John Kilcullen and John Scott, 2 vols. (Lewiston, NY: Edwin Mellen Press, 2001), 234.

12. G. A. Cohen disavows common dominion because he equates it with joint ownership, in which each person has a full set of private property claims over everything on the earth, while Mathias Risse equates common dominion with common ownership in his own work on global justice. G. A. Cohen, *Self-Ownership, Freedom, and Equality* (Cambridge:

of what common dominion refers to, why it is of such concern morally, and why it matters for the establishment of property regimes. If we take Huguccio's approach from the previous chapter, common dominion does not refer primarily to a state in which anything is available for anyone's use, but rather to the moral claim that the things of the material order are first ordered for the use of each person. But humans use the material order, *must* use the material order, in order to exercise their nascent powers of self-direction. Indeed, for Aquinas, one could say that humans use the parts of their bodies and their individual faculties in coordinated ways to achieve self-direction. In much the same way that humans use their bodies for self-direction and to achieve their own flourishing, they must also use the things of the earth to achieve those same purposes.[13] The moral significance of common dominion has much less to do with strict material equality, and almost everything to do with the equal claim of each person to be able to act in ways proper to a human: to equitably and freely direct her own actions and to pursue her own flourishing. Common dominion matters for property regimes because to the extent that the division of property restricts each person's access to the material order, it implicates each person's ability to exercise her directive dominion and pursue her flourishing. This concern is apparent in what follows and becomes crystallized in scholastic discourse on liberty and property.

What then of an approach like Rufinus's, which seems to discuss common dominion primarily as a state of common possession? The primary sense of common dominion is a theological framework. Rooted in the equality of humans as rational creatures, each possessing the *imago Dei*, and each alike the recipient of the grant of dominion over the earth from God, common dominion means that humans possess a proper power of self-directedness through the use of the material things of the earth. Nonetheless, the secondary sense of common dominion as a state of common possession is important for understanding scholastic thought, as it constitutes a base scenario or paradigm from which a "departure" from common dominion in the form of property can be understood. In contemporary economics, this is referred to more precisely as an open access

---

Cambridge University Press, 1995), 95–98; Mathias Risse, *On Global Justice* (Princeton: Princeton University Press, 2012).

13. A technical analysis of Aquinas's action theory shows that the use of external things is an extension of the use of one's own faculties and body to act. Brock, *Action and Conduct*, 29–33. For my own argument, what this suggests is that dominion over oneself is the root and of the same kind (directive dominion) as dominion over external things, or natural dominion.

regime, where everything is available for anyone's unregulated use.[14] Whether as a thought experiment or a purportedly historical account, scholastics refer to such a state of common possession to describe what is natural to humans with respect to the material world, the moral implications of that natural state, and how conventions of property depart from it. It is a useful place to examine the meaning of equity, equality, sufficiency, and liberty in the natural law of common dominion and how those principles relate to institutions of property.

The scholastics draw on the idea of a natural state of common possession to understand and legitimate property relations. Whether because of sin or because of the nature of being human in a world of scarce resources, a state of common possession entails certain serious liabilities. For a thinker like Aquinas, property is necessary simply to organize a multitude of persons and their relationships to the material world, without which a certain amount of disorder and waste would occur. For all three of our scholastics, postlapsarian humans in a state of common possession are likely to descend into a situation where the violent and greedy dominate the peaceable and meek, and the principles of equity, equality, liberty, and sufficiency find little if any room for expression. Seen in this light, property is an institution that has the potential to preserve and foster these moral principles, even if it does not express them perfectly. On the one hand, there is no way in which one can say that institutions of property do not curtail the expression of these natural principles in a state of common possession (especially an idealized state of common possession like the prelapsarian). Property of any form (common, collective, private) almost necessarily means that some have more, and some less, a discrepancy that is, strictly speaking, unequal and will also likely lead to divergent possibilities for self-direction and, thus, liberty.

At their best, however, and in comparison to any postlapsarian state of common possession, institutions of property can be said to foster and preserve and, so, express these principles in a different way, one suited to the conditions, limitations, and aspirations of the society in which they are established. It is precisely through their own curtailment that the principles of equity, equality, sufficiency, and liberty, considered in the human relationship to the material world, can find expression in postlapsarian society. And it is precisely in the tension between the curtailment and preservation of these principles that the

14. Importantly, in economic literature, open access is juxtaposed with a common governance regime. The "tragedy of the commons," first described by Garrett Hardin, is really a tragedy of open access regimes, and not common governance regimes, a point detailed by Elinor Ostrom in *Governing the Commons: The Evolution of Institutions for Collective Action* (Cambridge: Cambridge University Press, 1990). See also Hardin's original essay, "The Tragedy of the Commons," *Science* 162, no. 3859 (1968): 1243–48.

The Principles of Property

normativity of common dominion, its role as a legitimating and limiting institution for property, can be understood.

Natural and Civic Equity

The jurists focus their discussion of common dominion and property around the principle of equity. As Rudolf Weigand notes in his discussion of the Roman law foundations of the medieval civilian tradition, in Roman and scholastic jurisprudence equity has both a regulative and generative function. On the one hand, it is "the overarching, common measure for all individual laws and each individual norm." Laws ought to generally track the best understanding of equity in whatever society they are passed. On the other hand, equity "also determines, from the inside of the law out, so to speak, the respective *suum ius*, what is due to each individually here and now, what he has to claim or to perform."[15] For the scholastic jurists, civilians as well as canonists, a paramount feature of justice was precisely the upholding of each one's due.

To get an adequate sense of the meaning of equity in the jurists' discussions of common dominion and property, we must look at both the civilian and canonist traditions, in part because the civilian tradition discusses in more detail a key distinction between natural and civic equity. In practical terms, natural equity partly fleshes out in claims of right that can be made on the basis of nature or the natural law. For Irnerius, an early civilian, one paradigmatic example is the honoring of pacts and agreements.[16] Another civilian, Hugolinus, writes that it is contrary to natural equity to enrich oneself at the expense of one's neighbor. Nonetheless, Hugolinus identifies a law that contravenes this precept of natural equity: the law of usucapion entitles someone who occupies another's property unimpeded for a certain amount of time (in Roman law, for example, several years), to legitimately claim that property as his own, even at the expense of his neighbor who might have previously owned the land.[17]

---

15. Rudolf Weigand, *Die Naturrechtslehre der Legisten und Dekretisten von Irnerius bis Accursius und von Gratian bis Johannes Teutonicus* (Munich: Max Hueber, 1967), p. 11.

16. Weigand, *Die Naturrechtslehre*, 17 (p. 20). Today this remains an important principle of international law (*pacta sunt servanda*) and enjoys the status of *jus cogens*, which are peremptory norms that stand prior to and above customary law and international treaties. *Jus cogens*, including this example of honoring pacts, retains a similar status as being a part of natural equity or the natural law today as in the medieval period.

17. See further discussion of *usucapion* in Peter Birks and Grant McLeod, trans., *Justinian's Institutes* (Ithaca, NY: Cornell University Press, 1987), 2.6 (p. 63).

What justifies this violation of natural equity is precisely another form of equity noted by the civilians, civic equity. When the rightful owner fails to visit or attend to his property for a long enough period of time and that same property is taken under the care of a nonowner, the ownership of that thing can become disputable. Can the absent owner claim back the thing that the nonowner has tended to, perhaps by improving or at least preventing disrepair? Such uncertainty is liable to introduce conflict in society. The rule of usucapion is a prescription of civil law intended to prevent just this uncertainty of ownership. And this rule of prescription accords with civic equity. As Hugolinus writes, "a rigor contrary to natural equity has been instituted for a purpose and for the sake of peace or society."[18] Where natural equity lacks something conducive to the peace of society, civic equity can introduce prescriptions that are in some way, or at least appear to be, contrary to it.

The question that immediately comes to mind is what role natural equity plays in the shaping of prescriptions of civic equity. The norm against gaining at one's neighbor's expense is still relevant, as usucapion is prescribed to place limits on such gain in the context of various societal exigencies, like the problem of long vacant but exclusionary (and potentially productive) spaces. The rigor is perhaps contrary to natural equity strictly speaking, in that it allows for gain at the expense of another, but it is certainly not a prescription or rule whose formal principle is "gain at one's neighbor's expense." In its Roman origins, it was likely a response to alleviate tension and conflict among neighbors and absentee landholders in a way that recognized both the problems of vacancy for those who live nearby and some sort of fairness to owners who may have legitimate reasons to be absent. It might be more accurate to say that civic equity is that equity that aims at the preservation of fairness in the context of other salient societal considerations, much like the *ius gentium* functions in Aquinas. In this case, natural equity is not opposed to civic equity but sets a *telos* for the balance of considerations that must be weighed in resolving civic questions. Civic equity preserves some sense of natural equity in the face of societal forces that would overwhelm, disintegrate, or make such equity unsustainable without laws that balance competing claims and needs by building considerations of fairness into those laws. Such an approach sets equity as an overarching standard for law and, as Weigand notes, establishes equity as the ground of certain right claims. Indeed, the very language of balance indicates

---

18. Sir R. W. Carlyle and A. J. Carlyle, *A History of Medieval Political Theory in the West*, vol. 2 (New York: Barnes & Noble, 1950), 48.

that the process of finding civic equity is itself shaped and motivated by a more general, preconventional equity.

Such a discussion is relevant for the scholastic discussion of property because the civilians and canonists discuss property in terms that, even if they do not always reference the divide between civic and natural equity explicitly, seem to make use of the divide to establish the legitimacy of the convention of property. In canonistic discussion, the natural law and, specifically, the natural law of common dominion are often equated with natural equity. In his gloss of the *Decretum*, Johannes Teutonicus writes that in order to understand Gratian's comments on the natural law in D. 1 c. 7, the reader must "note that the word 'nature' is used in many ways." The three ways correspond to different levels of living beings—plants, animals, and rational creatures. The first way is the simple force that moves things to growth and reproduction; the second is the movement in pursuit of physical desire and the movements of the sensitive appetites. Teutonicus writes that in the third way "nature means an instinct of nature proceeding from reason. Law proceeding from nature in this sense is called natural equity. According to this law of nature, all things are called common."[19] He makes the same comparison later, saying that "natural law in the sense of natural equity existed from eternity" and equating natural equity with the "essence" of natural law.[20]

It is similarly the case that just as common possession is identified with natural equity, the institution of private property is seen as, to use Hugolinus's language, introducing a rigor contrary to natural equity. Recall from chapter 1 Gratian's use of the Pseudo-Clementine text in C. 12 q. 1 c. 2, which claims that "through iniquity [*per iniquitatem*], one said this was his, and another that, and thus division was made among mortals."[21] In their *Summae*, several canonists gloss this passage by arguing that what is meant by "iniquity" is "inequity." Here we can look to Huguccio's commentary on D. 8 c. 1 to establish the equivalence between natural law and natural equity, on the one hand, and *ius gentium* (and civil law) and "inequity," on the other. Referencing the discussion in C. 12 q. 1 c. 2, he writes, "by iniquity, that is by the *ius gentium* or civil law that is iniquity, that is, inequity, that is, contrary in this to natural

---

19. Gratian and Johannes Teutonicus, *Treatise on Laws (Decretum DD. 1–20) with the Ordinary Gloss*, trans. Augustine Thompson, OP, and James Gordley, Studies in Medieval and Early Modern Canon Law (Washington, DC: Catholic University of America Press, 1993), 6.

20. In a gloss of D. 5 c. 1. See Gratian and Johannes Teutonicus, *Treatise on Laws*, 16.

21. Gratian, *Corpus Iuris Canonici: Pars Prior: Decretum Magistri Gratiani*, ed. Aemliius Friedberg (Graz, Austria: Akademische Druck-U. Verlagsanstalt, 1959).

equity."[22] This explanation found its way into the jurisprudence of the Bolognese, Frankish, and Anglo-Norman schools, and thus became a more widely held principle, given expression in Teutonicus's gloss to C. 12 q. 1 c. 2.[23]

How does this inequity relate to the civilians' civic equity? In a way, the canonists are constrained to specifically introduce the term "inequity" in their attempts to meliorate the condemnation by Pseudo-Clement. In other words, while the language of inequity seems to erode the legitimacy of the institution, it is in fact utilized to bolster its legitimacy by weakening the connection between sin (iniquity) and property. Though their language is distinct, the canonists' arguments resemble the civilians' arguments in important ways. Much as the civilians think that natural equity can be curtailed or modified through the introduction of civic equity, which is, one might say, a derivative but distinct form of equity, the canonists also evidently think that the departure from natural equity is legitimate. This position is held broadly across canonistic thought. Alanus provides one of the clearest statements of the relationship between natural law (as natural equity) and civil law (as civic equity). He notes that by natural law all things are common; nevertheless, "since in positive law there is a command not to usurp someone else's good, the one who does the opposite is found wanting and unexcused by the natural law." The natural law does not excuse or legitimate theft, Alanus says, because "positive law always judges before the natural law," which seems to mean that actions first fall under the jurisdiction of positive law structured through civic equity, though perhaps where such law is silent one may appeal to natural law or natural equity.[24]

Rufinus and the canonists who followed him resolved the contrast between natural and civic equity through the idea of demonstrations. Again, though the language is distinct, this method of resolution largely resembles the approach of the civilians to natural and civic equity. Recall from the previous chapter how Rufinus argues that the demonstrations of the natural law show what is good without commanding it. Nonetheless, civil laws that depart from the demonstrations of the natural law must still refer back to the natural law. Ru-

---

22. Huguccio, *Summa Decretorum: Tom. I: Distinctiones I–XX*, ed. Oldřich Přerovský (Vatican City: Biblioteca Apostolica Vaticana, 2006), 127.

23. See the discussion in Weigand, *Die Naturrechtslehre*, pp. 340–41, for more sources and their commentary on natural law and natural equity and the *ius gentium* and inequity. Teutonicus writes, "*per iniquitatem*: that is, by the convention of *ius gentium*, namely, what is contrary to natural equity."

24. Weigand, *Die Naturrechtslehre*, 537 (p. 318). See Weigand's commentary on this, especially on 319: positive law "always takes precedence to the natural law, as Alanus understands it, namely, [natural law] as pure equity."

finus's example is slavery: the violation of the demonstration of one freedom is permitted to the extent that violence and lawlessness are curbed and peace and humility cultivated through the institution. Though Rufinus does not make the argument explicit, the institution of slavery can refer back to one freedom: to the extent that freedom cannot be enjoyed in a state of violence and lawlessness (by either the victims or the perpetrators), then the attenuation of such vices through the institution of slavery helps to foster the conditions in which freedom can be enjoyed (again, by both parties). Rufinus's discussion of slavery might best be characterized as a discussion of a penal institution, and, either way, it is subject to significant critique. Nonetheless, it provides a helpful starting point for thinking about the place of natural equity in natural and civil law. Similar lines of reasoning would show that Huguccio's permissions and Aquinas's additions to the natural law are other ways of navigating between a pure, natural equity and an equity developed to function in the midst of societal exigencies.

As noted in chapter 2, not every demonstration relates to principles of justice like natural equity, but those that do remain normative for the civil institutions that depart from them. Some demonstrations, like one freedom, seem to express a principle of justice—the expression might be fungible but the principle is binding. In a world in which the freedom of some is threatened by the violence of others, the institution of a penal institution may curb or remove the freedom of some on account of their violation of the freedom of others. The natural law of common dominion seems to be another such demonstration. Natural law shows that all things are possessed by all in common. This is according to natural equity, as on the scholastic account there are no natural means by which anyone may appropriate the things of the earth. However, in a state of common possession (especially a postlapsarian state), the violence and greed of some will impinge on this common possession. Some will be dispossessed of access to common possession while others seize or usurp whatever they can. Rufinus draws a likeness between the seizure of property and the first act of enslavement. Though the first enslavement, attributed by Rufinus and other Decretists to the tyrant Nimrod, was done through oppression and iniquity, it has over time come to be "administered not by the perversity of iniquity but by the law of custom." So the seizure of property "was done initially through the burning desire for things, which, nevertheless, after long usage and by the enactment of laws is [now] judged irreprehensible."[25] The

---

25. Rufinus, *Summa Decretorum*, ed. Heinrich Singer (Paderborn, Germany: Scientia-Verl. Aalen, 1963), 21. See my critique of Rufinus on slavery in chapter 2, above.

iniquity of slavery and property is rectified through the introduction of law, which refers such institutions back to the equity (e.g., the one freedom) of the natural law even though, in the context of societal exigencies, these institutions also curtail or modify that equity (and so admit of inequity). To apply the language of the civilians here, the institutions have become products not of strict iniquity nor natural equity but of civic equity.

The equity of institutions of property is different from but derivative of the natural equity of common possession. In a state of common possession, equity means open access. Recall Huguccio's reasoning: when one sees how there is one Creator, one earth, one sun and sky common to all, the judgment of reason dictates that all the rest—the resources and creatures of the earth—ought also to be treated as common to all. But, for example, for the sun to be common to all simply means that no one can impede another's use of the sun. Even ancient Rome, where private property was firmly protected, made laws against infringing upon one's neighbor's sunlight by building too high on one's own property.[26] The natural equity of the natural law of common dominion represents a sort of free and unimpeded access to the things of the earth.

Here, one could adduce at least two considerations that warrant departing from the state of natural equity. The first is the example Rufinus has already provided: the threat that a tyrant or groups of individuals usurp what is common for themselves. In such circumstances, natural equity is evidently undermined. Laws and conventions are introduced, as Augustine noted, to restrain evildoers. And such laws and conventions, to the extent that they divide and restrict access to the things of the earth, necessarily depart from natural equity. Some will, through no fault of their own, find that some portion of their property becomes worth less over time, as when the real estate in a certain region declines in value. Others will find that a trade or craft they pursue becomes valueless in their society, while others become fabulously wealthy by pursuing the right trade or purchasing the right real estate at the right time. Some laws might be introduced to pursue alternative forms of equity, as to ensure that a greater share of resources accumulates to industrious individuals, for example. Under such laws, an individual who pursues a leisurely life would have less access to the things of the earth than an industrious individual. In all of these cases, access to the things of the earth becomes restricted and unequal for the sake of ensuring that those restrictions and that inequality accord with some alternative standard of equity (such as proportionate reward for labor)

---

26. Peter Birks, "The Roman Law Concept of Dominium and the Idea of Absolute Ownership," *Acta Juridica* 1 (1985): 16–17.

and that they remain within certain limits (limits that might otherwise be obliterated in a context without laws and conventions). What those limits are must be decided in accord with civic equity, that standard that departs from natural equity even while seeking to preserve its logic in the context of societal exigencies.

The departure from natural equity need not occur only on account of the sinful nature of humans, though. As Elinor Ostrom showed, open access regimes with scarce resources entail a host of problems. A fishery that has no rules, customs, or expectations regarding what each individual may harvest will soon face shortages and perhaps extinction, imposing high and long-term costs on all. One need not suppose that some tyrant or group will collude to usurp the fishery and exclude all the others to realize that this sort of natural equity (meaning open access) will soon deplete the fishery merely through the steady increase of population and uncoordinated action.[27] Rules and customs that structure and limit access necessarily depart from the standard of natural equity even while preserving its logic: that each person has access to the things of the earth, grounded in the will of God that the earth and all that is on it be for the sustenance and use of each and all alike. In a situation in which open access will necessarily undermine the ability of the things of the earth to be for the sustenance and use of each person, conventions that administer and protect those resources preserve the possibility that the things of the earth remain available for the sustenance and use of all. Again, such conventions introduce inequality and differential access depending on the rationale used by society and the choices it makes. The rationale might be egalitarian: that each individual or group has access to the same amount of fish (though even here, luck and differential preferences will drive different levels of success and harvest). This might entail that individuals with larger ships have briefer access to the fishery than individuals with smaller ships. On the other hand, a society might use a different logic that prioritizes something like efficiency: individuals with a larger capacity to harvest fish may be permitted to harvest more than individuals with a smaller capacity. In every case, the logic of natural equity must be preserved, even if civic equity still departs from natural equity through the introduction of differential access and other inequalities.

27. This, it seems to me, is closer to Aquinas's position, following Aristotle. It does not invalidate Rufinus's focus on usurpation, as it is certainly the case that usurpation is also a risk of open access regimes. My point in emphasizing Aquinas's position is that one need not appeal to the limit case (the tyrant) to see that more generally uncoordinated action by individuals creates strong reasons to generate conventions precisely to coordinate their activities.

CHAPTER THREE

Liam Murphy and Thomas Nagel demonstrate this very method of reasoning with a central and disputed topic for societies today: wealth, income, and taxation. They start by establishing that they will treat property, including wealth and income flows, as a legal convention with no independent standing over against tax law, itself an integral part of the property regime. By doing so, they are able to evaluate and argue for different understandings of equity, and other principles of justice like equality and liberty, not as constrained by a prior conception of property but as themselves generative of a set of property laws that give expression (ideally) to the most compelling articulation of those principles. Without suggesting that they would endorse the natural law theory of property as I present it here, this is a mode of reasoning that is, to my mind, very much commensurate with what might emerge from a scholastic natural law framework.[28]

In concrete terms, for the canonists, the departure from natural equity found one limit at the level of subsistence for the twelfth-century peasant. Despite the oppressive nature of the feudal system, Brian Tierney notes that it persisted not simply because of the intransigent domination of manor and liege lords but also because of the limits of contemporary agricultural technology and economic organization.[29] In a context in which the path out of the feudal system and a subsistence lifestyle (and one of servitude) for the majority was not clear, insisting on laws that protected the subsistence of each individual was one way of ensuring that, in the absence of viable alternatives, peasants could at least access as much as they needed to endure, say, a time of famine or illness and maintain their capacity to subsist on their own in the future.

Medieval jurists, both civilians and canonists, though, demonstrate other limits on the departure from natural equity. For instance, the law that if a peasant could escape to a town for a year and a day he would be freed from his obligations to his lord (and, thus, become free) introduces a standard of equity that fosters the movement away from a feudal and toward a commercial society. The introduction of such laws and conventions involves trade-offs: the peasant-turned-artisan may freely pursue a life beyond subsistence through the competency of a craft, but he also loses his claim to the parcel of land that provided his subsistence. In other words, the peasant-turned-artisan becomes free of the claims of his lord and free to pursue a livelihood beyond subsis-

---

28. Liam Murphy and Thomas Nagel, *The Myth of Ownership: Taxes and Justice* (New York: Oxford University Press, 2002).

29. Brian Tierney, *Medieval Poor Law: A Sketch of Canonical Theory and Its Application in England* (Berkeley: University of California Press, 1959), 22–23.

The Principles of Property

tence, but he also loses his power to claim his right to the land against his lord. The canonists continued to insist that artisans had access to the poor relief of the church and rights of subsistence, even though they had lost their access to the land.[30] The logic of natural equity—to preserve the use of the things of the earth for each person—is preserved under both systems. What changes are the other values and principles that shape civic equity: guaranteed subsistence and the ostensible protection of a manor lord, on the one hand, and the freedom to pursue meaningful work beyond subsistence and the life of freedom in a town, on the other. These and other laws are intelligible at least partially in reference to the logic of natural equity and show how different facets of natural equity can be at work in the same law, as the laws freeing peasants from their lords can be intelligibly related to both the logic of common dominion (in terms of greater access to the things of the earth) and the logic of one freedom (in terms of freedom from feudal obligations and servitude to the manor lord).

We can connect this account with the substantive account of common dominion as common powers of self-direction. The use of the things of the earth for each person is not simply for mere survival, but also for the exercise of self-direction proper to humans as free and rational creatures. In a feudal society, this self-direction is severely limited for the peasant majority. The feudal peasant received time away from manor chores and subsistence farming on Sundays and a handful of feast days. Peasants were in principle free to marry whom they would and to pursue religious life. Beyond these freedoms, the feudal peasant's life was immersed in cycles of farmwork and hard labor.[31] Further, these freedoms were enjoyed only at the goodwill of the manor lord. For the peasant of a harsh lord, they could only be enjoyed relative to the effectiveness of the local church in coercing the lord to recognize the peasants' privileges.

---

30. Commercial society evidently brought about great good for a great many in Europe (including for those who remained peasants, whose labor became scarcer and thus whose services were more willingly exchanged for greater concessions, including the end of servile burdens), but it also led to new forms of poverty, creating problems of unemployment and vagrancy that became significant across Europe in the fourteenth and fifteenth centuries. Though canonists continued to insist on a right of subsistence, this right was not as well suited to the new realities of the emerging mercantile society as it was to the feudal society. This led to a time of transition over the course of the thirteenth to the sixteenth centuries, when the civil law and civil institutions began to assume a greater role in poor relief on account of the inertia in canon law and ecclesial institutions to develop new responses to new challenges. See Tierney, *Medieval Poor Law*, chap. 6.

31. On the life of medieval peasants, see Brian Tierney and Sidney Painter, *Western Europe in the Middle Ages: 300–1475*, 6th ed. (New York: McGraw-Hill, 1998), 285–92.

CHAPTER THREE

The peasant life had, without a doubt, only a very diminished level of self-direction. But it also provided a relative degree of certainty and stability. Peasants' lands could not be taken from them, and, in principle, neither could any of the other few freedoms they enjoyed. The artisan, meanwhile, enjoyed a greater degree of self-direction, pursuing a craft that offered opportunities for existence beyond subsistence. The enjoyment of Sundays and feast days as well as the ability to travel and move between towns were not restricted by a manor lord. The formation of guilds even began to give the artisans some collective power to wrest favorable tax terms and political recognition from the local lords. Indeed, this power was in part due to the very freedom of mobility that the artisans and merchants enjoyed—if a lord did not give them favorable terms, they could threaten to leave to establish themselves (and all the associated benefits of their presence) in another town.[32] This level of self-direction evidently exceeded that of the peasant, but despite the safeguards offered by the church, the artisan's self-direction was also enjoyed with a lesser degree of certainty. Unlike the peasant, the artisan did not possess an inalienable claim to his means of production nor to his place as a supplier of goods. The damage to an artisan's tools through flood or fire, or an illness that kept him from work for a significant amount of time, for example, could end his ability to practice his craft. From the thirteenth through the sixteenth centuries, however, social agreements such as the formation of guilds helped to attenuate some of this uncertainty.[33] In either case, to the extent that natural equity means

---

32. Tierney and Painter, *Western Europe in the Middle Ages*, 276–82.

33. This stability was once again thrown into upheaval with the processes of enclosure and the establishment of capitalism, which involved the steady removal of political protection of the guilds from competition and the creation of both an urban and rural proletariat. Over the course of three centuries (seventeenth to nineteenth), the safeguards of the old world (claims to the land or the protection of guilds) were abrogated, leading to the tumultuous nineteenth century and the slow establishment of new regimes of labor in order to recover and protect a new set of safeguards in a new system. See Tierney, *Medieval Poor Law*, 112–14; Robert Heilbroner, *The Worldly Philosophers: The Lives, Times, and Ideas of the Great Economic Thinkers*, 7th ed. (New York: Simon & Schuster, 1999), chap. 1. Since the late twentieth century, the globalization of capital has created another shift in societal and economic conditions and raised questions of how to safeguard what we might call here natural equity. On labor and globalization, see Brian Langille, "General Reflections on the Relationship of Trade and Labour," in *Fair Trade and Harmonization*, vol. 2, *Legal Analysis*, ed. Jagdish N. Bhagwati and Robert E. Hudec (Cambridge, MA: MIT Press, 1996); Joseph Stiglitz, *Globalization and Its Discontents Revisited: Anti-Globalization in the Era of Trump* (New York: Norton, 2017), esp. part 1. A recent approach that finds a positive correlation between globalization and labor conditions is Robert J. Flanagan, *Globalization and Labor*

open access to the things one needs for a life of self-direction, both of these systems, the feudal and the commercial, can be understood in light of trade-offs for the preservation and guarantee of some degree of access through the very curtailment of open access. Not only can these systems be understood through reference to natural equity and the power of self-direction, they also can be evaluated and compared by reference to such principles, so that, though various property regimes might all be legitimate, one might be preferable in terms of its ability to achieve principles of justice and other important moral and societal goods.

Despite being understood partially in reference to natural equity, however, these laws can also only be fully comprehended in terms of the free judgment of a society to pursue certain ways of life and forgo others. In chapter 1 I noted how the usefulness of property for the pursuit of this or that good means that property could only be understood in terms of its usefulness for the pursuit of more basic moral and political ends and other sets of societal values. Property does not have its own end; its ends are set by the natural law and the judgment of society. But this is just to say that in the departure from, in this case, natural equity to civic equity, we witness not just the limits and logic of the natural law in the establishment of diverse regimes of property, but also the will of the community to pursue this or that set of values or societal ends. This is a dynamism that, on the one hand, shows that the conventionality of property is always tied to the natural law. But in this conventionality a horizon of freedom also opens for society, in which through the determination of conventions it is free to pursue distinctive forms of life.

As the example of natural equity shows, property is both called forth by and bound to natural principles to the extent that its legitimacy depends on fostering and protecting those principles in situations where they would otherwise be severely undermined. On the other hand, to the extent that the manner and mode of the protection of those natural principles are indeterminate, society must draw on other stores of value and judgment in order to decide its manner of fostering those natural principles. And this means that society will aim through or beyond these natural principles in the establishment of property regimes. Property is thus a twofold expression of the political nature of the human. On the one hand, it is proper to the political nature of humans that their relations be equitable. On the other hand, it is proper to the political nature of humans that they choose and pursue diverse forms of societal organization and

---

Conditions: Working Conditions and Worker Rights in a Global Economy (Oxford: Oxford University Press, 2006).

life. This further connects to the substantive meaning of common dominion as a common power of self-direction. Natural equity means things are available for the exercise of self-direction, while civic equity means that limits are placed upon that availability for two reasons. The first is that the lack of conventions will threaten some individuals' abilities to exercise this self-directedness; the second is that the conventions themselves can augment the individual's flourishing by coordinating and giving expression to the aspirations of the political society of which she is a part.[34] Natural equity insists that civic equity prioritize access for each individual, but natural equity also warrants the structuring and limitation of that access for the sake of social and political life.

Natural Equality and Material Inequality

With such a full discussion of equity, less needs to be said about the role of equality in scholastic reflections on property. Equality and equity function similarly in the framework of common dominion and legitimate property regimes. Indeed, equity might best be articulated as one instantiation of the principle of equality: equality before the law. The fairness in legal and political processes that defines equity takes its ground in the more basic conviction of the natural equality of all persons. If conventions introduce a rigor contrary to natural equity, the resultant civic equity must at least ensure that each individual is treated the same under the same law and that no law target individuals in a way that violates the honor due to each person as a result of his claim to equality with each other person. This is necessary for civil law to uphold the *equity* of civic equity.

That said, the meaning of equality is not restricted to equality before the law, and the question of property presents two significant reasons to explore the role of this principle in scholastic reflection. First, a distinctive issue in the morality of property is whether material inequality is tolerable, which depends to some extent on the meaning of equality in the natural law of common dominion and the expression of that equality in distinct regimes of property. Second, in contemporary political philosophy (especially that concerned with wealth and property), equality plays a central and disputed role. A deeper understanding of the role of equality in scholastic thought offers a concrete point of intersection with contemporary political philosophy, suggesting areas

---

34. On the link between the values of a community and individual freedom and flourishing, see Jean Porter, *Ministers of the Law: A Natural Law Theory of Legal Authority* (Grand Rapids: Eerdmans, 2010), 150–66.

of convergence and divergence and perhaps an opportunity to analyze some of the convictions and disputes of contemporary political philosophy through the lens of scholastic thought.

The kind of equality at stake in Aquinas's framework of common dominion is natural equality—the equal moral regard due to each person. But what is the relation of natural equality to material equality? Aquinas has little to say about equality at all in a state of common possession: the state of common possession is simply of nature because nature did not introduce the contrary, not because nature inclines humans to the pursuit of such a state. It seems reasonable to presuppose a state of material equality in a state of common possession, though for Aquinas this has as little normative significance (which is to say none) as the state of common possession itself. From the ancient and patristic sources for whom natural equality was also a central and normative principle we can infer a state of material equality in the Golden Age. For Seneca, "the boundaries of nature lay open to all, for men's indiscriminate use."[35] Accompanying Golden Age thinking is the idea that prior to cordoning off parcels of land and things of the earth, the earth was more bountiful and its harvests more abundant. Still, in the Stoics and the church father closest to their thought, Ambrose, the discussion of material equality can only be inferred from their thought on a primordial Golden Age of common possession. The focal point is less equality than the openness of the earth for the use and sustenance of all. And this is very similar to the canonists—in the Golden Age, the equality that counts vis-à-vis the earth and the things of the earth is equality of access. If material equality is presupposed and of any concern, it is most certainly secondary to equality of access.

Nonetheless, there are a number of reasons why a regime of open access would presuppose something like material equality. Beyond the rather obvious fact that no one could claim ownership of anything (the typical measure of wealth), the attribution of wealth-value to things is largely predicated on their division. Not only could no one claim a set of resources, and thus some amount of wealth-value, as her own, no wealth-value would attach to things to tally up their societal worth anyway. There could be no wealth, as commodities or as resources convertible to money, since wealth as a measure of value depends on the right of exclusion and the creation of scarcity.[36] The economic historian and theorist Robert Heilbroner is worth quoting at length on this point:

---

35. Seneca, Letter 90, cited in Peter Garnsey, *Thinking about Property: From Antiquity to the Age of Revolution* (Cambridge: Cambridge University Press, 2007), 124.

36. Francisco Suárez, a defender of the possibility of property in the state of innocence,

Wealth is therefore a social category inseparable from power. In simple egalitarian societies, where all have access to the resources needed for the maintenance of a conventional way of life, wealth cannot exist, although prestige objects can. Per contra, wealth can only come into existence when the right of access of all members of society to an independent livelihood no longer prevails, so that control over this access becomes of life-giving importance. The corollary is that wealth cannot exist unless there also exists a condition of scarcity—not insufficiency of resources themselves, but insufficiency of means of access to resources. As Adam Smith put it, "Wherever there is great property, there is great inequality. For one very rich man, there must be at least five hundred poor, and the affluence of the rich supposes the indigence of the many."[37]

In chapter 1, we saw Basil, Ambrose, and Chrysostom claiming that rich and poor are created by the very institution of property itself. Their point should not simply be reduced to a rhetorical flourish. It is key, however, that none of them saw inequality as a problem that obviates the value of property—for each of these thinkers, property remains a legitimate and useful institution in the present state of sin. However, for these and other patristic theologians, while any primordial material equality may be deviated from, some access to what is necessary for life must always be preserved. In both patristic and scholastic discourse, the focus in the state of innocence is not on material equality per se, despite its necessary and *de facto* presupposition in a state of open access, but on that open access itself.

---

makes a thought-provoking comment that connects with this point. He writes that in the state of innocence, property would count as nothing, so that while one can posit the existence of property in the state of innocence, one really can have no certainty about its nature and significance. Francisco Suárez, "On the Work of Six Days: Book 5, on the State That Wayfarers Would Have Had in This World If the First Parents Did Not Sin; Chapter 7, What Kind of Corporeal or Political Life Men Would Have Professed in the State of Innocence," trans. Matthew T. Gaetano, *Journal of Markets and Morality* 15, no. 2 (2012): 560. The point is plausible, and it opens the door for thinking about how property could be introduced in a state of innocence without, in fact, material or resource inequality. If property is counted as nothing, it has no wealth-value and, lacking wealth-value, provides no way of tallying up relative inequality in terms of the diverse levels of possessions of different groups and individuals. This, of course, resonates with a certain intuition regarding the nature of the state of innocence, which is that none would lack access to the resources needed to sustain her own flourishing nor exert the sort of dominance over others that wealth and status afford.

37. Robert Heilbroner, *The Nature and Logic of Capitalism* (New York: Norton, 1985), 45–46.

Aquinas elsewhere discusses accidental inequalities that further suggest material equality would not have been a principle of direct concern for him. In several questions on the state of innocence, Aquinas asks whether one human would have been master over another in that state.[38] He answers in the affirmative. With respect to inequality among humans, he writes that there would have been natural differences in terms of age, righteousness, knowledge, and body. Such diversity, however, is a necessary part of establishing an order that can better show forth the goodness and beauty that creation is meant to reflect of the Creator.[39] This is, indeed, a part of the reason that in the state of innocence one human would have been ruler over others, in the sense of a political authority proper to free persons. Given that humans naturally live in society and that society needs some authority to direct the activities of diverse individuals toward the common good, political authority is a natural occurrence, even in the state of innocence. Secondly, the diverse gifts of humans in mind and body are most fitting when they are used for the benefit of others, one way in which inequality can manifest beauty and goodness. But one way of manifesting this providential use of one's gifts is to command, Aquinas quotes Augustine, "not by the lust for dominating, but by the service of offering counsel."[40] Though Aquinas does not discuss material inequality specifically, it is clear how one could extrapolate from the usefulness and goodness of inequality in general to the usefulness and goodness of certain levels of material inequality, which might better manifest order and beauty in humans' providential ordering of the material world. So, for example, the wealth of those who choose to cultivate fields could provide for the needs of those who dedicate their lives to the contemplation and preaching of the divine mysteries.[41]

Contemporary thought on material inequality largely corresponds to the approach seen in scholastic thought, where inequality is less of a concern than

---

38. *ST* I 96.3–4.

39. See also Thomas Aquinas, *Summa contra Gentiles, Book 2: Creation*, trans. James F. Anderson (Notre Dame: University of Notre Dame Press, 1975), chap. 45 (pp. 136–39).

40. Aquinas, *ST* I 96.4.

41. This is a Thomistic way of framing something that might resonate with a Rawlsian approach. Rawls admits of inequality for the sake of raising the standard of living of all members of society, and thus implements his difference principle precisely for ensuring that the only acceptable increase in inequality is one that makes the least advantaged better off. Rawls would have no doubt found any idea of a providential social order in Aquinas, in which persons appear destined for certain roles in society, objectionable. Nonetheless, both Rawls and Aquinas recognize the division of labor and disparities in wealth as potentially conducive not simply to the greatest good but to each individual's good. See John Rawls, *A Theory of Justice* (Cambridge, MA: Harvard University Press, 1971), 60–75.

CHAPTER THREE

sufficiency and the negative effects that certain levels of inequality might have on individual and societal well-being. Two powerful and recent statements of this position come in the thought of Harry Frankfurt and Thomas Scanlon. Frankfurt lays out an intentionally provocative thesis: that the fact of wealth inequality is morally neutral and contemporary society's focus on it is detrimental to its own well-being. What ought to concern society, Frankfurt argues, is that everyone be able to attain an adequate level of *sufficiency*, by which he means the material resources necessary to lead not simply a subsisting but a good life, based on reasonable expectations in any given society. Though he emphasizes the primacy of the principle of sufficiency and the moral neutrality of wealth inequality in what we might call economic ethics, Frankfurt does note that wealth inequality can have morally deleterious side effects, such as political disempowerment for those who have little, that warrant it being the direct attention of social ethics.[42]

This is a point on which Scanlon elaborates, who also thinks that in the abstract wealth inequality itself is not morally objectionable. Scanlon lists six potential results of inequality (especially great levels of inequality) that render inequality an object of moral concern: that those with less would be regarded as essentially inferior and less worthy of respect; that those with more would have "an unacceptable degree of control over the lives of others";[43] that it would lead to dramatically different opportunities between children whose families have more and those who have less; that the influence of wealth in many aspects of political life and institutions would undermine the fairness of political institutions; that political authority would show different levels of concern to some rather than others; and that dramatic enough levels of inequality would perpetuate further inequality by granting those with certain social roles the power to divert more rewards to those social roles than others (what Scanlon calls unfairness in distribution of income).[44]

Kate Ward's work presents a challenge to these contemporary philosophical approaches to inequality. Material inequality is a concern not simply because

---

42. Harry G. Frankfurt, *On Inequality* (Princeton: Princeton University Press, 2015).

43. On this point Scanlon writes in more detail: "If, for example, a small number of people control almost all of the wealth in a society, this can give them an unacceptable degree of control over where and how others can work, what is available for them to buy, and in general what their lives will be like." T. M. Scanlon, *Why Does Inequality Matter?* (Oxford: Oxford University Press, 2018), 5–6. The point is corroborated by Heilbroner, who describes the power of the capitalist as just this kind of noncoercive domination in *Nature and Logic of Capitalism*, 40.

44. Scanlon briefly discusses each of these in the introduction. See *Why Does Inequality Matter?*, 4–9.

of the possibility of unsettling imbalances of social and political power, but because of the morally deleterious effects inequality, especially the kind of stark inequality in the United States today, has on every person.[45] In conversation with contemporary virtue and womanist thought, Ward notes the effects that poverty can have not just in impeding the pursuit of virtue but also in burdening the possession of virtues so that, even when achieved by the poor, they are incomplete expressions of the virtues due to the social and economic exigencies of poverty.[46] More challenging to liberal political philosophy, Ward argues that any amount of wealth can instill the kind of callousness and entitlement contrary to the virtues that a democratic and free society, as well as the Christian tradition from which Ward writes, espouses as part of a good life.[47] Ward's focus on the achievement of virtue suggests a greater affinity with the perfectionist political philosophy of Joseph Raz, for example, than Frankfurt or Scanlon. Nonetheless, the juxtaposition between Frankfurt and Scanlon, on the one hand, and Ward on the other helpfully shows how diverse interpretations of the principles of property (like equality) can lead to diverse sets of property laws, which can focus either on inequality indirectly by addressing its effects or on inequality directly through, for example, a much more aggressive taxation of upper incomes, inheritance, and capital gains.[48]

Not every contemporary philosopher sees equality in these terms. Ronald Dworkin begins his political philosophy with the claim that the legitimacy of a government depends on its showing equal concern to each member of the political community and that this equal political concern is best achieved through equality of resources.[49] While Dworkin is ultimately concerned about the same moral issues as Frankfurt and Scanlon (especially discrepancies in political power and access to what is necessary for sufficiency), he argues that the most effective and principled way to address the negative effects of inequality is to

---

45. Additionally, Ward documents studies that argue for not just correlation but also causation between inequality and increasing social, epidemiological, and economic ills. Kate Ward, *Wealth, Virtue, and Moral Luck: Christian Ethics in an Age of Inequality* (Washington, DC: Georgetown University Press, 2021), 15–29.

46. Ward compares the philosophical tradition on moral luck and burdened virtue with womanist thought in *Wealth, Virtue, and Moral Luck*, 94–99 and 105–10.

47. Ward only distinguishes between "enough" and "not enough," but it seems to me the Christian tradition more commonly distinguishes, as David Cloutier does in his contemporary analysis of these distinctions, between "not enough," "enough" (decency/comfort), and "more than enough" (riches/luxury). Cloutier, *Vice of Luxury*, chap. 7.

48. Ward, *Wealth, Virtue, and Moral Luck*, 214–17.

49. Ronald Dworkin, *Sovereign Virtue: The Theory and Practice of Equality* (Cambridge, MA: Harvard University Press, 2000).

address that inequality itself. So, for example, rather than introduce legislation to limit campaign contributions, Dworkin thinks (at least in theory) that the problem tackled by such legislation can be resolved through mechanisms that ensure that each person has equal access to the same amount of resources.

Dworkin provides another contemporary example of a philosophy that clearly employs the conventionality of property. In Dworkin's theory, property is distributed by political authority for the sake of upholding the principle of equal concern through the equal distribution of resources. Further, Dworkin thinks that equality of resources is the primary vehicle through which the principle of equal concern ought to be instantiated—this sort of material equality is itself an object of moral concern. But in arguing for equality of resources, Dworkin does not argue for wealth equality as an end-state distribution. His claim is rather that government ought to institute redistributive programs that approximate the kinds of institutions that would develop in an idealized society of rationally self-interested persons who each begin with equal resources. Some might choose to use these resources to fund a leisurely life and others an industrious life, and so the distribution patterns in society will lead to wealth inequality. So long as society insures against the kind of deprivations that rationally self-interested individuals would insure against, it can be said to fulfill the demands of equality of resources even though inequality exists. Dworkin's argument provides some nuance regarding the moral importance of material equality, even while confirming that it is not end-state or patterned distributions within society but rather issues of equal consideration and sufficiency that are direct objects of moral concern. The full power of Dworkin's proposal can only be understood with reference to its potential to satisfy the ubiquitous concern for sufficiency, though, and I return to Dworkin after discussing subsistence, sufficiency, and rights of extreme necessity.

Subsistence and Sufficiency

Though the scholastics and contemporary philosophers exhibit a similar pattern of concern, which focuses less on end-state material equality and more on ameliorating the negative effects of inequality, they seem to differ in the way they describe what is due to each individual with respect to his access to material goods. In contrast to the contemporary language of sufficiency, enough to lead a good or decent life, the scholastics establish the apparently more austere measure of subsistence as what is due to each person. What should one make of the distinction between *subsistence* in scholastic sources and *sufficiency* in

The Principles of Property

contemporary sources? While the idea of subsistence might seem to differ from the way Frankfurt discusses sufficiency, Tierney's analysis in *Medieval Poor Laws* helps to show that in a feudal society, the condition of sufficiency was nearly equivalent to the condition of subsistence in terms of general expectations for peasant life. Societal life largely followed the agricultural cycle, and standards of living tracked agricultural subsistence. In a feudal society, the limits of sufficiency track not only the social but also economic organization and technological availability, which correspond significantly with the condition of subsistence.[50] For the medieval peasant, sufficiency is subsistence (with an attached set of rights to rest also defended by the church).

The comparison between sufficiency and subsistence gains clarity by putting what is at stake not in terms of material possessions, but in terms of having access to what is necessary to exercise one's powers of self-direction. The state of common possession ensures open access to the resources and things necessary to embodied and self-directed action in the world in accordance with natural equity and equality. In property regimes, curtailed access to these resources must still allow at least some acceptable level of self-directedness in the context of the society in which the regime exists. That is, the principles of natural equity and equality, and their implications for what is due each person in terms of exercising powers of self-direction, place limits on the amount one's self-directedness can be curtailed through the establishment of property and the concomitant restriction of access to material resources.

These limits, however, are always determined in part by the prevailing social, economic, and technological context. Subsistence is a quite permissive limit on how far one's self-directedness can be constricted, but in the twelfth and thirteenth centuries, it tracked the limits of social, economic, and technological organization that offered few prospects for a life beyond subsistence. Today, the moral limits on how far one's self-directedness can be curtailed are stricter and require, among other things, access to education, health care, and the internet.[51] This is certainly (and thankfully) more than subsistence, but when placed in a wider context of social and economic possibilities and expectations, subsistence looks to be just the specification of sufficiency in the twelfth and thirteenth centuries.

If the rough equivalency between subsistence and sufficiency holds, then what are the implications for the scholastic right of subsistence today? If up

---

50. Tierney, *Medieval Poor Law*, 22–23.
51. This is, at least, how philosophers like Frankfurt and Mathias Risse construe sufficiency, which I believe is correct.

to the fourteenth century the idea of sufficiency could be adequately captured by subsistence, can one make an argument today that there is a more general right of sufficiency that tracks the powers associated with the medieval right of subsistence? Could an individual who did not have "enough" to lead a satisfactory life simply take from what he deemed to be the surplus of a neighbor (or a big box store) who, on his reckoning, had more than enough?

At first glance we might be inclined to think there is something especially compelling about subsistence that distinguishes it from sufficiency, and that if the two happened to overlap in the medieval era they have since come apart and the same claim rights (to a neighbor's surplus) and immunity rights (from prosecution for taking that surplus) do not apply to sufficiency as they might to subsistence. While it is true that, for instance, in the contemporary United States there seems to be no feasible way of attaching such powers to a right of sufficiency, it need not be simply because the moral significance of sufficiency is less exigent than subsistence. Though that certainly seems to be the case, the apparent moral divide between subsistence and sufficiency might be fairly narrow: access to the internet, health care, and mobile communication are all essential in societies like the United States to securing basic needs.

However, the rights of subsistence were also enforced in a low-mobility, small-scale, and economically limited society where social expectations and what counts as "enough" were relatively well defined. In a mobile, large, and wealthy (though dramatically unequal) society like the United States, the enforcement of rights of sufficiency would be almost impossible to adjudicate. If legitimate claims to the possession of a phone (or access to the internet, health care, or childcare products like diapers) were to be exercised by simple taking, courts and investigators would be overwhelmed trying to determine what was taken out of legitimate need to maintain sufficiency and what was taken for whatever other reason.[52] It seems plausible, then, that though there may be moral differences between stealing bread because one is starving and stealing a phone to secure a job, those differences are less significant than the logistical challenges to rights of sufficiency in the United States today. There may be a case for such rights, but we lack either a feasible way of instituting them (a technical problem), a political or cultural will to do so (a moral problem), or both. Indeed, simply reasserting the same solutions (e.g., a right of taking) to problems of sufficiency that twelfth- and thirteenth-century canon-

---

52. Programs like this have been tried at the district level. Catherine Marfin, "Texas Prosecutors Want to Keep Low-Level Criminals out of Overcrowded Jails. Top Republicans and Police Aren't Happy," *Texas Tribune*, May 21, 2019, https://tinyurl.com/49znvc4m.

ists developed is what led to the obsolescence of canon law in poor law in the fourteenth and fifteenth centuries and, as this analysis suggests, would lead to similar irrelevance today.[53] A concern for sufficiency means thinking of creative ways to satisfy it beyond mere rights of taking that seem in multiple ways unrealistic in contemporary society.

From both a technical and moral perspective, Dworkin's thought presents a compelling way of addressing the issue of sufficiency through equality. "Equality of resources" utilizes political instruments of distribution to try to minimize and preempt the dire need that would drive one to exercise a right of sufficiency, much as the charitable instruments of the church and the social support among peasants of the same manor were intended to do under feudalism. It does so through a formal principle: if everyone (in principle) has access to the same amount of resources, sufficiency is essentially guaranteed, at least in an idealized society. In real societies, universal sufficiency would be approximated through the development of institutions according to this formal principle. This is for two related reasons, but it is worth explicating them separately. First, and more obviously, equal access to resources means forestalling the objective insufficiency that occurs in countries like the United States today. Second, and related to this, since sufficiency is a relative term, equal access to resources would establish clear and reasonable expectations for what counts as "enough" in a society. In a highly stratified society, in which access to resources is dramatically unequal, not only do many have significantly less than a few, but what the many can reasonably expect is skewed by the excessive capture of resources by the few. A recent, thorough analysis by David Cloutier, for example, shows that the problem is not finding reasonable and objective barometers of sufficiency in contemporary society (which in absolute terms *has* made sufficiency more widely available than prior eras), but that the stratification of contemporary society distorts the subjective perception of sufficiency and, in fact, can conceal just how many individuals have attained well more than sufficiency.[54]

In absolute and relative terms, equality of resources makes the attainment of sufficiency much more certain. In the real world, there will still be instances of need, though far fewer than in the contemporary United States, and perhaps at such a level that in fact something like rights of sufficiency could be exercised without logistically overwhelming the legal system. This is an issue

---

53. Tierney, *Medieval Poor Law*, chap. 6.
54. David Cloutier, *The Vice of Luxury: Economic Excess in a Consumer Age* (Washington, DC: Georgetown University Press, 2015), chap. 6, esp. 194–204.

whose resolution remains beyond the scope of this section, but it is enough to note at this point that bringing together this area of scholastic thought with contemporary political philosophy prompts some discussion about the morality and feasibility of rights of sufficiency along with (*pace* Frankfurt) the intrinsic relationship between equality and sufficiency.[55]

Less theoretically, Catholic social thinkers have been sketching policy proposals for sufficiency that presuppose the idea that property is instrumental to human flourishing. Some proposals, indeed, may reflect the kinds of institutions that a society that takes equality of resources seriously would devise. Recently, Christine Hinze has sketched a proposal for what she calls radical sufficiency, taking inspiration from early twentieth-century Catholic social thinker John Ryan, and aiming at what one might call a decent or flourishing life for all, which for Hinze, as with the above thinkers, does not require strict material equality.[56] Her argument draws attention to dynamics of race, gender, and class, the latter a category that has fallen out of use in Catholic social teaching and liberal political philosophy, for both defining sufficiency and analyzing problems of insufficiency. While her proposals regarding economic policy, labor law, and social services all deserve close attention, what I want to highlight here is how Hinze's approach, alongside Dworkin's and Murphy's and Nagel's, presupposes that the material order is in the service of the principle of sufficiency, and then asks what that means for economic policy, labor law, social services, and, implicit to many of those proposals, property itself. Property, in this case, becomes intelligible in part because of a desire to ensure the establishment of sufficiency as a principle of justice.

While the scholastic position tracks much contemporary social ethics in the insistence on subsistence or sufficiency over strict material equality, the twelfth- and thirteenth-century canonists and theologians also converge with contemporary scholars like Dworkin, Hinze, Scanlon, and Ward on how inequality itself can cause other morally problematic outcomes within a society. One of the secondary effects of material inequality that preoccupies scholastic thinkers is the differences in social standing and power that such inequality introduces into society. This concern is apparent as early as the twelfth century in Gratian's *Decretum*, and in the solicitousness the canonists show for securing extensive privileges for the poor in ecclesiastical courts. By the fourteenth century, the Franciscans adopt this concern as central to their theological and social

---

55. Frankfurt denies any connection between sufficiency and equality—for Frankfurt, what is "enough" can and ought to be defined independent of one's neighbors.

56. Christine Firer Hinze, *Radical Sufficiency: Work, Livelihood, and a US Catholic Economic Ethic* (Washington, DC: Georgetown University Press, 2021).

thought and practice. This concern, though, is best discussed not in the context of equality or sufficiency but in the context of the principle of liberty.

Use and the Meaning of Liberty

The principle at the foundation of the scholastic approach to common dominion is liberty: the power of self-direction. The scholastic discussion of *dominium* over oneself and *dominium* over external things, a relationship that a Thomistic account shows is in some sense coextensive or at least integral, intersects with questions about freedom, noncoercion, and autonomy in capitalist societies today. It is the medieval mendicants—the Dominicans and Franciscans—who explicate the relationship between these two modes of dominion: dominion over oneself manifests itself in dominion over external things, while the curtailment of dominion over external things correspondingly constricts one's powers of self-direction. The implicit claim in this discourse is that though a person may always retain the free exercise of her will, a theoretical conception of freedom of the will can never be divorced from the practical ability to exercise one's will through the use of external things. I first recount scholastic discussions of liberty, related to both self-dominion *and* dominion over material resources. I show how this intersects with a discussion about the insufficiency of noncoercion as a standard of liberty in G. A. Cohen, and how Cohen's account of autonomy construed as both noncoercion and access to material goods resonates with scholastic discourse. I conclude this section by documenting how the canonists responded concretely to the relationship between poverty and powerlessness in their crafting and interpretation of canon law.

The basic claim in the Thomistic account of common dominion is perhaps uncontroversial, but at the same time it is a truth that does not receive a great deal of explicit attention. Humans act by using the material things of the world. Not every act requires material things, but the very power to act in the first place requires the use of external goods. One can dedicate oneself to a life of contemplation, but only after one has eaten, slept, and had the time and space to observe the world and digest one's observations. As Aquinas notes in his defense of poverty, though a life with few wants and minimal needs is conducive to a life of contemplation, it is also important that one can be relatively carefree about securing these wants and needs, as the mendicant orders generally are.[57]

---

57. Thomas Aquinas, *Summa contra Gentiles, Book 3: Providence Part II*, trans. Vernon J. Bourke (Notre Dame: University of Notre Dame Press, 1975), 133.4 (pp. 178–79).

So, humans act by using the things of the world, but, at least in a Thomistic framework, humans also determine themselves through their actions—that is, by and through the use of external things. To be free to determine oneself through action, one must be able to use the material resources of the world.

Unlike the state of common possession, which is, as it were, the paradigmatic state of the natural law of common dominion, the scholastics do not describe a "state" of perfect liberty, free of any obligations or responsibilities. Rather, they define the one freedom of the natural law in contrast to the servile conventions of their society. Certainly it is in contrast to any institution of perpetual slavery (which had mostly disappeared by the tenth century), but also to the servile obligations of the manorial system.[58] The natural freedom that we ought to associate with a state of common possession, then, is not complete detachment from the responsibilities and obligations that pertain between individuals on account of their equal status, within families, and toward the other members of society. It is rather the freedom to determine oneself through the exercise of reason and will within the parameters of an orderly and decent society. And this corresponds quite closely with the Thomistic account of common dominion, in that the use of the things of the world for one's own advantage is intrinsically bound to considerations of justice and the common good, as each of these is a part of the good of the individual.

The basic notion of freedom is the freedom to direct one's actions through the use of reason and will to one's own advantage, and not in service to burdensome feudal or manorial obligations. Again, the contrast between servitude and freedom corresponds to Thomas's account of dominion over one's actions. Humans are free when they direct their actions to freely chosen ends; they are correspondingly less free when their actions must be directed toward ends that are not freely chosen, especially ends that correspond to the good of another, such as the manor lord. Servile obligations still allow space for freely chosen actions, such as the freedom of marriage guaranteed in medieval law, and Thomas denies that the full scope of the action of even a human bound in perpetual slavery is entirely devoted to the ends of his master.[59] For Aquinas

---

58. Weigand, *Die Naturrechtslehre*, pp. 259–82.

59. Antonia Bocarius Sahaydachny, "The Marriage of Unfree Persons: Twelfth Century Decretals and Letters," in *De Iure Canonico Medii Aevi: Festschrift für Rudolf Weigand*, ed. Peter Landau, Studia Gratiana 27 (Rome: Libreria Ateneo Salesiano, 1996), 483–506. Jean Porter summarizes this feature of Aquinas's discussion of slavery in *Justice as a Virtue: A Thomistic Perspective* (Grand Rapids: Eerdmans, 2016), 129.

and the canonists, there is a basic freedom of will that remains even in the most degrading of human conditions.

Even this basic freedom of will, though, exists on a continuum in which, in the Middle Ages, two variables are vital: office or status and access to resources. Liberty is directly correlated with both of these variables. The exemplar of freedom is the person whose actions are entirely his own, which in the Middle Ages corresponded to the feudal lords who could, through their control of property (in the form of land and fortifications), marshal the largest retinue and command the greatest feudal and manorial obligations.⁶⁰ The antithesis of freedom is the person whose actions are least his own, which at this time corresponded to the peasants who controlled few resources and were widely subject to manorial obligations. Self-direction can never fully be eliminated, but it can, as both the canonists and civilians put it, be covered over or obscured by conditions of servitude.⁶¹ On this account, manumission is tantamount to the rediscovery or uncovering of the freedom one possesses by natural law.

The relationship between self-direction and use raises questions about the relationship of metaphysical freedom, or freedom of the will, and freedom to use material resources (or the degree and extent of control one has over external things). The Mendicants, though, make little of this distinction. Their theology seems rather to highlight and emphasize the connection and not the distinction between these freedoms.⁶² In his tract *De perfectione spiritualis vitae*, Aquinas connects the relinquishment of external goods and the relinquishment of oneself (and, correspondingly, one's liberty). The "liberty of one's

---

60. T. N. Bisson describes the "quest for status" in feudal society in this way: knights and nobles "needed servants, dependents, suppliants; needed to dominate proprietorially." See T. N. Bisson, "The 'Feudal Revolution,'" *Past & Present* 142, no. 1 (February 1994): 18–19. Wendy Davis and Paul Fouracre note that power in the early Middle Ages did not entirely reduce to land, but was a function of both land and office. In this case, *dominium* aptly describes both the *de iure* power of one's office and the *de facto* power of control of land and bodies. Wendy Davis and Paul Fouracre, eds., *Property and Power in the Early Middle Ages* (Cambridge: Cambridge University Press, 1995), 245.

61. Weigand, *Die Naturrechtslehre*, pp. 280–82.

62. As Annabel Brett notes, the division between the Dominican and Franciscan orders on the theological significance of poverty and the legitimacy of property is not broached until the fourteenth century. On more general reflections on the legitimacy of mendicant poverty and its relationship to the relinquishment of *dominium*, the orders have a common cause until the end of the thirteenth century. Annabel S. Brett, *Liberty, Right, and Nature: Individual Rights in Later Scholastic Thought* (Cambridge: Cambridge University Press, 1997), 11n3.

own will" is among the highest desires of a human. It is by such liberty that the human "is a human and *dominus* over other things, by this that one can use and enjoy them, by this even that one masters one's own actions."[63] The relinquishment of *dominium* of self to God entails also the relinquishment of the *dominium* of external objects.

The Franciscans take the relinquishment of external objects to its most acute form: they do not possess (let alone own) the alms they receive. Recall that in the classical and medieval understanding, possession can be understood as a power of use that lacks the rights of ownership. But, as we saw above, use in its fullest sense is the external manifestation of *dominium*, the ordering of the things of the world to one's freely chosen ends through one's reason and will. The Franciscan relinquishment of such possession is grounded in the idea that those who give them alms also decide the use of those alms. The lesser friar receives food and eats it because the one who gives him the food intends that to be its use, likewise with clothing and housing.[64] Thus, Pecham writes, the Franciscan friar cannot receive the *dominium* of external objects (in this case, money), "so that it is subject to the full power of the brother, so that he may use it fully and at whim."[65] The clearest sign of the relinquishment of one's own liberty (for the sake of Christ) is the relinquishment of the power to use and direct external objects toward one's own end. The medieval mendicants clarify and sharpen the full relationship between *dominium* of one's own actions and *dominium* over external objects: the latter is not only an extension of the former, but the former also depends on the latter. Each is a necessary condition of the other.

The question about the relationship between liberty and the freedom to use external things manifests itself in contemporary political philosophy in the language of self-ownership, and a brief examination of one approach to the question might clarify the issues at stake. Most of the discussion around this takes place in the Lockean language of self-ownership, which in its own way parallels and

---

63. Cited in Brett, *Liberty, Right, and Nature*, 14.

64. Hence the contentions in the Franciscan order about the reception of money, the use of which is indeterminate and seems to call forth some exercise of prudential judgment on the part of the friar, and the subsequent institution in the thirteenth century of the procurator, who can receive and deploy monetary donations on behalf of the friars. See Gregory IX's discussion of procurators in section V of *Quo Elongati* (1230), in *Francis of Assisi: Early Documents*, vol. 1, *The Saint*, ed. Regis Armstrong, J. Wayne Hellmann, and William J. Short, 3 vols. (Hyde Park, NY: New City, 1999), 570–75.

65. Cited in Brett, *Liberty, Right, and Nature*, 17. The thirteenth-century controversy that set the Franciscan order in disarray had to do with just this question of the poor use of alms. See chapter 1, note 75.

diverges from medieval understandings of self-dominion. Much as the scholastic theologians and canonists understood dominion over external things to be grounded in self-dominion, the Lockean theory of property establishes ownership on the idea of self-ownership—ownership of one's own actions and person. And like the scholastic account of *dominium*, the ideal of self-ownership is generally construed as the ground of freedom: one owns one's own actions and so exercises a sort of power of exclusion over them. No one can force someone to do something that she does not want to do, which is just what the power of exclusion over one's own actions constitutes. The freedom of self-ownership is a negative freedom, a freedom from coercion and not a freedom to act in a certain way. Since *dominium* over one's own actions is the ground of *dominium* of external things, and since self-ownership is the ground of ownership, one question that suggests itself is whether ownership and self-ownership are also in a reciprocal relationship, whether ownership is also necessary for self-ownership, as *dominium* of external things is necessary for *dominium* over oneself.

One way of construing the libertarian account is by arguing that the freedom self-ownership entails is sufficiently secured by the absence of coercion. On this account, the property-less worker exercises the same self-ownership as the owner of productive goods. This is G. A. Cohen's way of construing Nozick's arguments in *Anarchy, State, and Utopia*.[66] This, however, only seems to make sense if one considers active coercion. No one may threaten with force a worker to take this or that job at this or that wage, but in a job market in which the owners have sufficient power and the workers few enough protections, hunger is enough to drive the worker to take perhaps an undesirable job for an insufficient wage. If this sense of self-ownership constitutes a power of exclusion over others directing one's actions, it is only in a very formal and thin sense.

Cohen's full engagement with Nozick is problematic but illuminative for illustrating the relationship between freedom of the will (as self-ownership) and access to external goods.[67] Cohen suggests that we consider a two-person world (person A and person B), in which A appropriates all and offers B the opportunity to labor on A's appropriated goods. A does not explicitly coerce, by manipulation, force, or threat of force, so in the very formal sense described above, B's self-ownership is not violated. Cohen's point is, nonetheless, the scope of free action and the free exercise of B's will is severely curtailed, so that it is hard to think of B as being free in any substantive sense precisely because

---

66. G. A. Cohen, *Self-Ownership, Freedom, and Equality* (Cambridge: Cambridge University Press, 1995), 80. For his arguments on autonomy and self-ownership, see 101–2 and 236–38.
67. Cohen, *Self-Ownership, Freedom, and Equality*, 67–102.

of B's lack of access to material goods (at least on B's own and not A's terms).[68] Cohen's argument against Nozick is that by construing liberty as freedom from violent coercion, he ignores the dimension of freedom that entails the power to act, which requires access to the materials by which one might act. On Cohen's reading, for Nozick a property-less individual is free because no one tells him what to do, but, as Cohen notes, lacking access to property, he also has few, if any, choices. The absence of coercion, in other words, does not entail the presence of the robust freedom that Cohen calls autonomy.

As a critique of Nozick's theory, this falls short. Nozick has two obvious replies. First, A's actions violate the Lockean proviso that one may appropriate so long as good and enough is left over for everyone else. Nozick admittedly does not interpret this as a proviso that anything need be left for someone to appropriate, as long as by the opportunity to work they are able to live better than in a completely unowned world.[69] In a two-person world, B can easily be seen to be made worse off by A's appropriation, as a single owner and single laborer clearly set the conditions for unjust exploitation. Nozick can show how in Cohen's example A violates the Lockean proviso. Nozick's second reply relates to this. In contemporary capitalist societies, a competitive marketplace affords labor some space for negotiating power that a two-person world would not. Labor, despite not having strict access to the means of production, still can exercise its freedom of will over and against capital by self-ownership, specifically, the ownership of labor power that it can withhold from capital.

What is key for this section, though, is not the adequacy of Cohen's critique or the power of Nozick's reply, but a similar recognition that freedom of self-direction depends to some extent on access to material goods. Nozick and other libertarians think that the loss of access to material goods is balanced by the retaining of one's labor power, but this will only be a sufficient balance when the labor market is adequately structured and regulated—when the labor market is subject to some mechanism of societal direction. It is also vital to see that Nozick, or at least my construal of Nozick, does not simply think that the ownership of one's own labor power in itself suffices; rather, it suffices as that by which the laborer gains access to those material goods. Self-ownership and freedom are not reduced to access to and use of material goods, but access to or use of material goods is a necessary condition of free self-direction, and up to a point, greater access or ability to use is correlative to greater degrees of freedom of self-direction. If I have access to more things, I can more freely and

---

68. Cohen, *Self-Ownership, Freedom, and Equality*, 67–68.
69. Nozick, *Anarchy, State, and Utopia*, 176.

capaciously exert my will, what Ward, adapting a term first coined in sociology, refers to as "hyperagency."[70]

The claim, then, in this first part is that access to material goods is a *sine qua non* of free self-direction and, to a point, directly related to the freedom of the will. Freedom of the will does not reduce to free access to material goods, but neither can they be separated, and, in the relevant terms here, the introduction of inequality of access to material goods will introduce inequality in the scope of free self-direction. As with the material inequality discussed above, it is not necessarily the case that inequality of free self-direction is morally problematic, but it is nonetheless a feature of the introduction of property regimes that must be recognized and accounted for to ensure that it does not become so.

The recognition of this relationship shaped canonistic discourse as much as mendicant theology. As Annabel S. Brett notes, the disparities in power between the lord and the pauper are manifest in the legal arena: "The *pauper* . . . was also the impotent, the socially insignificant . . . , he who required protection against the power of lords. Poverty thus came to have in addition a juridical dimension in the sense of absence of legal standing."[71] In this context, the scholastic canonists developed privileges to ameliorate the powerlessness of poverty precisely as it manifested itself in the difficulties court processes and procedures present for the poor. We can look at three different sources to get a better sense of the way in which the canonists understand and address this problem.[72]

As early as the *Decretum*, canon law shows an awareness and sensitivity to the challenges the poor face in achieving justice in courts. In Distinction 87 of the *Decretum*, Gratian affirms that the church ought to provide free legal counsel to the poor and vulnerable, including widows and orphans. They are granted refuge in the church from persecution and legal defense by the church for their court cases. This distinction provides an important example of how the issues of poverty and liberty inhabit the same conceptual space in scholastic thought. In canonistic jurisprudence, the natural laws of common

---

70. This is not to deny that possession carries with it certain threats to one's freedom, as was especially clear in the patristic discourse I examined in chapter 1. One can "become a slave to one's possessions," e.g., so that one's freedom of will is curtailed by an excessive desire to retain or grow one's possessions, what Ward argues is an interference with the development of the virtue of prudence. More expansively, Ward argues that the "hyperagency" enabled by excess wealth can also undermine the development of key virtues like justice, fidelity, and temperance in *Wealth, Virtue, and Moral Luck*, chap. 5.

71. Brett, *Liberty, Right, and Nature*, 12.

72. I rely on Brian Tierney's discussion of canon law and privileges for the impoverished in *Medieval Poor Law*, 13–15, for the sources I discuss and my general approach to the topic.

CHAPTER THREE

dominion and one freedom are often—almost always—placed side by side. In the practical discourse of Distinction 87, which addresses legal counsel for widows, orphans, and those without means (D. 87 cc.1–5), Gratian also introduces provisions for ecclesial protection for those who have been recently manumitted, whether from threats to their newfound liberty or from the seizure of "their small bit of property" (D. 87 cc. 7–8).

Throughout the thirteenth century, the legal protections the church afforded to widows, orphans, the poor, and the recently freed (collectively, *miserabiles personae*) underwent significant clarification in the *Decretals* of Gregory IX (*Liber extra*) and its commentaries and glosses, as Brian Tierney documents.[73] In the *Liber extra*, several cases of *miserabiles personae* were examined. The general trend is to divide and order the category of *miserabiles personae*, giving the most preferential treatment to the condition of poverty. Though, for example, widows still receive some privileges from the church, canon law begins to clarify that the most expansive benefits of the church are to be geared specifically toward the poor. An ecclesiastical court declined to hear the case of a widow suing over property rights, because although she was a widow, she was well-off. This and several other cases are clarified in Innocent IV's commentary on the *Liber extra*, which notes that though the general class of *miserabiles personae* may receive some expedited treatment in ecclesiastical courts after their case is tried in a civil court, only those who are truly poor may bring their cases before ecclesiastical courts without first attempting to secure justice in a civil court. The efforts of the canonists augment the power of the poor in court by virtually augmenting their material resources, whether it is through the forgiveness of payments or the free provision of legal services.[74] It is this very practical focus that constitutes the primary point of connection between liberty and access to material goods in scholastic canon law.

The analysis of property in terms of freedom demonstrates the values at stake in the institution of property much more starkly than an appeal to the principle of equality. One might, in other words, be more willing to concede the legitimate introduction of inequality of possession in a society for the sake of the pursuit of values like efficiency than the introduction of differences in freedom. Nonetheless, the claim here is that by introducing inequality society thereby introduces differential levels of freedom. And the legitimations for introducing inequity

---

73. Tierney, *Medieval Poor Law*, chap. 1.

74. Leo XIII observes the same powerlessness of the poor in defending their rights but, in a sign of the changed legal landscape, appeals to the special care and protection of the state for the poor. Pope Leo XIII, *Rerum Novarum*, encyclical letter, §37, Vatican, May 15, 1891, https://tinyurl.com/8t6sxdf4. Thanks to Catherine Osborne for pointing out this connection.

and inequality into human access to the material world—to preserve and foster some level of equity and equality by curtailing their natural expression—apply in the same way to liberty. A system in which individuals could lose their access to material resources through the deprivation imposed by a tyrant or the dearth created by uncoordinated action means that individuals could correspondingly lose their liberty. If in an idealized rendering of scholastic thought (the scholastics themselves never put it in this way, in part because, as I noted above, the scholastics never theorized about an abstract state of perfect liberty) equality of access is the state that corresponds to one or perfectly equal liberty, then the curtailment of access in the service of ordering and preserving access is thus also a modification of liberty. In the service of ordering and preserving some exercise of liberty for all, society orders and limits access to the things of the earth.

This point is especially pertinent to contemporary capitalist economies. The idea that one significant advantage capitalist social systems have over other regimes is the greater degree of freedom—brought about by the self-organization of the marketplace according to the free activities of its participants—appears to overstate the case in light of the connection between liberty and the use of material things. It would seem more accurate to say, as a general claim about freedom in capitalist societies, that the distribution of liberty shifts in a manner proportionate to the distribution of capital. However one frames it, even in capitalist regimes that emphasize noncoercion, liberty is evidently a principle whose expression is curtailed through the introduction of property, precisely through the introduction of unequal access and ownership. As with equality and equity, the principle functions as a regulative principle: any regime of property is answerable to the manner in which it distributes and protects liberty as self-direction through free action and use of the material world. And, as with equality and equity, it is a principle that functions alongside other sets of values and principles that different societies, through their exercise of their proper judgment, choose to instantiate in diverse regimes of property.

Conclusion

Property is a convention that gives expression to the social and political nature of humans. It does this in two ways. First, for property to be an expression of the political nature of humans requires that any given property regime sustain, in some form, the moral principles of equity, equality, sufficiency, and liberty. According to the Christian tradition, each of these principles reflects some basic truth about humans, and their abrogation always constitutes a violation of justice antithetical to social and political life. In some way or another, property, along with other social and political conventions, must respect certain standards of each of these moral principles in the way that it structures and governs human life together. Nonetheless, scholastic argument does not treat these principles as univocal in their expression. They are, rather, fungible, and this allows for diverse legal, social, and political organization. In addition to securing the principles necessary to human society, property also enables the exercise of self-determination proper to humans at both the individual and the societal level. No society is bound to hold property in this way or that, but every society is bound to respect the principles of equality, equity, sufficiency, and liberty in whatever way it judges to hold property.

Seen in this light, the natural law of common dominion provides both the moral framework and the anthropological warrant for the diversity of property institutions. From the early church to contemporary Catholic social thought, common dominion is a theological claim regarding one end of the material world. To the extent that the material world is for the use of humans, it is for the use of each and every human alike, without prejudice or discrimination. It is in the use of the things of the world that each human is able to give expression to that freedom and self-direction proper to her as a rational creature and a creature made in the image of God. On account of our equal status, then, each human may lay claim to this liberty, which is also intrinsically oriented toward just relations with others and the common good of each individual's society. The self-determination of individuals, further, is manifest in society, so that individuals together may properly decide to pursue certain ways of life, which entails a diversity of customs, laws, and social organization and, thus, a diversity of property regimes.

Besides flouting the principles of equality, equity, sufficiency, and liberty, a theory of property can transgress the framework of common dominion in two ways. First, it can claim property as a natural right, and thus a preconventional feature or extension of human life. By nature, each human has a claim to the use of all the things of the world, and thus there can be no appropriation of the world, only division through convention. The natural right that accords with this claim of the natural law of common dominion is a natural right of use, not of ownership. Second, and what is perhaps the same as flouting these central political principles, it can subordinate political values to the economic values of efficiency, productivity, and development. On the basis of a Christian anthropology, economic values are always subordinate to political values as *instrumental* to those values. In the final two chapters, these two transgressions offer key points of critique for a Lockean theory of property and raise questions of interpretation for contemporary Catholic social teaching on property.

FOUR

Critiquing Locke

PART OF THE PAYOFF OF THE RECOVERY of the scholastic theory of property is that it provides a compelling lens for interpreting papal teachings on property in contemporary Catholic social teaching. Any argument about property in papal teaching, though, has to deal with its Lockean elements, expounded right at the start of this tradition in Leo XIII's *Rerum Novarum*. Since Leo's use of something like Locke's labor-mixing argument to affirm a natural right to private property, the tradition has been relatively silent on whether to accept or reject such an approach to property. The popes seem to prefer either a creative or selective reinterpretation of their predecessors' thought or to pass over any divergences in silence. This is partly the case with Leo's points on property, which I discuss in the next chapter.

At least in Anglophone political thought, the lack of alternative systematic theories of property that are not utilitarian has encouraged some scholars of Catholic social thought to incorporate or baptize the Lockean theory of property. Arnold McKee goes so far, for instance, as to argue that a natural right to private property is a development of Catholic social doctrine.[1] Subtler approaches have simply endeavored to show a broad compatibility between Locke's theory and the Christian tradition, papal teachings included.[2] The question is paramount for this project, since on key points, like whether property is natural or a convention, Locke's and the scholastic approaches to property fundamentally diverge.

The primary focus of this chapter is a threefold critique of Locke's labor-mixing theory of property, which is one version of a broader set of what I call agriculturalist theories of property in early modernity. The first issue I

---

1. Arnold F. McKee, "The 'Natural' Right to Private Property," *Review of Social Economy* 49, no. 4 (1991): 483–501, https://tinyurl.com/2mjfu9b3.

2. B. Andrew Lustig, "Natural Law, Property, and Justice: The General Justification of Property in John Locke," *Journal of Religious Ethics* 19, no. 1 (1991): 119–49.

raise is philosophical and relates to an internal critique of Locke's theory. Key philosophers who exegete Locke's labor-mixing theory of property, many of whom are at least very sympathetic to Locke, find it incoherent. The second critique discusses the practical implications of theories of property that locate the origin and fullness of property rights in some form of settled agriculture. While this discussion raises theoretical questions for this model, I focus on its practical colonial implications—or, more specifically, the kinds of concrete activities of acquisition and dispossession that this theory legitimates—since it is evident that they run counter to the stated aspirations of papal teaching for the self-determination of peoples. Here the discussion allows for a brief examination of and comparison with scholastic theory in early modern Spain. Finally, I raise a theological critique, demonstrating how Locke's theory of property foregrounds the power of private use, which runs contrary to the fundamental conviction of the patristic and medieval traditions that property is not morally speaking a power of private use but a power of distribution. After a brief summary of Locke's theory of property, I take each of these three points in turn.

Chapter 5 of the Second Treatise

Locke's theory is characterized by the development of tradition. History is usually helpful, but the history I have covered so far largely bypasses the tradition that Locke primarily inherits and develops. It is no doubt important that Locke preserves rights of subsistence and duties of charity, which can be traced back to the canonist and theological traditions.[3] But when Locke writes that common things must first be appropriated and owned by someone before they can be of any use to him, he is operating in the tradition that runs from Roman law to the civilian tradition and through Pope John XXII. The most useful history for understanding Locke in relation to the Christian tradition is the history of Roman law, the scholastic civil lawyers (the "civilians"), and the Michaelist disputes of the early fourteenth century. Though this discussion deserves a much richer historical treatment, I can cover the key points where Locke inherits and develops prior tradition and examine how these developments open him to the kinds of philosophical and theological critiques that follow.

3. See Scott G. Swanson, "The Medieval Foundations of John Locke's Theory of Natural Rights: Rights of Subsistence and the Principle of Extreme Necessity," *History of Political Thought* 18, no. 3 (1997): 399–456.

Critiquing Locke

The natural law of occupation is a key part of the tradition that Locke inherits. According to Roman law, transmitted through Justinian's *Institutes* (and cited in the *Decretum* D. 1 c. 7): "Wild animals, birds and fish, the creatures of land, sea and sky, become the property of the taker as soon as they are caught. Where something has no owner, it is reasonable that the person who takes it should have it."[4] In Roman law, appropriation applies to what the civilians call "movables," objects and items that can be taken from one place to another. As I showed in chapter 2, the main lines of the canonist and theological traditions hold that property is from positive law, whether civil or the law of nations. As such, these traditions assign the law of occupation to the law of nations, those positive laws conducive to the peaceful coexistence of humans and adopted by the preponderance of known nations. The civilian tradition holds to an alternative division of natural law and *ius gentium*, and the place of natural appropriation within that tradition is more complicated. As John Kilcullen documents, some of the most prominent transmitters of the civilian tradition synthesize Roman and canonist sources to claim that the appropriation of movables (birds and fish, fruit, etc.) is by natural law while taking property in immovables like land can only be done by the sanction of the law of nations.[5]

One further aspect of the tradition that draws on Roman law helps to show how Locke inherits and innovates. It is a specification of the relationship between use and ownership that the secular theologian Gerard of Abbeville first raises in his criticism of the Franciscans. The Franciscans claim that they own nothing, not even the bread they eat and the water they drink. In his criticism, occasioned by disputes over the Franciscans' place (and displacement of secular theologians) at the University of Paris, Gerard questions how one can destroy something in use without owning it.[6] If the Franciscan friar who eats a loaf of bread, so that it is of no more use to anyone except him, does not own it, then who does? Surely, to say that the benefactor continued to own it up until

---

4. Peter Birks and Grant McLeod, trans., *Justinian's Institutes* (Ithaca, NY: Cornell University Press, 1987), 2.1 (p. 55).

5. John Kilcullen, "The Origin of Property: Ockham, Grotius, Pufendorf, and Some Others," in *A Translation of Ockham's Work of Ninety Days*, vol. 2 (Lewiston, NY: Edwin Mellen Press, 2001), 905–11. A. J. Carlyle provides a brief summary of earlier, twelfth- and thirteenth-century jurists up to Accursius, noting that they seem less certain about how to locate property in the major divisions of law. See *A History of Medieval Political Thought in the West*, 6 vols. (New York: Barnes & Noble, 1950), 2:41–49.

6. Lambert summarizes Gerard's position and its context in *Franciscan Poverty: The Doctrine of Absolute Poverty of Christ and the Apostles in the Franciscan Order, 1210–1323* (St. Bonaventure, NY: St. Bonaventure University Press, 1998), 133–41.

CHAPTER FOUR

it was destroyed seems like legal fiction. Gerard's point is that the Franciscans seem to be stretching the limits of belief to bolster their claim that they practice the most perfect form of life. The question of "using up" (*consumptus* or, sometimes, *abusus*) and ownership had not been raised in either the civilian or the canonist traditions until this point in the thirteenth century, in part because no one had ever made such a radical claim as the Franciscans.[7] This becomes a part of the civilian tradition (though never ubiquitously held) when John XXII, himself a civil lawyer, revives Gerard's argument in the fourteenth century to repudiate William of Ockham and the Michaelist Franciscans: one must have ownership in things that one destroys in use.

Locke inherits the civilian tradition and develops it in important respects. The foundation of Locke's argument comes in section 26 of chapter 5 of the *Second Treatise*, which is worth quoting at length here:

> Nobody has originally a private dominion, exclusive of the rest of mankind . . . yet, being given for the use of men, there must of necessity be a means to appropriate [plants and animals] some way or other before they can be of any use, or at all beneficial to any particular man. The fruit or venison which nourishes the wild Indian, who knows no enclosure, and is still a tenant in common, must be his, and so his (i.e. a part of him) that another can no longer have any right to it, before it can do him any good for the support of his life.[8]

Locke is evidently discussing "movables"—fruits and wild animals—at this point. We can briefly compare his thought with Ockham and John XXII.[9] For Ockham, who works most closely with the canonists, Scripture, and Thomas Aquinas, it is enough that everyone has a natural right of use to make use of the things of the world.[10] John XXII's argument seems to imply that in

---

7. In Roman law, it was certain that one could not have usufruct in things one consumed in use. Birks and McLeod, *Justinian's Institutes*, 2.4.2 (p. 61). But, elsewhere, Roman law delineates a "simple right of use" of agricultural goods that remains clearly separate from the powers of ownership. See Birks and McLeod, 2.5 (p. 63).

8. John Locke, *The Second Treatise of Government*, in *John Locke: Political Writings*, ed. David Wootton (Indianapolis: Hackett, 2003), 5.26 (p. 274).

9. For a detailed examination of the dispute that captures the importance of the natural right of using and the nuances of misunderstanding between John XXII and the Michaelists, with a focus on Ockham's confrere Bonagratia of Bergamo, see Virpi Mäkinen, *Property Rights in the Late Medieval Discussion on Franciscan Poverty* (Leuven: Peeters, 2001), 164–89.

10. On Ockham's sources, see Brian Tierney, *The Idea of Natural Rights: Studies on Natural Rights, Natural Law, and Church Law, 1150–1625* (Grand Rapids: Eerdmans, 2001), 101–3. On

things that are consumed in use, one must have *dominium* in the proprietary sense or a property right in the thing itself. This latter *dominium* is referred to in the fourteenth-century disputes as *dominium proprium*. Locke adopts the latter, civilian (and, in this case, Johannine) position. The things of the field must be the Indian's to the exclusion of others—must be the Indian's *dominium proprium*. Use of consumables requires a property claim in the thing consumed.

It is at this point that Locke first innovates within the civilian tradition. No one from within the Roman law or civilian tradition seems to offer a precise account of the mechanism by which something that is common may morally become private by appropriation. Civilians like Castro and Vázquez argue that in the beginning there was *dominium commune* in all things, which is altered by the occupation of movables that natural law permits. No detailed mechanism, aside from occupation, is offered for how *dominium commune* becomes *dominia propria* or *distincta*.[11] As the quote above shows, Locke is committed to the prior commonness of all things. But he is unwilling to simply posit occupation as a legitimate means of moving from common dominion to distinct dominions. This is in part because he takes seriously Robert Filmer's argument that moving from common dominion to distinct dominions would seem to demand the unanimous consent of the whole world. If taking something as one's own prejudices everyone else (now, after all, no one else can eat that venison), then, Filmer claims, to do so rightfully one must secure the consent of everyone else. Filmer argues that things were never held in common but all things were given in the beginning as the private property of Adam and have passed down patriarchally through succession to the monarchs of the world.

Locke needs to provide some moral and philosophical argument by which things can go from being common to being private without needing universal consent or prejudicing the right of another:[12]

> Though the earth and all inferior creatures be common to all men, yet every man has a property in his own person. This nobody has any right to but himself. The labor of his body, and the work of his hands, we may say, are

---

the natural right of use, see William Ockham, *A Translation of William of Ockham's Work of Ninety Days (Early 1330s)*, trans. John Kilcullen and John Scott (Lewiston, NY: Edwin Mellen Press, 2001), e.g., 415–16, 436–47.

11. Kilcullen, "The Origin of Property," 908–9.

12. Waldron has a helpful summary of the background of consent theories and Filmer's criticism of them in *The Right to Private Property* (Oxford: Clarendon, 1988), 148–53.

properly his. Whatsoever, then, he removes out of the state that nature hath provided and left it in, he hath mixed his labor with, and joined to it something that is his own, and thereby makes it his property.... It hath by this labor something annexed to it that excludes the common right of other men.[13]

This is the clear statement of Locke's labor-mixing theory of property.[14] It is of central interest here for two reasons. First, it is one innovation he makes to the tradition that he received, where he elaborates a theoretical mechanism of natural appropriation (of movables). More importantly, it is the locus of philosophical incoherence in Locke's theory of property.

Before I examine the critiques of Locke's theory of property, it is worth laying out a second innovation to the civilian approach to property that Locke takes up from Alberico Gentili.[15] For the civilians, though less clearly for Roman law, natural appropriation was restricted to movables and did not apply to immovables like land.[16] After discussing in detail the mechanisms and his two provisos on the appropriation of movable things from the common store, Locke provides a symmetrical account for how the same mechanisms and provisos that apply to movables apply to immovables, specifically land.[17] This is a

---

13. Locke, *The Second Treatise*, 5.27 (p. 274).

14. Locke could have taken a different approach, namely, where common dominion constitutes a freedom to use rather than discrete claim-rights and, thus, where property could be established precisely by convention. This would have brought him closer to the scholastic tradition. It is simply worth mentioning an important reason why he did not take this alternative. According to Waldron: "Locke... has a reason for wanting to avoid consent theories.... If an individual's property rights were conventional, then they would be vulnerable in principle to the claim that the demands which the magistrate made upon them in fact fairly reflected the terms of their conventional establishment. In itself, conventionalism provides no defense against oppression or absolutism" (*Right to Private Property*, 152–53).

15. Gentili proposes this in his 1598 work *De iure belli*. For more on Gentili, Thomas More, and the emerging idea that one could appropriate land privately by natural law, see David Lantigua, *Infidels and Empires in a New World Order: Early Modern Spanish Contributions to International Legal Thought* (New York: Cambridge University Press, 2020), 226–29.

16. Andrew Fitzmaurice notes that "the distinction between land and movable goods was not as important in Roman law as it would be in modern European law." At least in popular argumentation, the idea of occupation was applied to land in ancient Rome. Andrew Fitzmaurice, *Sovereignty, Property, and Empire, 1500–2000* (Cambridge: Cambridge University Press, 2014), 35. See, however, Lauren Benton and Benjamin Straumann, "Acquiring Empire by Law: From Roman Doctrine to Early Modern European Practice," *Law and History Review* 28, no. 1 (2010): 15, who show that at least in strict legal terms Roman law did not allow for the taking of land by occupation.

17. Locke, *The Second Treatise*, 5.27–31, is his discussion of movables and the two provisos.

central concern for Locke in chapter 5: "But the chief matter of property being now not the fruits of the earth, and the beasts that subsist on it, but the earth itself... I think it is plain that property in that too is acquired as the former. As much land as a man tills, plants, improves, cultivates, and can use the product of, so much is his property. He by his labor does, as it were, enclose it from the common."[18] Land, also, is acquired under the labor-mixing theory. Here, and throughout chapter 5, the norm for Locke is private cultivation and enclosure and the exception is land left common by compact (for common cultivation), a point that is important for placing Locke in relation to the prevailing rhetoric of enclosure in seventeenth-century England as well as its intrinsic prejudice against societies that rely mostly on common cultivation.[19]

For both movables and immovables, the sufficiency and spoilation provisos apply. These provisos are vital in contemporary usages of Locke, which tend to focus on the provisos and not on labor mixing to legitimate natural appropriation, but also for understanding the colonial implications of Locke's theory. Briefly stated, the sufficiency proviso allows an individual to appropriate as much as she can use, "at least where there is enough and as good left in common for others." The spoilation proviso states that one may appropriate "as much as anyone can make use of to any advantage of life before it spoils." The material limitations of each proviso are both transcended through improvement, trade, and the use of money.[20] With the extension of natural appropriation to land, Locke, following Gentili, places himself outside of all three medieval European traditions on property: civilian, canonist, and theological.

The importance of land at this time, and why it might have been a central concern for Locke, can be seen in prevailing legal and social shifts of seventeenth-century England. Locke's defense of enclosure, his presumption in favor of private cultivation and against common cultivation, and his largely economic justifications of that enclosure movement reiterate judicial and social arguments that had been made since the end of the sixteenth century and were achieving a sort of critical impact in the years 1660–1690. Charles Reid Jr. describes how the prevailing sentiment against enclosure in the sixteenth century did an about-face over the course of the seventeenth century, led by Parliamentarians like Sir Walter Raleigh and driven by a "rhetoric of

---

18. Locke, *The Second Treatise*, 5.32 (p. 276).
19. Locke, *The Second Treatise*, 5.35 (pp. 277–78).
20. The sufficiency proviso (Locke, *The Second Treatise*, 5.27 [p. 274]) and the spoilation proviso (5.31 [p. 276]). On improvement, trade, and money in relation to the provisos, see Locke, *The Second Treatise*, 5.36–37, 40–51.

improvement."[21] A series of tracts in the early seventeenth century argued that the economic benefits of enclosure would accrue to both the commonwealth and the poor.[22] In 1660, the restoration of Charles II solidified the enclosure movement: "From about [1660] writers . . . in general no longer argue the pros and cons of enclosure, or for that matter of engrossing, or of converting the peasant proprietor into a wage-earning labourer. All three alike are in general taken for granted."[23] Parliamentary enclosure continued to rapidly increase after the Glorious Revolution of 1688 and the establishment of the Parliamentary monarchy. Locke's concern with improvement on the basis of enclosed private cultivation was quite in line with the prevailing economic and political movement of enclosure establishing itself in England, which argued from the improvement brought by efficiency to abrogation of common rights and common land.[24]

Two facets of Locke's theory bear reiteration. First, property holding begins in the state of nature, prior to the creation of a state and political society. Property is, in the most explicit sense, natural and preconventional. Second, the conditions on appropriation change with the introduction of money, which *also* occurs in the state of nature, though its origins are not natural but based on tacit consent.[25] With the introduction of money, the limits on acquisition imposed by the spoilation proviso are transcended to a degree. Certainly, one may still not hoard acorns and let them rot, nor enclose land and let it go to waste. In a money economy, though, one may gather acorns and sell them for money—money that does not spoil no matter how long it sits idly in someone's chest. The limits on appropriation have subtly shifted and are no longer a matter of how much one can reasonably use. Rather, one may appropriate as much as one may expect to sell or, in the case of land, lease or hire labor to work. As Locke says, an appropriator in the state of nature "invaded not the right of others: he might heap up as much of these durable things as he pleased."[26]

---

21. Charles Reid Jr., "The Seventeenth-Century Revolution in the English Land Law," *Cleveland State Law Review* 43 (1995): 252–60.

22. Polanyi cites an official document of 1607 for the Lords as arguing the following: "The poor man shall be satisfied in his end: Habitation; and the gentleman not hindered in his desire: Improvement." Karl Polanyi, *The Great Transformation: The Political and Economic Origins of Our Time* (Boston: Beacon, 1944), 36.

23. W. E. Tate, *The English Village Community and the Enclosure Movements* (London: Gollancz, 1967), 78–79, cited in Reid, "The Seventeenth-Century Revolution," 258.

24. Reid, "The Seventeenth-Century Revolution," 261.

25. Locke, *The Second Treatise*, 5.48–50 (p. 285).

26. Locke, *The Second Treatise*, 5.46 (p. 284).

In this way, Locke not only explains the natural and prepolitical origins of property, he also explains the prepolitical origins of large-scale accumulation and inequality, rooted in natural right.[27]

Is Locke's Theory Coherent? Analytic Critiques

With this background in place, I can evaluate the Lockean theory of property. What arguments exist for or against using the Lockean theory to make sense of papal teaching on property, especially in light of its significant presence in at least two encyclicals? The labor-mixing aspect of Locke's theory has largely fallen out of favor in political theory and political economy, even among those who hold significant commitments to other elements of Lockean and liberal theory.[28] In and of itself, this is not a reason to dismiss the theory, but this desuetude is rooted in two significant theoretical arguments against the labor-mixing theory of property itself. Both have to do with the coherence of two parts of the argument: the construal of one's relation to one's "person" as one of ownership and the claim that one "mixes" one's labor with an unowned object. Given that it is the labor-mixing aspect of this theory of property that initially appears in the papal encyclicals, incoherence here provides a compelling reason against using this theory to drive the hermeneutic by which papal teaching is interpreted.

Jeremy Waldron systematically presents both critiques of the labor-mixing theory of property.[29] Locke thinks he must give an account of how an individual can legitimately appropriate things—animals, plants, land—from the common store without committing any injustice against the others who make use of that store. Locke begins his argument by claiming that "every man has a property in his own person. This nobody has any right to but himself. The labor of his body,

---

27. C. B. Macpherson, *The Political Theory of Possessive Individualism* (New York: Oxford University Press, 1962), 199; Michael Zuckert, *Natural Rights and the New Republicanism* (Princeton: Princeton University Press, 1994), 269, https://tinyurl.com/4yeu7yfm; Jeremy Waldron, "Disproportionate and Unequal Possession," in *God, Locke, and Equality: Christian Foundations of Locke's Political Thought* (Cambridge: Cambridge University Press, 2002), 151–87.

28. Even libertarians like Robert Nozick, whom I discuss below, and David Schmidtz hold only to the provisos of Lockean theory, and not the labor-mixing concept that is influential for Leo XIII's *Rerum Novarum*. For Schmidtz's view, see David Schmidtz, "The Institution of Property," *Social Philosophy and Policy* 11, no. 2 (1994): 42–62, https://tinyurl.com/mr3m9stb.

29. Waldron, *Right to Private Property*, 177–91.

and the work of his hands, we may say, are properly his." James Tully provides a helpful summary of Locke's account of "person" in the *Essay concerning the Human Understanding* in order to explain what Locke means here.[30] For Locke, a person is defined by consciousness of the self, which extends backward in time, to the present, and to the future. The actions of a person are those she is conscious of having intended and performed. And intentional or deliberate action is action that is deliberated upon by the reason and consciously willed.

In Locke, a property right arises from the act of making: "in respect of God the Maker of Heaven and Earth, who is sole Lord and Proprietor of the whole World, Mans Propriety in the Creatures is nothing but that *Liberty to use them*, which God has permitted."[31] Citing the maker's right, Locke refutes the idea that each person has a property in his life and limb, or in his children's life and limb, since each person only brings forth and does not, properly speaking, make his own or his child's body: "If any one thinks himself an artist at this, let him number up the parts of his child's body, which he hath made, tell me their uses and operations . . . if he made it, let him, when it is out of order, mend it, at least tell wherein the defects lie."[32] It is this sort of maker's right, though, that Locke claims each person has in her own person and in her own intentional actions or labor. Tully notes a problem here, that consciousness "is not made; it is something for which a man is obliquely responsible in virtue of thinking and acting."[33] This attempt to apply property or proprietary dominion to one's own person is a philosophical difficulty I return to below. However, if we distinguish between one's "person" and actions, it is easier to see how one might have something like a maker's right in one's actions: one applies one's own will and reason freely to act in this way or that. At least on the order of secondary causation, the human is the "maker" of her own actions in a way that she is not of her own body or her children's bodies.

Though the idea of a "maker's right" might appear more straightforward in the case of action or labor, it is precisely here where yet another problem of incoherence arises. Tully writes this: "To own one's actions is equivalent to being the proprietor of them. Although man makes not himself nor the world, he makes the actions of his person and so has a natural and exclusive maker's right in them."[34]

---

30. The following draws from James Tully, *A Discourse on Property: John Locke and His Adversaries* (Cambridge: Cambridge University Press, 1980), 106–8.

31. The quotation is from the *First Treatise*. See John Locke, *Two Treatises of Government*, ed. Peter Laslett (Cambridge: Cambridge University Press, 1960), 1.4.39 (p. 168).

32. Locke, *Two Treatises*, 1.6.53 (p. 179).

33. Tully, *A Discourse on Property*, 109.

34. Tully, *A Discourse on Property*, 108.

What exactly does Locke mean by having a property in one's own actions? In the *Essay*, he writes that the "personality extends itself beyond present existence to what is past ... where it becomes concerned and *accountable*, owns and *imputes* to itself past actions."[35] Though it is tempting to elide a strict sense of ownership, one characterized by powers of use, exclusion, and alienability, with this loose sense of ownership, in which I "take responsibility for" or "own up to" certain of my actions, it will not help make sense of Locke's argument. Tully never presses Locke on this, taking for granted that to "own" one's actions as Locke describes in the *Essay*, to be accountable or impute them to oneself, is sufficient to ground the kind of ownership that originates over an unowned object as a result of mixing one's labor with it. If Locke's labor-mixing argument is to follow, however, he must mean instead that each person has something like strict property rights in and over his freely chosen actions, especially rights of exclusion.

This is a problem that Waldron recognizes and, likewise, insists on facing: the "claim that the *suum* ... the sphere of inviolable personality defined ... by the boundaries of one's body ... can be extended by unilateral appropriation is controversial: both Filmer and Pufendorf deny it. Locke's claim that one has property in one's own person and actions is supposed to be the first step in an *argument* to this effect."[36] To "own" one's actions, in the sense of taking responsibility for them, will not achieve the end that Locke aims for. If this sort of ownership were the basis for original appropriation, "it would entail only that a thief should refrain from claiming credit for another's production."[37] If the end result is the powers of ownership that Locke claims (use, exclusion, and alienability),[38] then the grounds must also be a similar set of powers over one's own actions that engender these powers in an external object.[39]

How exactly can one construe labor—more basically, freely chosen actions—as something that one can own, in this strict proprietary sense?[40] Simply equating labor with discrete acts is ruled out, since there is no coherent way of thinking about excluding, alienating, or even possessing those acts in a way even

---

35. John Locke, *An Essay concerning Human Understanding*, ed. Peter Nidditch (Oxford: Clarendon, 1975), 2.27.26. Cited in Tully, *A Discourse on Property*, 108.
36. Waldron, *Right to Private Property*, 183.
37. Waldron, *Right to Private Property*, 181.
38. These are the powers of property Locke attends to in the *Second Treatise*: use (5.26, 31, et al.), exclusion (5.32, 34, et al.), alienation (5.46).
39. In addition to Jeremy Waldron, this is a problem J. P. Day raises in "Locke on Property," *Philosophical Quarterly* 16, no. 64 (1966): 207–20. Waldron engages with Day extensively in his section on Lockean self-ownership.
40. The following comes from Waldron, *Right to Private Property*, 182–83.

CHAPTER FOUR

analogous to property. One could think of Marx's labor-power or capacity to labor as a compelling way of making sense of this. I can sell my capacity to labor, for instance. But, as Waldron notes, someone "may take an [unowned] object I have labored on, but still leave me with my [full] capacity to labor." In this way it is hard to see how any of one's "capacity to labor" is transferred to the object on which the labor is expended. There seems to be no intelligible way to understand how one can own one's labor, or freely chosen actions, or at least no way that can do the work that Locke requires for his labor-mixing theory of property.[41]

This connects directly with the second critique Waldron makes of Locke's theory of property, which is that when it comes to mixing labor and an unowned object, the action or argument seems to be missing a term. Waldron's extensive argument can be summarized in the following way.[42] If I mix an egg and milk, there are three components to the mixing: the egg, the milk, and the act of mixing. Without any one of these components—if I only have one object or do not engage in the act of mixing—it is not clear how I can speak of mixing things together. Locke describes the process like this: "The labor of his body, and the work of his hands, we may say, are properly his. Whatsoever, then, he removes out of the state that nature hath provided and left it in, he hath mixed his labor with, and joined to it something that is his own, and thereby makes it his property.... It has by this labor something annexed to it that excludes the common right of other men."[43] In another place: "The labor that was mine, removing them out of that common state they were in, hath fixed my property in them."[44] Land is acquired in the same way, repeating the quotation from above: "As much land as a man tills, plants, improves, cultivates, and can use the product of, so much is his property. He by his labor does, as it were, enclose it from the common."[45] What are the terms of Locke's labor-mixing theory? On Waldron's reading, there are only two terms where three are needed: there is one's labor and there is an unowned object. One can treat one's labor as the process by which the mixing occurs, but then one is only left with an unowned object and nothing to mix with it. One can treat one's labor as an object that will be mixed with the unowned object, but then one lacks any action by which the two are mixed. This latter option also seems clearly antithetical to the way in which Locke consistently uses "labor" to describe *actions* of improvement, development, etc. Labor refers consistently to action-words in chapter 5.[46]

41. This discussion can be found in Waldron, *Right to Private Property*, 187–88.
42. Waldron, *Right to Private Property*, 184–91.
43. Locke, *The Second Treatise*, 5.27 (p. 274).
44. Locke, *The Second Treatise*, 5.28 (p. 275).
45. Locke, *The Second Treatise*, 5.32 (p. 276).
46. Tully, *A Discourse on Property*, 109.

Among libertarians who appropriate aspects of Locke's theory of property, few, if any, make explicit use of the labor-mixing component, focusing instead on the two provisos as the grounds of "no harm" theories of accumulation.[47] In *Anarchy, State, and Utopia*, Robert Nozick ostensibly adopts Locke's theory of property to stake out a sort of immunity to taxation without the property holder's consent. The point here, though, is not the details of Nozick's theory of property and taxation but the nature of his engagement with Locke. Nozick's initial discussion gives the impression that he will adopt a thoroughly Lockean approach. He construes the products of one's labors as equivalent in some way with one's person understood as one's free actions.[48] So far, so Lockean. Nozick's next move, however, suggests a critique rather than appropriation of Locke's labor-mixing theory. He raises a host of problematic questions for Locke's theory of appropriation:

> Can virgin land (for the purposes of ecological investigation by high-flying airplane) come under ownership by a Lockean process? Building a fence around a territory presumably would make one the owner of only the fence (and the land immediately underneath it). Why does mixing one's labor with something make one the owner of it? . . . But why isn't mixing what I own with what I don't a way of losing what I own rather than a way of gaining what I don't? . . . Why should one's entitlement extend to the whole object rather than just to the *added value* one's labor has produced?[49]

Nozick does not have good answers to these questions, so he comes to the conclusion that the "crucial point is whether appropriation of an unowned object worsens the situation of others."[50] I call this Nozick's "no-harm theory of acquisition and ownership."

---

47. See, for another example, David Schmidtz's "The Institution of Property."
48. Robert Nozick, *Anarchy, State, and Utopia* (New York: Basic Books, 2013), 172.
49. Nozick, *Anarchy, State, and Utopia*, 174–75. To this last point, Locke might presumably respond that the value added by labor constitutes 99.9 percent of the value of the product. See Locke, *The Second Treatise*, 5.37, 40, 43. In response to this, G. A. Cohen offers a helpful critique, suggesting that Locke mistakes marginal value with total value. The laborer adds 99.9 percent of the marginal value to the product (so that, say, a plot that did not grow crops now does) but can hardly claim to have created 99.9 percent of the value in that product by his labor (the soil, minerals, water, microbial life, exposure to sunlight, all necessary to grow those crops). In Cohen's words: "It will often be true that: (1) the application of labor makes virgin land produce ten times what it did before. But it does not follow that, in such a case: (2) labor produces 90 per cent of the product of applying it to virgin land." See G. A. Cohen, *Self-Ownership, Freedom, and Equality* (Cambridge: Cambridge University Press, 1995), 183.
50. Nozick, *Anarchy, State, and Utopia*, 175.

Nozick has abandoned any claims about the natural mechanism by which things can be taken from the common store. His critique is less systematic than Waldron's but seems to come to the same conclusion: the labor-mixing theory of property does not stand up to closer scrutiny. However, it is not clear on the basis of this theory whether he can maintain his earlier and central claim that seizing "the results of someone's labor is equivalent to seizing hours from him and directing him to carry on various activities. . . . It gives them a property right in you."[51] This claim, it seems to me, is so dependent on the equivalence of the products of one's labor with one's person or free action, that in order to retain it he must also retain some explanation of that equivalence. This is the role of labor mixing for Locke, but after Nozick sets aside the labor-mixing theory, he offers no alternative explanation for this equivalence. It seems then that even contemporary philosophers who want to maintain the strictest interpretation of Locke's conclusions about the inviolability of property do not find the labor-mixing theory compelling grounds for their conclusions. On the other hand, it is precisely the labor-mixing mechanism that establishes the libertarian inviolability of property. Locke's recognition of the metaphysical relationship between personality and labor and the moral correlation between labor and property distribution are salutary, but his attempts to reduce those patterns narrowly to natural appropriation with private property rights fail on logical grounds, suggesting a compelling reason to be circumspect in using a Lockean lens to understand, explain, and advance papal teaching or the more general field of Catholic social thought.

Is Locke's Theory Imperialist? Decolonial Critiques

The analysis of the nature of European territorial acquisition in the Americas, and Locke's place within that colonial enterprise, is both extensive and complex. It is the latter attribute, the complexity and inconclusive nature of this area of research, which reflects the complexity of European-Amerindian economic and political interactions, that shapes my approach in this section. To reflect the convoluted nature of the historical encounter as well as current scholarship, and to avoid getting embroiled in contentious disputes about what did happen and what kinds of arguments and legal concepts were used to justify what, I will be circumspect with my claims.

---

51. Nozick, *Anarchy, State, and Utopia*, 172. Michael Otsuka makes the same critique in *Libertarianism without Inequality* (Oxford: Clarendon, 2003), 20.

I intend to make no causal claims about Locke's theory of property and late seventeenth- through nineteenth-century dispossession of the Amerindians by English colonists and US settlers. The current state of research indicates that the acquisition of land proceeded along a variety of economic, legal, and extralegal pathways, and the ill or good intentions of those acquiring and, in some cases, expropriating the land from the Amerindians are not always perspicuous. There is no evidence that English and US settlers were waving the *Second Treatise* and proclaiming the land waste as they continually encroached westward on the Amerindians. The most recent discussions suggest that arguments about the Americas being *terra nullius* or *vacuum domicilium* are but one part of a more comprehensive approach to the English and US acquisition of land that employed a variety of legal arguments and precedents but was likely driven by raw economic calculus more than anything.[52] Indeed, Locke's is but one argument defending the agricultural appropriation of waste land, and is neither the earliest nor the most trenchant version nor, perhaps, the most influential for later international thought.[53] Nonetheless, any evaluation of Locke's theory of property must understand its place within this broader sweep of international thought and ask about its theoretical implications for international thought and practice today.

I begin by situating Locke's thought within a broader historical context. The first section of this chapter emphasized the context and history of Locke's *Second Treatise ad intra*, with special attention to the civil and canon law influences on Locke and the changing domestic economy in England. Over the past fifty years, historians have been steadily building the case that the *Second*

---

52. Pagden notes that a variety of claims—including discovery, prescription, and *res nullius*—were made depending on audience and context as part of a broader project of gaining international legitimation and recognition for imperial claims. Anthony Pagden, "Law, Colonization, Legitimation, and the European Background," in *The Cambridge History of Law in America*, vol. 1, *Early America (1580–1815)*, ed. Christopher Tomlins and Michael Grossberg, Cambridge History of Law in America (Cambridge: Cambridge University Press, 2008), 1–31, https://tinyurl.com/yrknbp3m. Through extensive historical documentation, Stuart Banner shows how land acquisitions were less ideologically than economically motivated, and the cheapest path for settling land most often involved land purchases and not explicit dispossession or expropriation. Stuart Banner, *How the Indians Lost Their Land: Law and Power on the Frontier* (Cambridge, MA: Belknap Press of Harvard University Press, 2005).

53. The last claim is of course merely speculative, but Emer de Vattel's codifying of a similar argument in his book (1758) on the *ius gentium*, deemed a classic of international law in the early twentieth century, indicates that the agriculturalist argument had its own influential proponents in international thought who may or may not have been influenced by its articulation in Locke.

Treatise must also be read in light of the context and history of England *ad extra*—disputes in the New World between colonies, colonists and their lords proprietors, and colonists and the Amerindians, as well as the broader context of seventeenth-century international thought.[54] Examining European international as well as colonial discourse before and after Locke situates Locke's theory as part of a trajectory of thought—at times theological, legal, or blatantly imperialist—that grounded property and eventually (full or true) sovereignty in agricultural improvement and a monetary economy, what I call the agriculturalist argument or agriculturalism.

Placing Locke within this agriculturalist trajectory of thought enables me to ask two questions. First, what, if any, contribution does Locke's theory offer to this trajectory of thought? If my argument is correct, then Locke is one of the first to systematize and ground genuine political society, and thus full sovereignty, in the system of property that emerges from agricultural cultivation. In this, he departs from the legal scholars Alberico Gentili and Grotius and joins what were two separate arguments in the English colonizers' discourse about waste land and the lack of Amerindian territorial sovereignty. Second, what, if any, are the theoretical and practical implications of this agriculturalist argument, both historically and today? Though this agriculturalist argument played a part in enabling and apologizing for English land acquisition and continues to play a similar role in the interaction between corporations, states, and indigenous peoples today under the language of development, my argument does not depend on a precise causal explanation of the role of the agriculturalist argument in historical and contemporary dispossession. Nonetheless, I do claim that the evidence suggests that both practically and theoretically, the agriculturalist/developmentalist approach has significant liabilities that the scholastic approach does not have. The practical implications of the agriculturalist approach run directly counter to the explicit aspirations of an international order in Catholic social teaching, at least since John XXIII, in a way that the natural law theory does not, offering another reason to use the natural law and not the Lockean lens for interpreting papal teaching and for political and economic ethics more generally.

I begin by recounting the historiography that connects Locke concretely with English colonialism. Since the 1970s, scholars have resituated the *Second Treatise* within its seventeenth-century context. Two basic historical findings are relevant here. First, the traditional dating of the *Second Treatise* to 1689 has been revised

---

54. For more, see Barbara Arneil, *John Locke and America: The Defence of English Colonialism* (New York: Oxford University Press, 1996), chap. 4.

to the years of 1679–1682.⁵⁵ The second set of historical findings—extensive documentation of Locke's involvement with the Carolina colony and the English Board of Trade—intersects with this first finding at numerous points. By 1682, Locke had had significant involvement with the Carolina colony, of which the Earl of Shaftesbury was a lord proprietor. Locke is attributed with drafting at least significant portions of the *Fundamental Constitutions* of Carolina. A trail of letters and personal documents has also placed Locke at the nexus of day-to-day administration and oversight of the colony from 1668 to 1675.⁵⁶ Though Locke was ostensibly several years removed from his work in the Carolina colony when he drafted the *Second Treatise*, more recent evidence places him in the Earl of Shaftesbury's house in 1682, redrafting the *Fundamental Constitutions* in response to disputes between colonists and the lords proprietors.⁵⁷ At the same time Locke was drafting the *Second Treatise*, he was also engaged in his work supporting and advancing the Carolina model of plantation colonialism.

There is compelling evidence that Locke's chapter on property is written specifically with the American context in mind.⁵⁸ Armitage suggests that chapter 5 of the *Second Treatise* may have been the last chapter drafted, placing its drafting squarely in the summer of 1682 when Locke was residing with the Earl of Shaftesbury and redrafting the *Fundamental Constitutions*, and added after the fact into the main text. Textual evidence corroborates that chapter 5 is written, if not exclusively to address the concerns of English colonialism, with these concerns in mind.⁵⁹ The twenty-six paragraphs of chapter 5 contain half the references to

---

55. This was first established by Peter Laslett. J. R. Milton and Richard Tuck provided further evidence that the *Second Treatise* was composed sometime in 1681–1682. David Armitage, *Foundations of Modern International Thought* (New York: Cambridge University Press, 2013), 94.

56. Arneil, *John Locke and America*, chap. 5.

57. David Armitage, "John Locke, Carolina, and the Two Treatises of Government," *Political Theory* 32, no. 5 (2004): 602–27.

58. In addition to Armitage and Arneil, see, for example, Herman Lebovics, "The Uses of America in Locke's Second Treatise on Government," *Journal of the History of Ideas* 47, no. 4 (1986): 567–82; Francisco Castilla Urbino, "El indio americano en la filosofía política de John Locke," *Revista de Indias* 46, no. 178 (1986): 421–51; James Tully, "Rediscovering America: The Two Treatises and Aboriginal Rights," in *Locke's Philosophy: Content and Context*, ed. G. A. J. Rogers (Oxford: Clarendon, 1994), 165–96; Anthony Pagden, "The Struggle for Legitimacy and the Image of Empire in the Atlantic to c. 1700," in *The Oxford History of the British Empire*, vol. 1, *The Origins of Empire*, ed. Nicholas Canny (Oxford: Oxford University Press, 1998), 42–47; Richard Tuck, *The Rights of War and Peace: Political Thought and the International Order from Grotius to Kant* (Oxford: Oxford University Press, 1999), 177–78.

59. Though Zuckert argues that the chapter is written as a coherent part of the *Second Treatise* and aims to explain master-servant relations, directly after a chapter on master-slave

America or the Amerindians in the *Second Treatise*. Arneil points out that many of the concrete examples Locke uses to illustrate his point are "crops native to America." Sections 36, 37, 43, and 48 speak of corn; section 40 of "tobacco, the most important crop of New England, and sugar, the staple crop of Barbados, in which Locke invested in 1673."[60] It is insufficient to see the *Second Treatise*, even chapter 5 in isolation, as motivated exclusively by English colonialism, but the historiographical and textual evidence suggests that understanding Locke's theory of property, and its implications, demands understanding it as part of and influenced by colonial history and European international thought.

As he does with other traditions of thought, Locke inherits and develops the emerging ideas of agriculturalism in international thought, specifically the work of Alberico Gentili and Hugo Grotius, by grounding not just property but also territorial sovereignty in agricultural development. Gentili and Grotius both maintain that unused land can be open to private appropriation, but that in so appropriating one places oneself under the laws of the sovereign within whose territory that land lies. As I noted above, Gentili was one of the jurists, if not the first jurist, to find the private possession of land (immovables) as part of the natural law: "The seizure of vacant places is regarded as a law of nature. So it was when the world was young."[61] Gentili also appeals to divine law, quoting the prophet Isaiah's description of God's intentions for the earth: "Not as an empty waste did he create it, but designing it to be lived in."[62] Anthony Pagden claims that Gentili permits waste land to be settled without transferring sovereignty over that land in reference to this passage: "Things which are common to all so far as their use is concerned are the property of no one; their jurisdiction and protection [however] belong to the sovereign."[63]

In *De jure belli ac pacis*, Grotius follows Gentili on the appropriation of unused land. Unused land could indeed be subject to the sovereignty of a people; nonetheless, it was also open to cultivation and, through cultivation, appropriation by anyone, sovereign subject or stranger.[64] The dominion gained in

---

relations and before a chapter on paternal-filial relations. Zuckert, *Natural Rights and the New Republicanism*, 247–48.

60. Arneil, *John Locke and America*, 139.

61. Alberico Gentili, *De iure belli* 1.17, cited in Lantigua, *Infidels and Empires*, 226.

62. Isa. 45:18. Cited in Lantigua, 227.

63. Gentili, *De iure belli* 1.19, cited in Anthony Pagden, "Gentili, Vitoria, and the Fabrication of a 'Natural Law of Nations,'" in *The Roman Foundations of the Law of Nations: Alberico Gentili and the Justice of Empire*, ed. Benedict Kingsbury and Benjamin Straumann (Oxford: Oxford University Press, 2010), 359.

64. Grotius applies the Roman law of *res nullius* here, which allowed for the acquisition

this land by the cultivator was, however, still subject to the original sovereign: "Uncultivated land ought not to be considered as occupied except in respect to sovereignty, which remains unimpaired in favor of the original people."[65] However, more than Gentili, Grotius gives detailed specifications about what constitutes unused land. As David Lantigua notes, though Grotius's thought was not directed at the Americas, he supplies key pieces of the colonial agriculturalist argument when he states that "the primary indicator of barren or vacant land . . . depended on its lack of cultivation and unboundedness" and that taking possession of vacant land necessitated "acts of bounding, fencing off, and marking the land."[66]

At the same time the agriculturalist argument was gaining steam among jurists, English colonizers were deploying it in a more ad hoc manner to justify the acquisition of land in the Americas. These arguments were deployed specifically in response to ethical challenges to settlement from other English citizens, in both the colonies and at home, and draw on the same rhetoric of improvement and economic gain that ushered in two centuries of large-scale enclosure in England. The arguments the colonists marshaled in defense of their acquisition of land bear striking resemblance to and at times important differences from chapter 5 of the *Second Treatise*. Whether or not Locke read any of the colonists I cite here, a similar set of principles animate both the colonists' arguments and Locke's *Second Treatise*.[67] These examples do not, nor need they, establish any sort of causal relation to place Locke within the broader history of these agriculturalist ideas and show that he is developing the same ideological stream as these colonists.

I look first, then, at some of the arguments of the pre–*Second Treatise* colonists. One of the organizers of the *Mayflower* expedition, Robert Cushman, wrote the following in a tract on "the Lawfulness of Removing Out of England into the Parts of America": "[The Indians are] not industrious, neither have art, science, skill or faculty to use either the land or the commodities of it; but

---

of movables by "Roman citizens and noncitizens (*peregrini*) alike," and extends it to land. On the right of strangers in the Roman law of *res nullius*, see Benton and Straumann, "Acquiring Empire by Law," 14.

65. Grotius, *De jure belli*, cited in Fitzmaurice, *Sovereignty, Property, and Empire*, 97.

66. Lantigua, *Infidels and Empires*, 228. Lantigua refers to this as a "nascent agricultural criterion."

67. That Locke's library contained John Smith, José de Acosta, Samuel Purchas, Cristóbal de Acuña, and William Wood likely underestimates the travelogues and colonial literature he would have had access to in Shaftesbury's library and the Council of Trade. John Locke, *Locke on Money*, ed. P. H. Kelly (Oxford: Oxford University Press, 1991), 97–98.

all spoils, rots, and is marred for want of manuring, gathering, ordering, etc. [They] do but run over the grass, as do also the foxes and wild beasts, [so their land is] spacious and void." We can see here several implicit connections with Locke's later argument. The Indians, as the colonists referred to them, did not use the land. In fact, "all spoils, rots, and is marred." This is due in part to a lack of industry, but also to a lack of requisite skills and knowledge to cultivate. At different points in his writing, Locke implicates the Amerindians as lacking both skill and industry. As Armitage notes, however, Locke never attributes a lack of any "faculty," especially the key faculty of reason, to the Amerindians.[68] Nor does Locke ever directly disparage the Amerindians as savages or beasts.

The question of how far these points go in distinguishing Locke from the colonists' agriculturalist arguments, though, turns on what qualifies one for the private possession of land. Armitage infers that Locke attributing reason to the Amerindians is evidence he is not an English imperialist. However, it is not the faculty of reason but the activity of industry that secures possession in the land, and for Locke the Amerindians may evidently be rational and unindustrious. This is a point Locke emphasizes: asking whether "in the wild woods and uncultivated waste of America, *left to nature, without any improvement, tillage, or husbandry*, a thousand acres yield *the needy and wretched inhabitants* as many conveniences of life as ten acres of equally fertile land do in Devonshire, where they are well-cultivated."[69] Indeed, as Lantigua notes, a "chief assumption of Locke's view on property in the *Second Treatise* was that the natives did not exhibit the full potential of reason under the divine mandate to subdue the earth through industrious labor." With respect to the disparagement of the Amerindians, Lantigua points out that though "Locke did not explicitly call natives savages . . . their savage way of life could be inferred easily from their occupation of the state of nature."[70] The fact that Locke maintained the rationality of the Amerindians and never directly disparaged them as savages or animals should not obscure the fact that the structure of Locke's argument mirrors Cushman's: since (a) the land is uncultivated (according to English sensibilities) and (b) is spoiling for want of care (anticipating the spoilation proviso), the land is void, or vacant.

68. Armitage, *Foundations*, 129.
69. Locke, *The Second Treatise*, 5.37 (pp. 279–80) (emphasis added). Locke, in the *Essay*, also notes how there are "whole Nations . . . amongst whom . . . uncultivated Nature has been left to it self, without the help of Letters, and Discipline, and the Improvements of Arts and Sciences." Cited in Arneil, *John Locke and America*, 115.
70. Lantigua, *Infidels and Empires*, 240. See also 223 on the connotations of the use of "savage" in Locke.

Critiquing Locke

The Puritan leader John Winthrop, in his own defense of English colonization, makes a case even closer to the explicit language of Locke's labor theory and sufficiency proviso: "This savage people rules over many lands without title or property; for they enclose no ground, neither have they cattle to improve the land by.... And why may not Christians have liberty to go and dwell among them in their wastelands?" The Indians possess no title *because* they enclose no ground nor improve the land. Note the echo of the rhetoric of improvement that was also crucial to the enclosure movement in England. Having failed to improve the land, the Indians dwell in the Americas as on waste land, another claim and term that will prove central to Locke's argument. John Cotton completes the argument in anticipation of Locke's philosophical formulation. As Cushman and Winthrop have argued, America is waste, or vacant, and, Cotton adds, in "a vacant soil, he that taketh possession of it, and bestows culture and husbandry upon it, his right it is."[71] Even Locke's two celebrated provisos can be seen as emanating from and, to a certain extent, reinforcing the colonists' logic of denying Amerindian dominion over the land. Locke's sufficiency proviso was anticipated by Winthrop's defense of the Massachusetts Bay Colony's appropriation of land. After noting that the Indians did not enclose nor improve land—and thus possessed no more title to the land than a right to use it—he then provides a sufficiency proviso to further justify this appropriation: "so ... if we leave them [the Amerindians] sufficient for their use, we may lawfully take the rest, there being more than enough for them and us."[72]

Implicit to the activity and arguments of the colonists is a denial not just of Amerindian proprietary claims but simultaneously of Amerindian territorial sovereignty. Amerindian sovereignty, the curtailment of which is central to Locke's justification of the appropriation of waste land, was effectively denied by the English Crown and its agents by interpreting all land deeds not as treaties between sovereigns but as sales of land under colonial law. As William Cronon notes, "No question of an Indian village's own sanctions could arise [in the question of interpreting a land deed], for the simple reason that Indian sovereignty was not recognized. The Massachusetts Bay Company was careful very early to instruct its agents on this point, telling them 'to make composi-

---

71. These are widely cited. I take all three examples from William Cronon, *Changes in the Land: Indians, Colonists, and the Ecology of New England* (New York: Hill & Wang, 1983), 56–57. Tully adds Samuel Purchas (1625), John White (1630), and Francis Higginson (1629) to the list of those who employ or justify appropriation by cultivation and without consent. Tully, "Rediscovering America," 176n43.

72. Cited in Tully, "Rediscovering America," 178.

CHAPTER FOUR

tion with such of the savages as did pretend any title or lay claim to any of the land.' Indian rights were not real, but pretended, because the land had already been granted the company by the English crown." The question of interpretation of land deeds is significant, as Cronon suggests that the Amerindians would have understood many of the deeds granted to the English to be for use and usufruct rights to the goods of the land, and not the land itself.[73] This is one way the "perfidy" of which the Amerindians were accused in selling the same tract of land to multiple settlers can be explained.[74] Understood as sales of the right to exclusion and alienation, those rights cannot be sold multiple times to different parties. Understood as rights of use and usufruct, there is nothing necessarily incompatible with multiple parties holding the same or diverse rights in a single tract of land. But in English court, the deeds would come to be interpreted as granting property rights—the sale of a right of exclusion to the land itself. To resolve the issue of multiple sales, the general court of Massachusetts Bay restricted "purchasing of Indian land without approval from the court, which restricted not just settler activity but Indian rights as well."[75] Here we can see in practice the overturning of Gentili's and Grotius's earlier claims: the Amerindians were denied territorial sovereignty over their land by denying their right to deal with a foreigner according to their own law within their own territory.

If in English colonial arguments before Locke the explicit denial of property and the implicit denial of sovereignty were made separately or at least not systematically related, Locke does the work of systematically grounding true political society in true cultivation and agricultural improvement.[76] For Locke, political society emerges *because* of the inconveniences that develop

---

73. Cronon, *Changes in the Land*, chap. 4. Cronon emphasizes that "land as commodity" is entirely novel and unintelligible to the Amerindians within their social and political system. "Land as commodity" was also novel to the English social and political system and was a significant part of the great transformation that Polanyi describes. Polanyi, *The Great Transformation*, 72–74.

74. Tully notes that this is one of the primary arguments of the colonists against respecting the treaties and land deeds that had been agreed upon with the Amerindians. "Rediscovering America," 185–86.

75. Cronon, *Changes in the Land*, 67–70.

76. A further point implicit here is that cultivation in Locke is always treated as private and not communal cultivation. Waldron, *Right to Private Property*, 168–71. This has the further effect of diminishing recognition of Amerindian land tenure because, aside from family corn plots, the practices of cultivation employed by the Amerindians were at least not restricted to private property, entailed larger kinship networks, and at times may even have been more properly communal, even between tribes and villages who might work

156

when property is settled and trespasses against one's person are multiplied as one's property becomes a target of trespass and one's life a target on account of one's property. The settlement of property increases the appeal of trespass as, on Locke's account, cultivated land yields much more than what one might, by one's industry, gather of the spontaneous fruits of the earth. Further, the cultivation of property opens the door to a money economy, which increases the appeal of trespasses not only from the object side of the equation but also from the subject side, as the apparently limitless increases in possession that the money economy introduces stoke the desire for ever greater possessions. The Golden Age that Locke describes—"before the desire of having more than men needed altered the intrinsic value of things"—is not so much a eulogy to the "natural human" as an account of its naïveté.[77] In such an age, humans were content "with what unassisted nature offered."

Once people cultivated the land, increased their population, and introduced money (making the land scarce and of some value), the people settled the boundaries of their societies in "leagues that have been made between several states and kingdoms." This settled territorial sovereignty does not apply everywhere, though, including the Americas: "Yet there are still great tracts of ground to be found which (the inhabitants thereof not having joined with the rest of mankind in the consent of the use of their common money) lie waste . . . and so still lie in common. Tho' this can scarce happen amongst that part of mankind that have consented to the use of money."[78] This argument anticipates what Locke later makes explicit: the Amerindians lack true or full sovereignty, including territorial sovereignty. Once it is established that the Amerindians do not settle land and have no common agreement on money, Locke's philosophy shows that such peoples have not entered political society, since they would have had no cause for, nor settled their territories in ways that

---

together, say, at a fish spawning ground where the harvest was particularly abundant. See Cronon, *Changes in the Land*, 60–66.

77. Locke, *The Second Treatise*, 5.37 (p. 279). This, incidentally, overlaps with other Golden Age accounts, such as the one in Seneca, where the Golden Age was not so much characterized by virtue as by the absence of vice. Nonetheless, in Seneca, the Golden Age remains an ideal in terms of calling for the cultivation of virtues that the actions of the naïve inhabitants of that age spontaneously mirrored. See Peter Garnsey, *Thinking about Property: From Antiquity to the Age of Revolution* (Cambridge: Cambridge University Press, 2007), 123. In Locke, there is no celebration of the virtue of the Amerindians, only recognition of their naïveté.

78. Locke, *The Second Treatise*, 5.45 (pp. 283–84). If we have any doubt that Locke has the Americas in mind here—though he never specifically references them—we can look to 5.49: "In the beginning, all the world was America."

demand, sovereign respect. To the colonists' practical overturning of Grotius, Locke adds a theoretical argument that does the same: uncultivated or waste land cannot fall under a sovereign, unless it happens to be in the middle of an otherwise cultivated landscape and settled political state, because where the land in general lay in waste, there is no true sovereign.[79]

Locke explicates the nonpolitical state of the Amerindians later in 8.107–108, confirming the argument just inferred from his discussion of "settling the boundaries of states and kingdoms." In 107, Locke describes the beginning of political society in general terms: "The equality of a simple poor way of living confining their desires within the narrow bounds of each man's small property made few controversies, and so no need of many laws to decide them. And there wanted not of justice where there were but few trespasses, and few offenders. . . . 'Twas natural for them to put themselves under a frame of government . . . [choosing] the wisest and bravest man to conduct them in their wars, and lead them out against their enemies, and in this chiefly be their ruler." Confirming one's sense that Locke has the Amerindians in mind here, he writes in the very next section: "Thus we see that the kings of the Indians in America, which is still a pattern of the first ages in Asia and Europe, whilst the inhabitants were too few for the country, and want of people and money gave men no temptation to enlarge their possessions of land, or contest for wider extent of ground, are little more than generals of their armies."[80] Lacking the kinds of trespasses that spur humans into true political society because they lack the kinds of cultivated property and subjective desires brought about by a monied economy, the Amerindians have merely, on Locke's terms, an ad hoc political society that organizes and disperses as the need for convenient defense against aggressors dictates. Locke's theory provides a systematic grounding for the diminution of Amerindian sovereignty on the very basis of colonial arguments that the Amerindians did not improve the land, and so joins two apparently separate arguments in earlier colonial discourse. Lacking territorial sovereignty, the Amerindians could not claim the land they did not actively occupy (itself being waste and subject to spoilation); the land could be claimed by any (private or public) who left the Amerindians as good and enough for their own use and, should they choose, cultivation and appropriation.[81]

79. This argument seems to undermine attempts to defend Locke as only thinking "in terms of private law occupation, not occupation with effects on sovereignty." Benton and Straumann, "Acquiring Empire by Law," 26.
80. Locke, *The Second Treatise*, 8.107–108 (pp. 315–16).
81. The power of this denial of Amerindian sovereignty can be seen in the way it continues to influence interpretation today, as when Waldron attempts to find a claim of equality

Locke's philosophy reflects important shifts in both colonial discourse and international law. In eighteenth-century colonial discourse, the colonists begin to connect the denial of property with the denial of sovereignty in, for example, arguments against court cases that rule in favor of the Amerindians. Several scholars have noted that John Bulkley's reaction to an English court's decision that the colony of Connecticut must respect original territorial treaties made with the Mohegan tribe draws explicitly on Locke's argument in the *Second Treatise*. Bulkley, citing Locke, makes the same conceptual connection between the arguments about the Amerindians' limited property, rudimentary political society, and lack of monetary system to suggest that they had no desires beyond subsistence prior to the English arrival, thus left the land in waste, and, as such, the English had an equal right to settle and claim it without their consent (the treaty being merely convenient for peaceful relations).[82] The use of these arguments to diminish or cast doubt upon treaties and land sales made with the Amerindians and legal injunctions in their favor is an important point to understand the agriculturalist argument's role in Amerindian dispossession.

Before turning to that, though, we can note how in international law, the use of *res nullius* became one of empire's central justifications in the work of Emer de Vattel. In his *Le droit des gens* (1758), Vattel delivers the agriculturalist argument: "The cultivation of the soil . . . is . . . an obligation imposed upon man by nature." When the states of Europe come upon the land of nomads and nonagricultural peoples, "which the savages have no special need of and are making no present and continuous use of, they may lawfully take possession of them and establish colonies in them."[83] With this argument, Vattel pushes "territories inhabited by 'roaming' peoples rather than farming settlers into the realm of *res nullius*," codifying in eighteenth- and nineteenth-century international law the absence of territorial sovereignty outside of settled cultivation.[84] Whether or not Locke can be directly implicated in the strengthening and

---

in chapter 5 of the *Second Treatise*. He suggests that Locke's theory treats Amerindians equally (at least in a formal sense) in that they also may engage in the activities that lead to appropriation and so stake their claims to the land they dwell on. Though Waldron thinks Locke's argument poor, his interpretation never questions the colonial and Lockean premise that the Amerindians are better understood as separate families and individuals and not political societies, for which the more basic expression of equality would have been recognition and respect for territorial sovereignty. Waldron, "Disproportionate and Unequal Possession," 168–70.

82. Tully, "Rediscovering America," 193–94; Lantigua, *Infidels and Empires*, 249.

83. Emer de Vattel, *Le Droit des gens; ou, Principes de la loi naturelle* (1758), 1.8.81, 1.18.207–210, cited in Tully, "Rediscovering America," 194–95.

84. Benton and Straumann, "Acquiring Empire by Law," 26.

reification of agriculturalist arguments in colonial discourse and international thought (the former is evident, at least), my argument is simply that the imperialist implications of Locke's agriculturalist and labor-mixing theory of property can be plainly seen in the actions and thought of eighteenth-century imperialists. The centrality of the agriculturalist argument becomes all the more evident as empire expands to Australia, California, and British Columbia in the eighteenth and nineteenth centuries.[85]

The agriculturalist argument runs in theoretical and practical opposition to the explicit aspiration for the self-determination of peoples in Catholic social thought. On the other hand, the scholastic theory of property can function as a bulwark for that same aspiration. Like the scholastics, Locke thinks that God gave the world to humans in common. In contrast to Locke (and Gentili), however, the scholastic canon lawyers and theologians think that property only emerges under the *ius gentium*, a form of positive law, and not under natural law. Recall from chapter 2, in Aquinas's thought, how property as a sort of principle of stewardship, of taking responsibility for, managing, and governing the things of the earth, is a part of the *ius gentium*. This principle is thus recognized as in part constitutive of human society, but it only takes concrete and determinative form through the customs, traditions, and enactments of each society. There is no presumption in favor of settled agriculture (or any other property regime) as the natural form of property in scholastic thought. Diverse forms of property are rather determined through usage, custom, and enacted law. There is ample room in the scholastic theory for the kinds of common, flexible, and mobile land tenure that the Amerindians exercised and that many indigenous peoples continue to exercise today.

The Spanish scholastics who wrote at the time of and in response to Spanish imperial activities in the Americas can provide a point of comparison for the natural law and Lockean theories of property. Does the natural law theory of property (and my claims about its theoretical space for diverse property regimes) manifest a different tendency than the Lockean theory? While I cannot fully examine the scholastic sources here, the divergent conclusions of the Spanish scholastics with respect to property can be readily demonstrated.[86] The *ius gentium* (a category missing from Locke) emerges from human rationality as such, and not the standards of "civilized peoples," as, following Ulpian, the early modern jurists characterized it. Despite its connection to

85. Stuart Banner, *Possessing the Pacific: Land, Settlers, and Indigenous People from Australia to Alaska* (Cambridge, MA: Harvard University Press, 2007).
86. The following discussion follows Lantigua, *Infidels and Empires*, 254–70.

reason, however, it is established through positive mechanisms, be they usage, custom, or enacted laws. As Vitoria writes, it represents "the common consent of all peoples."[87] In the encounter with the peoples of the Americas, the Spanish were encountering other peoples and, between them, the principles and norms of the *ius gentium* applied.

Lantigua shows how this tension between the rational and positive character of the *ius gentium* generates a productive set of principles and reflections on the character and nature of difference between peoples in political practices, religious practices, and the division of goods or property. Though Vitoria can be demonstrated to be mostly commensurate with later thinkers on this point, it is Domingo de Soto, Bartolomé de Las Casas, and Francisco Suárez who establish the clear legitimacy of diverse divisions of goods between peoples. For each of these thinkers, the *ius gentium* refers to laws and customs that are conducive to preserving and fostering human sociability, which, as Soto states, "are ordained to a determined end and deliberated through specific circumstances."[88] Different laws and customs are intelligible as ways of organizing human social life but are determined according to the "specific circumstances" of different peoples. Notice two points about this way of conceiving of property. First, it is quite clearly an explicit representation of the claim that I make in previous chapters that for the scholastics, property, as a part of the *ius gentium*, is one expression of the political nature of humans. Second, it inverts the agriculturalist arguments given above: true or full sovereignty is not dependent upon certain forms of cultivation and the introduction of bullionist monetary systems; rather, it emerges from the social and rational character of humans, who express that sovereignty in part through different modes or regimes of property. The concrete implications of this in the Spanish scholastic rebuke of Spanish imperialism can be seen in Las Casas, who had firsthand experience with the alternative regimes of property and settlement among the Amerindians. Las Casas's third principle of interaction between peoples recognizes the sovereignty of peoples irrespective of any specific property regime, agriculturalist, private, or otherwise: "All nations and peoples, however much they be infidels, possess their separate lands and kingdoms, which they have inhabited originally. They are free peoples and do not recognize a political superior outside themselves, except their own."[89] That Spanish scholastic

---

87. Vitoria, *Comentarios*, 3:ad q. 57.3.3, cited in Lantigua, *Infidels and Empires*, 257.
88. Soto, *De justicia et jure*, lib. 3, q. 1, a. 3, cited in Lantigua, *Infidels and Empires*, 261.
89. Bartolomé de Las Casas, *Principia quaedam*, p. 1255, cited in Lantigua, *Infidels and Empires*, 269. Las Casas is addressing Spanish claims to subject the Amerindians on account

CHAPTER FOUR

thought had little practical impact on the policies and practices of the Spanish Empire and the *encomienda* system is not immaterial to this discussion but neither is it central. At least, it is no more central than the practical impact of Locke's theory in the colonization of North America. Contrary to Locke, Spanish scholastic thought reinforces Amerindian sovereignty, in part by (and partly as a consequence of) maintaining the legitimacy of alternative understandings of property and land tenure.

The practical implications of Locke's thought, however, are worth addressing. As is suggested in Cronon and Arneil and made explicit through extensive historical research in Stuart Banner's *How the Indians Lost Their Land*, most colonial land acquisition did *not* take place through unilateral acts of occupation and cultivation, but through land purchases.[90] If that is the case, then just how important is this agriculturalist argument, for which Locke's labor-mixing theory of property provides powerful justification, to English colonial and later US land acquisition? In the first case, as with the Spanish scholastics, I want to separate the evaluation of Locke's theory of property from whether or not agricultural settlement was the actual or primary mode of Amerindian dispossession. Locke's theory, taken on its own terms, licenses such dispossession, whether or not anyone actually utilizes this method of dispossession. Second, the theory, taken comprehensively, may not have done all the work of dispossession, but there is ample evidence it created an important framework for interpreting treaties, laws, and renegade acts of dispossession by disgruntled colonists, settlers, and later frontiersmen in a way that favored dispossession.

The nonpolitical status of the Amerindian and the categorization of their land as waste played a significant role in shaping what we might call the transatlantic social imaginary. As Eric Kades notes, the dispossession of Amerindians proceeded along a plurality of legal, extralegal, cultural, and environmental pathways, though it was almost always conducted under a "thin veneer of voluntariness (Indian deeds, treaties) covering a process that was, in large part, coercive."[91] One strategy was the disparagement or disregard of laws and rulings out of England (or, in later years, the East Coast) in favor of the Amerindians. Recall Bulkley's response to the Privy Council's ruling in favor of the Mohegan tribe in 1703, denying their political sovereignty and territo-

---

of their being infidels, but his argument can be extrapolated to the question and context that occupies the present section.

90. Banner, *How the Indians Lost Their Land*.

91. Eric Kades, "The 'Middle Ground' Perspective on the Expropriation of Indian Lands," *Law & Social Inquiry* 33, no. 3 (2008): 828.

rial rights. When the Privy Council reruled in favor of the Mohegan tribe in 1743, William Samuel Johnson went further, in general terms disparaging any agreement made between the colonists and Amerindians. The treaties made with the Amerindians had no force because the colonists were not treating with states (or political entities) but with "a company of lyons, wolves or bests whom the Indians but too nearly resembled."[92] The agriculturalist account need not directly impugn the Amerindians as savages to support this sort of depoliticization of them and, consequently, undermine the force of legal agreements made with them or legal rulings made in their favor.

A second strategy, impossible to reconcile with giving equal respect and territorial sovereignty to Amerindian society, was a variety of tactics to drive down the price of acquiring land.[93] The laws, enacted in every colony, restricting the purchase of Amerindian land to the colonial governments (or at least subject to the authorization of the colonial governments) would have driven down the price of land by turning a competitive market of many potential buyers into a monopolistic market of a single buyer.[94] Regardless of the reality on the ground, this position was codified in US law in Chief Justice Marshall's opinion in *Johnson v. M'Intosh* (1823), which "found that Indians (under the colonists' laws) had a limited title of occupancy that did not include free rights of alienability."

Another, more pernicious approach was to take advantage of how settlement alongside Amerindians tended to weaken their societies over a period of time through the spread of deadly disease and the alterations of their environment through the introduction of European flora and fauna. Diseases like smallpox that the Amerindians had no acquired resistance to could easily reach 90 percent kill rates, while creatures such as European pigs would often outcompete "Indian game animals for key foodstuffs (e.g., acorns and other seeds)."[95] A decimated Amerindian population living in an ever-more-foreign

92. William Samuel Johnson, cited in Tully, "Rediscovering America," 194.
93. The following is drawn from Kades, "The 'Middle Ground' Perspective on the Expropriation of Indian Lands." Most of this also reads as an almost complete confirmation of Tocqueville's account in *Democracy in America and Two Essays on America*, trans. Gerald E. Bevan (London: Penguin Books, 2003), 376–97.
94. Though Kades notes that Banner challenges this characterization of colonial land law, suggesting that many land transactions continued to occur informally and in, so to speak, an unregulated market between the Amerindians and the colonists. Kades argues that the question remains unsettled. See Kades, "The 'Middle Ground' Perspective," 835–38; Banner, *How the Indians Lost Their Land*, chap. 5.
95. Kades, "The 'Middle Ground' Perspective," 831. Tocqueville: "Half convinced and half compelled, the Indians move away to dwell in new deserts where the whites will not allow them to live ten years in peace. Thus it is that Americans acquired for next to nothing

environment would be in a weak bargaining position, making the land far cheaper to acquire than through initial land treaties or outright conquest. As early as the late eighteenth century, this strategy was given official recognition by US General Schuyler: as the settlers advanced, and game diminished, "[the Indians] dwindle comparatively to nothing, as all savages have done, who gain their sustenance by the chase, when compelled to live in the vicinity of civilized people, and thus leave us the country without the expense of purchase." George Washington affirmed Schuyler's position as "the cheapest as well as the least distressing way of dealing with them."[96] This was also the impetus behind many Homestead Acts in the mid-1800s, which encouraged settlers to advance toward the edges of nominally claimed (*de iure* under colonial law but not yet agreed with the Amerindian tribes) colonial territories to help bring *de facto* in line with *de iure* boundaries.[97]

What all of this suggests is that the agriculturalist argument did not exactly provide the mechanism for settling the land but did support important categories and assumptions devised by imperial agents about the political status of Amerindians and their claims to the land that undermined the laws that protected the Amerindians, legal rulings in their favor, and, in some cases, any sense of moral restrictions that would limit and constrain the acquisitive impulses of colonists and frontiersmen. The social imaginary created a situation in which Alexis de Tocqueville could state, with a great deal of irony, that while the Spanish had failed to exterminate the Indians, "the Americans of the United States have attained [this] with singular ease, quietly, legally . . . and with no violation to the great moral principles in the eyes of the world. Men could not be destroyed with more respect for the laws of humanity."[98] As moral and political justification, the agriculturalist argument embodied in Locke's theory may have enabled even many isolated acts of settlement and dispossession, but it did even more in creating a lens through which any mode of dispossession, through unfavorable or willfully misinterpreted treaties and land sales, for example, could be construed as justifiable by natural and divine law.

The argument in this section points to a much more general divergence between scholastic and early modern—mostly northern European—ideas of

---

whole provinces, which the richest monarchs of Europe could not afford to buy." *Democracy in America*, 381.

96. Schuyler, 1783, cited in Kades, "The 'Middle Ground' Perspective," 832–33.

97. Douglas W. Allen, "Homesteading and Property Rights; Or, 'How the West Was Really Won,'" *Journal of Law & Economics* 34, no. 1 (1991): 1–23.

98. Tocqueville, *Democracy in America*, 397.

property. Each view of property at least implicitly conveys a certain sense of the primary justification and teleological orientation of property. I have already argued extensively that it is primarily justified in scholastic thought as in some form instantiating and protecting basic norms of the human and political orders: equity, equality, sufficiency, and liberty. The agriculturalist approach—in the seventeenth century being just as theological as the scholastic approach—instead justifies one narrow conception of property: that which maximizes (at least apparently) the production of the goods useful to human society and well-being. That it responds to certain features of humans (their dependency on the material world) should not obscure that, whereas for the scholastic theory the basic principles are political, for the agriculturalist approach the basic principles are economic: development, productivity, and efficiency. The establishment of property is prepolitical, not aimed at wanton gain, but at alleviating the poverty of "natural" human life by developing land, making it in Locke's estimation one hundred or one thousand times more productive, and therefore making the satisfaction of human need far more efficient and secure an enterprise. It perhaps demonstrates Locke's quiet understanding of the moral ambivalence of an institution whose logic is reduced to the satisfaction of material want that by the end of chapter 5 of the *Second Treatise* humans no longer labor to satisfy material needs but rather labor only to satisfy ever-growing material desires and trade is connected not to the alleviation of need but to the pursuit of riches and power.[99]

In general terms, we can differentiate between the scholastic and agriculturalist approaches in two key ways. First, whereas in the scholastic approach the general end of governing the material world must be specified according to a variety of possible concrete determinations of that end (thus calling forth practical reasoning), in the agriculturalist approach the only way of specifying that general end is that which is most productive—to choose to hunt and gather when a society could develop and produce much more (much more efficiently) by settling and cultivating is to forgo claims to the land itself. Second, whereas in the scholastic approach economic considerations are secondary to the attainment of moral and political principles in the establishment of property law, in the agriculturalist approach property regimes are driven by economic considerations. For the agriculturalist approach, any other political values are realized not by the establishment of property regimes that positively instantiate those values but by the securing of laws that otherwise

---

99. Arneil, *John Locke and America*, 147. Here Arneil cites some of Locke's unpublished notes on trade: "The chief end of trade is riches and power."

restrict, limit, or curb the holding and acquisition of property. Political values are, in other words, extrinsic to the logic of property and, in the most extreme articulation of this approach, only moral limits on the primary task of politics, which is "the increase of lands and the right employing of them."[100]

The scholastic approach, at least in theory, precludes this conception of politics: economics is at the service of politics, and economic values, though genuine values, are secondary to political values, which brings us back to the need for practical reasoning in establishing property regimes. The scholastic approach connects with the most recent pronouncements of the magisterium that the economy must be at the service of the political order, and not vice versa.[101] It is evident that I do not want to simply reject Locke's theory of property here; I want to reject the whole shift in early modernity from thinking about property as a political institution to thinking about it as merely an economic institution, a commitment that both informs and is reinforced by the agriculturalist approach.

Locke and the Telos of Property: A Theological Critique

I conclude this chapter with a brief evaluation of Locke's theory of property in terms of the principle that I discussed in chapter 1: that in the Christian tradition, from the early church to today, property is understood as a power of distribution and not a power of personal use. This last critique picks up where the previous discussion left off and decidedly weighs in on a debate about the implications of Locke's theory of property that I have so far passed over. My analysis focuses narrowly on just what it means to contrast property as a power of distribution and property as a power of personal use. I differ from other prominent readings of Locke in that I do not attempt to attribute the implications of his view to his taking sides in an emerging class conflict, as in C. B. Macpherson, nor situate his theory of property within a grander project of undermining classical natural law with a novel account of natural rights, as in Michael Zuckert. Nonetheless, my contention is that, irrespective of Locke's intentions, social position, or religious and philosophical commitments, his

---

100. Locke, *The Second Treatise*, 5.42 (p. 282). Zuckert writes that "Locke thus becomes the first to define political economy as the central task of politics." *Natural Rights and the New Republicanism*, 272.

101. Francis, *Laudato Si'*, encyclical letter (Vatican City: Libreria Editrice Vaticana, 2015), §§54, 189.

Critiquing Locke

theory of property is an example of what A. J. Carlyle calls a power of personal use, and that this conception of property makes the economy the primary and first concern of politics. This is a view of politics untenable within the Catholic social tradition and provides a concluding point to my overarching argument against the use of Locke's theory of property to interpret that tradition.

The idea that in the Christian tradition property is a power of distribution (and not personal use), first put in these terms by Carlyle, raises questions about what exactly this assertion means. In what sense is property a power of distribution? Does this mean that I own property if and only if I have a power to distribute it? Does selling count as enacting this power of distribution? How does a power of personal use coexist with the power of distribution? Does any distribution count? If I am a wealthy individual and spread the wealth to my other wealthy friends, who do the same with me, are we enacting this power of distribution?[102]

Descriptively speaking, and at its most general formulation as a system of governing a society's material resources, no single power can be associated as characteristic of holding property. In Roman law, one could alienate the powers of use and usufruct, so that property did *not* entail a power of personal use. This is also the case today with, say, a residential building that one leases to someone else. Constraints on personal use likewise limit one's power to distribute: if I own but have already rented out a residential property, I cannot offer it to a neighbor who has just been evicted, no matter how well intentioned. The power to develop property can be restricted by a perpetual conservation easement, which is put in place to prevent the development of property around riparian resources. Under feudal law in Europe, a peasant's land was inalienable except by permission from the manorial lord. In New Zealand law today, alienation of Maori land is restricted by a right of refusal, wherein the seller must first offer to sell the land to those claiming Maori ancestry, and only if that right is refused may the land be sold outside of that population. When it comes to personal property, even the right of exclusion might be limited in areas where gleaning laws enable access to and use of private agricultural property at certain times of the season.[103] As a characteristic descriptive feature for property, use (and distribution), alienation, development, and exclusion could all apply, but none applies without certain conditions.[104] This is a reason that

---

102. Thanks to Paul Weithman for raising similar questions and directing my attention to this needed clarification.

103. See a contemporary example of this practice in France in *Les Glaneurs et La Glaneuse*, Documentary (Ciné Tamaris, 2000).

104. There is a good case to be made that in contemporary capitalist frameworks the right to exclusion is *the* characteristic of private property. On this, see Thomas W. Merrill, "Prop-

legal scholars tend to resist discussing property in general terms, preferring instead to specify the bundle of rights that pertain to person A (and perhaps other persons) with respect to object B.[105]

Nonetheless, as Jeremy Waldron argues, a property regime often has some organizing principle or principles that descriptively characterize ownership under it.[106] In private property regimes, not every object is privately held nor does every privately held object entail the exact same set of rights between owner A and object B, but in general, an individual within such a regime can expect that, absent some clear information to the contrary, the land and things she comes across in that society are privately held with powers of exclusion. Waldron does not make the analogy to the other regimes he considers, collective and communal, but one could imagine that in a communal property regime an individual can expect that, absent some clear understanding to the contrary, the land and things she comes across in that society are communally held with certain rules of use. According to William Cronon, Amerindian societies in New England prior to the arrival of Europeans would have functioned in just this way, with an understanding that with the exception of habitations and cornfields, lands, resources, and even the things of the community would have been available for common use to others in that society.[107] Private, collective, and communal are examples of descriptive organizing principles offered by Waldron. The principle of property as a power of distribution, though, is held in common across a prominent strand of the Christian tradition. Valid across Roman law, late antique, feudal, mercantile, and capitalist systems of property, this principle's application to a wide variety of property regimes resists the idea that this is a descriptive principle. The same is true for the power of personal use.

The contrast between property as a power of distribution and property as a power of personal use, then, is not a contrast of descriptive but of moral organizing principles. They function in a similar way to the descriptive, or what we might call functional, organizing principles that Waldron discusses. Neither "moral organizing principle" excludes the possibility of distribution or personal use within its property regime. Indeed, the scholastic argument

---

erty and the Right to Exclude," *Nebraska Law Review* 77, no. 4 (1998): 730–55; Thomas W. Merrill, "Property and the Right to Exclude II," *Brigham-Kanner Prop. Rts. Conf.* 3 (2014); Robert Heilbroner, *The Nature and Logic of Capitalism* (New York: Norton, 1985), 38.

105. Thomas C. Grey, "The Disintegration of Property," *Nomos* 22 (1980): 69–85; Anthony Honoré, *Making Law Bind: Essays Legal and Philosophical* (Oxford: Clarendon, 1987), chap. 8.

106. Waldron, *Right to Private Property*, 42–43.

107. Cronon, *Changes in the Land*, 60–67.

necessitates that a power of personal use attach to property. The scholastic argument as I have developed it over the previous chapters is that property is an institution for dividing the natural right of each person to use the things of the earth for his own sustenance, precisely for the purpose of preserving that natural right of use (in line with some measure of equity, sufficiency, and liberty) for each person. According to different sources, this might be because the ability of each person to make use of things held in common is threatened by sin or because of the simple problem that uncoordinated action will tend to threaten and undermine access and equitable distribution of the things of the earth, or both. The key point, though, is that, normatively speaking, property *must* entail a power of personal use in order to satisfy the arguments from the Christian sources we have examined about the problems a system of property is introduced to solve.

So, what does it mean to say that in this tradition property is a power of distribution and not a power of personal use? We have already seen various formulations of this principle in earlier chapters. In the early church, Chrysostom argues: "You too are stewards of your own possessions. . . . Everything belongs to God . . . he left these things in your hand, in order to 'give [the poor] their meat in due season.'"[108] For Aquinas, while powers like administering and managing property may be said to be private, use always remains in principle common, so that one "might readily share [her property] with others in their needs."[109] The logic here is the same as that which guarantees that personal use will be a power associated with property in this tradition. The whole point of a system of property in this approach is to guarantee and protect the access of each person (and not just myself) to the things of the world in accordance with the dictates of natural and divine law. The power of distribution as a moral organizing principle functions at both the level of the regime (the purpose of this regime is to ensure that material resources are distributed in accordance with and to preserve some measure of equity, sufficiency, and liberty) and the level of the individual. One way it could be said to pertain to the individual is that the power of personal use in this system is a power of personal distribution: in a private property system, I hold the powers of administration and distribution over certain things and I distribute these things first to myself for the satisfaction of my own needs. The perfect and moral possession of these

---

108. Chrysostom, *Homilies on the Gospel of Matthew*, in *Wealth and Poverty in Early Christianity*, ed. and trans. Helen Rhee (Minneapolis: Fortress, 2017), 96.

109. Thomas Aquinas, *Summa Theologiae [1265–1274]*, 9 vols. (Scotts Valley, CA: NovAntiqua, 2010), II-II 66.2.

things, though, requires that I be prepared to share them to provide for the needs of others and the community. It is in the sharing of property for the satisfaction of others' needs and, to some extent, for their flourishing, that the moral *telos* of property is achieved.

Charitable practices and the virtue of charity are intrinsic to and commensurate with the very logic of this conception of property. That property is according to its very logic a power of distribution does not undermine the development of virtues of charity, generosity, and magnanimity any more than, say, the claim that marriage is according to its very logic a monogamous institution undermines the development of virtues of fidelity and chastity. For one thing, the ease with which I distribute my property will tend to grow as I grow in charity, in part through a continued practice of being willing to distribute my property. For another, the degree of my distribution can also grow, so that I am willing not just to provide food to the indigent but am also willing to provide the use of my car to a neighbor or the use of my spacious lawn to local children for their softball games. The moral logic of an institution may indeed establish grounds for certain laws or rules (the right of extreme necessity in the medieval era or redistributive taxation today) while leaving ample space for the perfection of the individual through the development of virtue. The *telos* of property in the natural law approach includes then the moral development of the individual. The perfection of that development is achieved through growth in charity, not at the expense of other pursuits but as the organizing principle of an individual's various pursuits, including the use and deployment of the material resources available to him.[110]

Likewise, there is nothing antithetical between the principle of distribution, the development of individual virtue, and communal or collective property regimes. Even in communal property regimes there is often some degree of personal property that one can be disposed to share with others in their need and want. More than this, however, communal property creates the opportunity for a less individuated but no less personal disposition to share. Elinor Ostrom recounts a system of communal dams in the Philippines that are used to moderate water levels to large gardens over the course of the year. The gardens are divided into personal plots and the system is set up around a set of incentives, both carrots and sticks, to try to ensure that each member does her part to maintain the dam. But a member's willingness to contribute beyond the minimum of what is required to maintain or improve the dam increases

---

110. This provides an interesting point of comparison with a Hegelian approach to property, which Waldron explicates in *Right to Private Property*, chap. 10.

the distribution of the good to every member of the collective.[111] Additionally, another gardener might fall ill for the season, and the community can pick up both his communal duties as well as tend to his garden plot to ensure that his family receives food that season. Systems of private, collective, and communal property can each provide the conditions to exercise and foster moral growth and maintain the character of property as a power of distribution.

What does all this have to do with Locke? My contention here is that if we want an example of a theory in which, morally speaking, property is constituted by a power of personal use, we can look to Locke. For Locke, property is a power of personal use—this is its *telos*, clearly stated right at the beginning and then several times throughout his discussion of property in chapter 5. God gave the earth, and all that is therein, to humans in common, "yet, being given for the use of men, there must of necessity be a means to appropriate [the things of the earth] some way or other before they can be of any use."[112] Lacking a clear account of a natural right to use independent of proprietary rights, Locke establishes that property is the institution that enables just use. Consider the different foundations of the scholastic and Lockean approach. On the scholastic account, property is an institution whose end is the achievement of a certain set of moral and social goods—its *telos* is intrinsically distributive. On Locke's account, property is an institution whose end is the preservation of an individual's life and enjoyment of that life by making use of "as much as anyone can . . . to any advantage of life before [the property] spoils."[113] There is nothing intrinsically distributive in Locke's theory, and any distributive implications (such as the duly noted right of charity that he discusses in the *First Treatise*)[114] are extrinsic to the logic of the institution. It seems impossible to reconcile a strictly Lockean account of property with the dual social and individual character of property that becomes a mainstay in papal teaching.

To hold a Lockean position regarding movables (as the medieval civilians did, for example) need not reduce the whole of the institution to the logic of personal use, however. It is only with Locke's extension of this logic to land—being the chief matter of property "as that which takes in and carries all the rest"—that the power of personal use becomes the overwhelming rationale of all forms of property and becomes directly problematic for political society.

---

111. Elinor Ostrom, *Governing the Commons: The Evolution of Institutions for Collective Action* (Cambridge: Cambridge University Press, 1990), 82–86.
112. Locke, *The Second Treatise*, 5.26 (p. 274).
113. Locke, *The Second Treatise*, 5.31 (p. 276).
114. See note 118 below.

Why is this? In the first case, as Locke himself is at pains to explain, a system in which only movables can be appropriated places significant limits on the degrees of inequality and penury present within a society: "considering the plenty of natural provisions there was a long time in the world . . . there could then be little room for quarrels or contentions about property so established." The appropriation of land opens the door to the production of surplus, the introduction of money, and accumulation well beyond what could have been imagined in a state where only movables could be appropriated, and the prevailing logic for all of this surplus property and accumulation remains that upon which property in movables and land is founded.

In a situation in which property in land is agreed upon and distributed for the sake of preserving a certain measure of equity, sufficiency, and liberty in the use of the things of the earth (and the human goods that follow from such equitable access), the conventional system of property could be morally characterized by a power of distribution even if movables were and continue to be open to natural appropriation. In other words, one could conceive of how the scholastic civilians could have, for practical purposes, come to a very similar moral construal of property as the canonists and theologians. In Locke's theory, however, the appropriation of land is just as oriented toward personal use as the appropriation of movables (though, as Zuckert notes, the logic of "using up" or *consumptus* as the rationale of property in movables does not apply to land in the same way).[115] "As much land as a man . . . can use the product of, so much is his property." The natural and divine law that "man was under was rather *for* appropriating" land as much as anything else.[116] Again, Locke does not initially construe this as conducive to very much inequality. As he proceeds with his argument, he endeavors to show how, though oriented toward an individual's personal use, the appropriation of property in land has positive externalities that benefit all. The individual who cultivates and appropriates land "has a greater plenty of the conveniences of life from ten acres than he could have from an hundred . . . [and] may truly be said to give ninety acres to mankind." The surplus that eventually results from such cultivation leads to the division of labor; the introduction of conveniences like bread, wine, and clothing; and the creation of so much value that "a day-labourer in England" is clad better than "the king of a large and fruitful territory" in the Americas. Not only has no direct harm been done in the appropriation of land, according to Locke's account, but the cup of the property owners overflows, so to speak,

---

115. Zuckert, *Natural Rights and the New Republicanism*, 263.
116. The first quote is Locke, *The Second Treatise*, 5.32 (p. 276); the second, 5.35 (p. 278).

Critiquing Locke

to those who are not the owners of land but merely the owners of their own person and who must sell their labor to live.

The introduction of money (and durable goods in general) introduces the possibility that one "might heap up as much of these durable things as he pleased." The introduction of money is ostensibly achieved by mutual consent, but the consent is tacit and, as Waldron notes, "those who are likely to be most prejudiced by the inequality [introduced by the use of money] are those who (on account of their poverty) will be participating least in monetary conventions, and so least likely to be involved as tacit consenters in assigning conventional value to gold and silver."[117] In any case, though a monetary convention is needed to unleash the full potential of property in land, the logic of property remains the same: its only end is personal use, unrestricted by the natural limits of the sufficiency proviso (since the surplus of cultivation and a money economy make more available to even a day laborer than she would have in the state of nature) and the spoilation proviso (since the bounds of one's property were limited only by "the perishing of anything uselessly in it"). The only limit is the right of charity, established by natural and divine law, that "gives every man a title to so much out of another's plenty, as will keep him from extreme want when he has no means to subsist otherwise."[118]

My claim here is not that such a system is inherently inhumane or cruel. There are ways of making such a political system humane—ensuring that the virtues of charity, generosity, and magnanimity are well cultivated across the propertied class; instituting generous systems of poor relief; passing laws guaranteeing full employment; etc. My claim is only that it is impossible on such an understanding of property to say that humans are simply stewards of their own possessions, implying that others have a claim to how they are used and distributed (beyond extreme necessity), or that with respect to one's own possessions their use always remains common, taking into consideration the needs and wants of others in the utilization of one's property. It is unintelligible to speak of the "social mortgage" of property—the rightful claim others and society have on one's own property—in a system in which the moral organizing principle of property is one's own personal use.

Let us say that, in theory, one could construe how similarly humane societies could embrace either approach to property. What are the practical implications of this difference? Just this, it seems to me: that in the Lockean approach those without property are mere patients and beneficiaries when

---

117. Waldron, "Disproportionate and Unequal Possession," 176.
118. Locke, *Two Treatises*, 1.4.42 (p. 170).

CHAPTER FOUR

it comes to outlays of property that more than suffice to keep them out of extreme want. The provision of educational, cultural, and public recreational institutions; the fostering of generous national unemployment, health, and agricultural insurance programs; social security; the creation of institutions of worker retraining; the payment of a just wage that accords with cultural standards of dignity and not bare standards of subsistence; redistributive taxes; the imperative to aspire to universal property in durable goods within a society, etc., are not the intrinsic responsibility of society and its property holders, as the Catholic social tradition holds, but are the blessings that accrue to a society that is fortunate enough to have generous benefactors.[119] Non–property owners have no natural claim to this sort of distribution where the moral logic of property is a natural right of personal use, but must only be prepared to stand in gratitude for whatever of this distribution is made that alleviates the burden of wage earners in society and enables some greater degree of flourishing on their part. Barring such a magnanimous property-holding class or a legislature that can enact laws compelling redistribution (which perhaps may be the same thing), the ordinary means of alleviating the burdens of daily life for wage earners would be ever-increasing economic activity and the hope that out of that increase a bit more will overflow. This is one significant point of connection with the claim that, on such a conception of property, economics becomes the primary preoccupation of politics.

When, in the nineteenth and early twentieth centuries, successive popes reiterated with increasing scope and emphasis that the provision of these social services was something that all members of society had a claim to and that, as such, the provision of which were matters of justice and not liberality, they embraced an approach to property incompatible with the one articulated by Locke in chapter 5 of the *Second Treatise*. Indeed, with the exception of right libertarians, liberal political philosophy has also generally made use of theories of property incompatible with the Lockean approach.[120] That so much schol-

---

119. See Macpherson on Locke: "The traditional view that property and labour were social functions, and that the ownership of property involved social obligations, is thereby undermined." *Possessive Individualism*, 211. With these claims I cannot avoid taking sides with Macpherson and Strauss in the dispute over the implications of Locke's thought, at least to the extent that I see in him a philosophy that insulates a propertied class from social claims directed at its property.

120. This, at least, is my interpretation of the place of property in John Rawls, in which property relations are functionally conventional insofar as they are restricted to what would pass muster behind the veil of ignorance, though I might question whether Rawls's difference principle is the only one that could pass such a test. John Rawls, *A Theory of Justice*

arship has in practice repudiated this understanding of property still leaves the question of just what idea(s) of property informs them. Though I think that a full examination would demonstrate that the principles systematized in the scholastic approach to property could form an adequate and compatible ground of property across a number of political philosophers and theologians today, in the next chapter I restrict myself to showing how the scholastic approach offers a compelling lens for interpreting the theory of property that undergirds much of Catholic social teaching.

(Cambridge, MA: Harvard University Press, 1971). Ronald Dworkin even more obviously diverges from this point—property is distributed by political society in such a way that it must meet the standards of the "equality of resources" principle. Ronald Dworkin, *Sovereign Virtue: The Theory and Practice of Equality* (Cambridge, MA: Harvard University Press, 2000). Left libertarians also depart explicitly from this conception of property. Otsuka, *Libertarianism without Inequality*.

FIVE

Reception and Innovation in Catholic Social Teaching

I F, AS I HAVE ARGUED, the natural law theory specifies a widely held and deeply rooted approach to property that runs the length of the Christian tradition, then what has become of this tradition of property in the twenty-first century? Neither within nor outside of Christian political discourse today does one find much explicit attention to the conventionality of property nor the idea that property is fundamentally a political institution, oriented toward political values, and only secondarily an economic institution. In fact, one finds opposing ideas in both Christian and non-Christian political thought: that private property is a natural right or that it is justified primarily by the improvements it can bring about in efficiency, productivity, and development (or general utility). Concerns about equality, sufficiency, and liberty seem to be extrinsic to the idea of property. They are limiting values that check and restrict the institution and the accumulation of property, not values that inform and legitimate the institution itself. Has the approach to property that I present, which stretches back through many of the high points and most important thinkers across the Christian tradition, fallen into desuetude?

My claim in this chapter is that, if this approach has fallen out of use, it is primarily at the second-order level of theological reflection. Certainly not every Christian political theology embraces the approach to property I have outlined. Nonetheless, this approach need not be stated explicitly to be operative within a theology (or a political philosophy, for that matter), as I suggest in chapter 3. To demonstrate the contemporary significance of the scholastic approach to property today, I show that the first-order arguments and claims regarding property in Catholic social teaching (CST), one of the most prominent expressions of Christian political thought from the late nineteenth century to today, are best understood and interpreted through the natural law lens. Part of what makes this so interesting in CST is that the tradition's treatment of economic questions commences with a Lockean approach to property in Leo XIII's *Rerum Novarum*.

Though *Rerum Novarum* and its incorporation of Lockean ideas of property may seem to indicate a deviation from the scholastic natural law tradition, here I argue that in its exceptionality and reception it more so proves the relevance of that tradition for CST. Subsequent papal teaching, as I discuss, clarifies, passes over, or actively reinterprets Leo's teaching on property in *Rerum Novarum*, with the cumulative effect of rejecting a Lockean approach to property. The popes who follow Leo XIII ground their teachings on property in the same theological and moral principles that ground the natural law theory of property: that "the Earth and its fullness" are given to all in common and that, therefore, each person has a licit power to make use of the things of the earth for her own well-being. The natural law of common dominion—that all things are common to all—shows up in CST as the common or universal destination of material goods, and by the papacies of John Paul II and Francis receives explicit articulation as foundational for a just social order. From the restatement of these principles, the instrumentality and conventionality of property emerge in CST, though the former receives more frequent and explicit affirmation. The conventionality of property is recognized explicitly only once, and this feature of the natural law theory must more so be inferred from CST. Nonetheless, though CST focuses on the realm of the plausible and possible and so never clearly articulates that regimes other than private property are legitimate, I suggest that it leaves the door open to alternative forms of property.

The scholastic natural law theory of property is characterized not only by reception but also by innovation. Here, again, CST demonstrates the vitality of the natural law approach. In the second part of this chapter, I show how subsequent popes utilize a small divergence between Leo and Locke in *Rerum Novarum* to incorporate a prominent modern, Hegelian theme of self-development as a key justification of property and a criterion of evaluating just property regimes. This is a development of the tradition that shows its ability to respond to new approaches to property, all while ultimately situating the new association of property and self-development within the general framework of property as conventional and instrumental to justice and the goals of society. Perhaps because of its theological presuppositions, CST holds together both instrumental and self-developmental ideas of property.[1] However, the differences between this tradition and Locke mean that CST manifests a much dif-

---

1. Alan Ryan, at least, thought that it was Locke's theological presuppositions that allowed him to hold together these two traditions that subsequent philosophers, from Rous-

CHAPTER FIVE

ferent way of holding these two approaches together—one that is also distinct from Hegelian theories, despite significant overlap. A key implication of this chapter, then, is that as CST carries forward the natural law theory of property, it engages critically and constructively with contemporary approaches to property and shows a path forward that is genuinely distinctive from but responsive to those approaches.

The grappling with Lockean themes in *Rerum Novarum* and Hegelian ideas in subsequent encyclicals shows Christian thinking on property to be very much alive and contested. There are, however, a number of ways to misread this contested space, as I discuss in this chapter. The first and most significant way is to interpret CST as introducing a Lockean natural right as a development of this Christian tradition on property. The idea of a natural right of appropriation is a clear violation of the natural law tradition that I chart in this project. Additionally, though, such a reading ignores the historical context of *Rerum Novarum* itself as well as its reception in subsequent encyclicals. A second way to misread this space is to claim that CST is simply an economic theory of distributivism. This claim ignores the principled openness of CST to less conservative and more radical ways of thinking about property. As one would expect in an inheritor of the natural law theory of property, CST preserves a level of generality in its thinking on property that allows for a variety of specifications. This generality allows it to prioritize the legitimate autonomy of peoples to form ways of life proper to their own history, culture, and environment. Though CST quite understandably never advocates for radical alternatives to private property, I suggest that its respect for peoples can accommodate other property regimes. These might include communal property regimes and certain modern approaches to collectivization so long as they can reasonably be said to preserve and even foster equity, equality, sufficiency, liberty, and, perhaps in a development of the natural law tradition, a principle of self-development.

Rerum Novarum *and Its Reception into a Natural Law Framework*

The social context of late nineteenth-century Europe was characterized by inequitable distribution of resources, extreme poverty, poor working conditions, and the relative political powerlessness of the proletariat, at least through

---

seau and Bentham to Hegel, Marx, and Mill, would separate. Alan Ryan, *Property and Political Theory* (Oxford: Blackwell, 1984).

any established channels of influence. Pope Leo XIII's *Rerum Novarum* (1891) addressed these challenges in a wide-ranging discussion that affirmed, among other things, the right to a just wage, the right of workers to organize, and the right to private property.[2] The right to a just wage and the right to organize stand out as compelling responses and perhaps developments, for example, of the tradition's emphasis on just price and support for medieval guilds.[3] On the question of property, Leo largely follows the work of nineteenth-century Catholic political economists, especially the Jesuit Luigi Taparelli. Of the various aspects of Thomistic thought that Taparelli recovered and put in conversation with contemporary political economy, Thomas's approach to property seems to have raised the most questions and misunderstandings.[4] Unable to resolve what he thought of as problems or inconsistencies in Thomas's thought, Taparelli adopts a Lockean position on property as a natural right, which Leo incorporates in the final draft of *Rerum Novarum*.

The use of the Lockean theory of property in *Rerum Novarum* raises important questions for the relatively recent tradition of magisterial Catholic social teaching, especially given the critiques I raised in the previous chapter. First, to what extent is the Leonine theory of property a fully fledged Lockean approach, or can the two be distinguished? Second, is this theory of property a legitimate development of, or a break with, prior Catholic political thought?[5]

---

2. Leo XIII, *Rerum Novarum*, encyclical letter, Vatican website, May 15, 1891, https://tinyurl.com/8t6sxdf4.

3. Catholic social thinkers of the period were divided over whether workers' associations should model the medieval guild or take the newer shape of the labor union. The final draft of *Rerum Novarum* includes a brief approbatory comment regarding the medieval guilds and modern worker associations, likely inserted by Leo, who redacted the final recension. It was vague enough to license either the guild or the union interpretation and as such became a standard if disputed text of papal support for labor unions. See Paul Misner, "The Predecessors of 'Rerum Novarum' within Catholicism," *Review of Social Economy* 49, no. 4 (1991): 452–53.

4. León de Sousberghe, "Propriété de 'droit naturel': Thèse néo-scolastique et tradition scolastique," *La nouvelle revue théologique* 72, no. 6 (1950): 590.

5. A number of sources treat a natural right to private property as a basic tenet of CST, with McKee arguing that it is a development of the tradition: Matthew Habiger, *Papal Teaching on Private Property, 1891 to 1981* (Lanham, MD: University Press of America, 1990), 329; Michael Lower, *Employee Participation in Governance: A Legal and Ethical Analysis* (Cambridge: Cambridge University Press, 2010), 50; Arnold McKee, "The 'Natural' Right to Private Property," *Review of Social Economy* 49, no. 4 (1991): 483–501, https://tinyurl.com/2mjfu9b3; A. M. C. Waterman, "Property Rights in John Locke and in Christian Social Teaching," *Review of Social Economy* 40, no. 2 (1982): 97–115, https://tinyurl.com/2fh589sb. Andrew Lustig sees a natural right in CST and Aquinas, a misreading that has historically

If the former, what new social organization or ideas warrant such a development? If it is a break, how are Catholics to interpret and evaluate it? In this section, I analyze Leo's approach to property, both in the wider context of the nineteenth century and in the narrower context of the encyclical itself. I then show how the reception of Leo's approach from Pius XI forward moves steadily away from treating property as a Lockean natural right and toward treating it as instrumental and conventional. Much of Locke's thought that appears in *Rerum Novarum* is not received by later CST as a development but is instead reinterpreted or jettisoned. Indeed, in John Paul II and Francis, one can find almost explicit restatements of the natural law theory of property and the natural law of common dominion, referred to as the "universal" or "common destination of material goods." And though private property regimes have been and remain presupposed as the norm in CST, this natural law reading of CST shows an openness in principle to other property regimes that receives explicit affirmation in John Paul II's *Laborem Exercens*.

The social and intellectual influence of Marx's analysis of political economy and property in nineteenth-century Europe is essential to understand Leo's analysis of private property. A cornerstone of Marxist thought is that private property, especially the private ownership of the means of production, stands in the way of more rational and egalitarian social and political structures defined by the social control of the means of production. This claim purports to be historicist: the erasure of private property in favor of the social ownership of the means of production is a part of a sort of natural progress toward higher, more rational, and more stable societies than the capitalist societies dominating contemporary social and economic organization. Marx also recognized that private property is a central pillar of capitalist political and economic organization, without which the whole structure falls. As Robert Heilbroner shows, the right of exclusion, specifically from the means of production, constitutes the core of the capitalist's power in society.[6] Capitalists can use the power of withholding the means of production (and thus access to the necessities of life) to secure preferable terms in the labor contract, especially with respect to wages. Labor is dependent on employment and laborers would find it difficult to survive "a week . . . a month . . . scarce any a year without em-

---

figured in Catholic social thought and might, at least post–*Rerum Novarum*, be attributed to reading Aquinas from the assumption of a natural right to property in CST. See B. Andrew Lustig, "Property and Justice in the Modern Encyclical Literature," *Harvard Theological Review* 83, no. 4 (1990): 415–46. On the historical misreading of Aquinas prior to *Rerum Novarum*, see Sousberghe, "Propriété de 'droit naturel,'" 580, 594.

6. Robert Heilbroner, *The Nature and Logic of Capitalism* (New York: Norton, 1985), 38.

ployment. In the long-run the workman may be as necessary to his master as his master is to him, but the necessity is not so immediate."[7] Though in theory laborers can withhold their work to exert their own pressure on the negotiations, the efficacy of that effort is closely related to prevailing labor laws and the social mores against which labor contracts are negotiated.[8] And by Leo's own account, the social mores of nineteenth-century Europe accommodated the exploitation of labor. In such a context, Marx and his followers saw the abolition of the right of exclusion especially from the means of production—and, more generally, the abolition of the right of private property—as the cure for the ailments of the proletariat and wider industrial society.

Against this, Leo argues that property is a natural right, something that cannot be eliminated or socialized without fundamentally contradicting human nature and the natural order of political society. In sections 6–11 of *Rerum Novarum*, Leo lays out his argument regarding the natural right of property. After claiming for each person "by nature the right to possess property as his own," Leo grounds this right in the natural tendency of humans to plan for the future through the exercise of reason. It must be within a human's right "to possess things not merely for temporary and momentary use, as other living things do, but to have and to hold them in stable and permanent possession."[9] That this right is *natural* Leo reiterates in the strongest terms, as compared with the preceding Catholic tradition: "There is no need to bring in the state. Man precedes the State, and possesses, prior to the formation of any State, the right of providing for the substance of his body." Without any context, there is no reason this statement could not align with the previous tradition.[10] Its novelty, though, is that Leo clearly does not equate the "right of providing for the substance" of one's body with a right of use but with a right of private possession and a bundle of rights, including exclusion, alienation, and private use, typically associated with private property. Property as a natural right is evidently inconsistent with the scholastic account of property as

---

7. Adam Smith, *Wealth of Nations*, 84, cited in Heilbroner, *Nature and Logic of Capitalism*, 41.

8. A study of the relative power of labor is beyond the scope of this project, but it fluctuates especially with major changes in economic systems. See chapter 3, note 33. Paul Misner, *Catholic Labor Movements in Europe* (Washington, DC: Catholic University of America Press, 2015), documents the efforts of Catholic labor movements to change working conditions through social and political action between World War I and World War II.

9. Leo XIII, *Rerum Novarum*, §6.

10. Charles Curran makes a similar point in a comparison of Leo and Aquinas on property in Charles E. Curran, *Catholic Social Teaching, 1891–Present: A Historical, Theological, and Ethical Analysis* (Washington, DC: Georgetown University Press, 2002), 176.

a convention, and contemporary commentaries on the encyclical confirm that conceptualizing property as a natural right emerged in Catholic social thought in the nineteenth century and only found its first authoritative expression in *Rerum Novarum*.[11]

Leo further strains tradition by drawing on an explicitly Lockean labor-mixing theory of property to bolster his account of property as a natural right. "When man thus turns the activity of his mind and the strength of his body toward procuring the fruits of nature," Leo writes, "by such act he makes his own that portion of nature's field which he cultivates."[12] Again: "That [sweat and labor] which has thus altered and improved the land becomes so truly part of himself as to be in great measure indistinguishable and inseparable from it."[13] When it comes to the moral limits of property, Leo combines both traditional and Lockean elements. In section 22, he quotes Thomas to note that one should hold one's possessions as common to all, but then adds a Lockean gloss that, save in cases of extreme necessity, the only duties that pertain to private property are duties of charity and not of justice. He ends this section with a restatement of the traditional principle that property is a power of distribution: "Whoever has received from the divine bounty a large share of temporal blessings, whether they be external and material, or gifts of the mind, has received them for the purpose of using them for the perfecting of his own nature, and, at the same time, that he may employ them, as the steward of God's providence, for the benefit of others." Leo presents a complex blend of theories of property, combining metaphysical and moral claims of the Lockean theory with the moral claims of the scholastic and early Christian traditions.

Despite Leo's claim that such conclusions about the origin of property in labor are "the common opinion of mankind . . . [and] found in the careful study of nature, and in the laws of nature," his argument is an otherwise close approximation of the theory that Locke first introduced in the seventeenth century.[14] It evidently differs from the Christian tradition examined in chapters 1 through 3 and preserved in key sixteenth-century scholastic sources, which holds that property is created and distributed by convention. While this tradition connects just distribution with patterns of labor, the act of laboring

---

11. Ernest Fortin, "'Sacred and Inviolable': *Rerum Novarum* and Natural Rights," *Theological Studies* 53, no. 2 (1992), https://tinyurl.com/592etjyv, 210–12; Sousberghe, "Propriété de 'droit naturel.'"
12. Leo XIII, *Rerum Novarum*, §9.
13. Leo XIII, *Rerum Novarum*, §10.
14. Leo XIII, *Rerum Novarum*, §12. Fortin, "'Sacred and Inviolable,'" 211–17.

is not held to be the grounds for a natural property right.[15] Further, though Leo's other prescriptions for alleviating the ills of the proletariat, such as a just wage and labor unions, presuppose the existence of private property, they do not depend on private property being a natural right. Thus, even if Leo's justification for private property is not preserved in later encyclicals, this does nothing to undermine the embrace of his other solutions for a just political and economic order.

Beginning with Pius XI, successive popes work steadily to shift away from a Lockean framework and recover a natural law framework for property. They do so by first articulating a wider nexus of rights and duties within which property ownership is embedded. This, again beginning with Pius XI, leads to an articulation of the natural law of common dominion that all things are common to all, which initiates an effort to articulate more clearly the instrumentality of property in service to each person's use of the world. And once the instrumentality of property is recovered, it is just another step toward recognizing that other regimes besides private property regimes can satisfy the instrumental end of property.

When Leo XIII discussed the relationship of the natural right to private property to other rights and duties, he insisted that any duties that impinged on the right to private property beyond sharing in times of extreme necessity were duties of charity and not of justice. In this, one can see yet another Lockean aspect of Leo XIII's thought. Though Locke articulated the sufficiency and spoilation provisos, scholars have recognized that the introduction of a monetary economy largely obviates the limits these provisos place on private acquisition—or at least substantially changes the meaning of their limits.[16] The remaining duties with respect to property that Locke articulates are twofold: a duty of justice to pay fair compensation for "honest industry" and a duty of charity to give from one's surplus to keep another from extreme necessity.[17]

---

15. Though the grounding of ownership in labor may have been anticipated in John of Paris. Janet Coleman, "Medieval Discussions of Property: 'Ratio' and 'Dominium' according to John of Paris and Marsilius of Padua," *History of Political Thought* 4, no. 2 (1983): 209–28; Janet Coleman, "Dominium in Thirteenth and Fourteenth-Century Political Thought and Its Seventeenth-Century Heirs: John of Paris and Locke," *Political Studies* 33 (1985): 73–100.

16. See, for example, Robert Nozick, *Anarchy, State, and Utopia* (New York: Basic Books, 2013), 174–76; Jeremy Waldron, "Disproportionate and Unequal Possession," in *God, Locke, and Equality: Christian Foundations of Locke's Political Thought* (Cambridge: Cambridge University Press, 2002), 151–87.

17. John Locke, *Two Treatises of Government*, ed. Peter Laslett (Cambridge: Cambridge University Press, 1960), 1.4.42 (p. 170). Locke frames these as rights, but they seem

Leo XIII's own articulation of the attending duties could almost draw from the *First Treatise* verbatim: "When what necessity demands has been supplied, and one's standing fairly taken thought for, it becomes a duty to give to the indigent out of what remains over . . . a duty, not of justice (save in extreme cases), but of Christian charity—a duty not enforced by human law."[18] Leo's encyclical, grounded firmly within the Christian tradition in its defense of workers' rights to a just wage, association, adequate rest, and work suitable to age, loses its footing at this crucial moment and neglects that the tradition demands much more in terms of justice both of individual owners and the institutions of society.[19]

With respect to property, later pontiffs articulate rights and duties, and especially distributive duties of justice, that recapture the important conviction of the Christian tradition that property is, morally, a power of distribution. Distribution beyond satisfying necessity, in other words, is not just a matter of Christian charity but a matter of what is due to others on the basis of an adequate construal of the material order and basic human moral equality, which opens the door to the legal enforcement of patterns or modes of distribution that accord with publicly articulated standards of what is due to each person. This aspect of property is grounded in what CST refers to as the "common destination of material goods," namely, that all things are common to or intended for the use of all. In the words of Pius XII,[20] "the goods which were created by God for all should flow to all alike, according to the principles of justice and charity."[21] And the principle that all things are common to all means that all ownership has a "twofold character," individual and social, which establishes its fundamentally distributive character. It is telling, with

---

self-evidently to be rights (to fair compensation and to another's surplus) that entail corresponding duties.

18. Leo XIII, *Rerum Novarum*, §22.

19. Thus, Aquinas does not limit justice in property to providing for another in extreme necessity in *Summa Theologiae* II-II 66.2, and canonists later articulated much more expansive duties beyond providing for another in extreme necessity. See chapter 1, note 103.

20. English translations of all of Pius XII's texts referenced in this chapter can be found in Pius XII, *The Major Addresses of Pope Pius XII*, ed. Vincent A. Yzermans, 2 vols. (St. Paul, MN: North Central Publishing Company, 1961). When no Vatican English translation is available, I often make use of these translations.

21. Pius XII, "On the 50th Anniversary of *Rerum Novarum*," radio address, Vatican website, June 1, 1941, https://tinyurl.com/4nmfv24j. Pius XII instructively references his encyclical *Sertum Laetitiae*, encyclical letter, Vatican website, November 1, 1939, https://tinyurl.com/ym43ce3t, §34: "The fundamental point of the social question is this, that the goods created by God for all men should in the same way reach all, justice guiding and charity helping."

reference to the latter, that Pius XI insists that Leo never denied nor questioned the twofold character of ownership, where the right of private ownership is given "not only that individuals may be able to provide for themselves and their families but also that the goods which the Creator destined for the entire family of mankind may through this institution truly serve this purpose."[22] The twofold individual and social character of ownership points toward the ultimate distributive purposes of ownership with the horizon of distribution being the common human family. These two principles of property, first clearly asserted in Pius XI, become mainstays of CST.

Duties of distribution apply both to individual owners and to political authority. Owners violate this duty of "social justice" when they excessively appropriate the returns of labor and development.[23] Though exact criteria for what would constitute an equitable distribution of the returns of labor and development are beyond the competency of CST to provide, grave inequality is at least one sign and symptom that the equitable distribution of material goods, in conformity with the norms of the common good and social justice, is being violated by individuals and is not being safeguarded by society (§§57–58, 60). This in no way sets aside duties of charity like almsgiving, beneficence, and munificence, but it also resists reducing the preponderance of duties associated with ownership to charity. Some duties of justice, like paying redistributive taxes, may be easy to define, while others are more difficult and so, while still duties of social justice, may not be enforceable by law (§47). With respect to the latter, one could imagine, for instance, the owners of a firm shifting from a wage contract to what Pius XI calls a partnership contract, where employees "become sharers in ownership or management or participate in some fashion in the profits received" (§§64–65). Where a partnership contract is conducive to the benefit of a firm, all things considered, such a transition may be a duty of justice (a distributive duty) that pertains to the owners of the firm. Even if such a duty cannot necessarily be enforced by law, it also seems clearly not to fall under duties of charity.

Political authority itself also has distributive duties and responsibilities. Since it is a matter of justice and not charity, the enforcement of distributive acts aimed at equity in distribution in conformity with the ends intended by the Creator is a task also of political society and its laws. Once again CST tends

---

22. Pius XI, *Quadragesimo Anno*, encyclical letter, Vatican website, May 15, 1931, §45, https://tinyurl.com/pep49ejv.

23. Pius XI, *Quadragesimo Anno*, §57. Hereafter, references from this work will be given in parentheses in the text.

to be silent on the details, given the multitude of possibilities associated with policy prescriptions to effect justice in distribution, but at the least one can infer several key principles with respect to ownership. First, taxation for the purposes of correcting injustices and inequities in the distribution of resources is certainly permitted. Indeed, since Leo XIII, the only limit on taxation clearly articulated in CST is that it not "exhaust private wealth through the weight of imposts and taxes" (§49). The "State is not permitted to discharge its duty" to distribute material resources in accordance with the common good "arbitrarily" (§49). Such a dictum could be taken right out of the natural law theory of property. And if, as many twentieth-century thinkers were to realize, private property were essential to a dignified life in a private property regime, then the state had at least one general obligation, howsoever it undertook to accomplish it: "To grant private ownership of property, if possible, to all."[24] John XXIII voices the same call to distribute property with additional focus on the distribution of resources that approximate property: social and agricultural insurance, social security, job training, etc.[25] As much as a strict concern to distribute property, this distribution of the kinds of resources important for social standing in contemporary society—education, job training, job security, health and other forms of social insurance, environmental resources, and a healthy environment—becomes a key concern of future popes and falls under a strict sense of social justice, in terms of what society owes its members.[26]

As with many of the scholastic canonists and theologians, the distributive duties grounded in the natural law of common dominion correspond to certain natural rights, such as rights of extreme necessity. In CST, the natural right to use the things of the world becomes prominent, eventually even displacing the natural right to private property entirely. The natural right to use finds clear and forceful expression in CST in Pope Pius XII, and has been a demand of every pope since.[27] In his address commemorating the anniversary of *Rerum Novarum*, Pius XII emphasizes the natural right of use, not that of property:

---

24. Pius XII, "Christmas Address, 1942," radio address, Vatican website, 1942, https://tinyurl.com/533eah5s.

25. John XXIII, *Mater et Magistra*, encyclical letter, Vatican website, May 15, 1961, esp. §§105–106 and 113–115, https://tinyurl.com/294awt43.

26. Among many examples, see John Paul II, *Centesimus Annus*, encyclical letter, Vatican website, May 1, 1991, §§19 and 34, https://tinyurl.com/59827buj; Francis, *Laudato Si'*, encyclical letter (Vatican City: Libreria Editrice Vaticana, 2015), §§25–52.

27. Though one might see Leo XIII's "right to procure what is required in order to live" as related to this more general right to make use of the things of the earth. *Rerum Novarum*, §44.

"Every human being, as a living being endowed with reason, has in fact the natural and fundamental right of using the material goods of the earth."[28] The very same principle is articulated in a series of encyclicals, with varying degrees of strength and specificity.[29] The natural right to use the things of the earth comes to steadily displace the natural right to private property, and even in encyclicals where the natural right to use is not explicitly articulated, private property is described not in an unqualified way as a natural right but as a right grounded in the natural order or possessing a "natural character."[30] In fact, though every pope since Pius XII has articulated clearly a natural right of use for each and every person, only John XXIII has articulated a natural right to property alongside that, and John XXIII's idea of a natural right to property differs in character from Leo's, as I discuss in the section below. What CST recovers that is basic about the human relationship to the material order is not the power of private ownership but the power of use, grounded in the conviction of the fundamental equality of each person and the grant of dominion given to each and all alike to make use of the world.[31]

The natural right of use does not merely displace any putative natural right to private property; it also explicitly subordinates and so instrumentalizes any right or form of property. More generally, this involves the commitment to subordinate the economic to the political order. Economic life must not be allowed to autonomously function according to the free competition of forces but must "be again subjected to and governed by . . . loftier and nobler principles—social justice and social charity." For the principle of social justice to be effective, society must "establish a juridical and social order which will, as it were, give form and shape to all economic life."[32] Property in particular, though, is singled out for its service to use. After noting that each person pos-

---

28. Though he places private property in the "natural order," he emphasizes that it is subordinate to and dependent on "the primary and fundamental right of use that is conceded to all." Pius XII, "On the 50th Anniversary of *Rerum Novarum*."

29. See, e.g., John XXIII, *Mater et Magistra*, §43; Paul VI, *Octogesima Adveniens*, encyclical letter, Vatican website, May 14, 1971, §14, https://tinyurl.com/4t73t8uj; Paul VI, *Populorum Progressio*, encyclical letter, Vatican website, March 26, 1967, §22, https://tinyurl.com/bdhb37dv; John Paul II, *Laborem Exercens*, encyclical letter, Vatican website, September 14, 1981, §14, https://tinyurl.com/4wmr3htn; Benedict XVI, *Caritas in Veritate*, encyclical letter, Vatican website, June 29, 2009, §27, https://tinyurl.com/3bwmewjz; Francis, *Laudato Si'*, §93.

30. John Paul II, *Centesimus Annus*, §30.

31. The latter consideration is especially prominent in John Paul II, *Laborem Exercens*, §§4–7.

32. Pius XI, *Quadragesimo Anno*, §88. The principle is evident as early as Pius XI but remains explicit across CST. See, e.g., Francis, *Laudato Si'*, §189.

sesses a right of use, Pius XII then states that property "should assist in making possible the actuation [of use] in conformity with its end."[33] And the language of instrumentality and subordination becomes ever more definitive: "All other rights ... including rights of property and free trade, are to be subordinated to [God's intention that the earth and everything in it be for the use of all human beings and peoples]."[34]

John Paul II offers a forceful, perhaps the most forceful, expression of this principle in his own social teaching.[35] One of the central principles of John Paul II's teaching in *Laborem Exercens* is "the principle of the priority of labor over capital," and the moral implications of this priority, including that capital is for the sake of labor and "should serve labor."[36] John Paul II is juxtaposing ownership (as capital) and use (as labor), where in the ordering of the material order use has a moral primacy over ownership. If we take labor here to mean *use*, then we can rewrite this central principle as "the priority of use over ownership." This reinterpretation coincides with John Paul II's own line of thought in §14, where, about ownership and use, he writes that the "Christian tradition ... has always understood [the right to private property] within the broader context of the right common to all to use the goods of the whole of creation: *the right to private property is subordinated to the right to common use*." Here, John Paul II offers an explicit restatement of the principle from chapter 2 that common dominion is the theological and moral framework of all property regimes. What matters in this restatement—"the priority of labor [or use] over ownership"—is that by understanding John Paul II in these terms we can also reframe what he says in §14 in the following way. Privately owned goods (especially the means of production) "cannot be *possessed against* [use], they cannot even be *possessed for possession's sake*, because the only legitimate title to their possession—whether in the form of private ownership or in the form of public or collective ownership—is *that they should serve* [use] and thus, by serving [use], that they should make possible the achievement of the first principle of this order, namely, the universal destination of goods and the right to common use of them."[37] By substituting "use" for "labor," one can see that

---

33. Pius XII, "On the 50th Anniversary of *Rerum Novarum*."
34. Paul VI, *Populorum Progressio*, §22.
35. Francis recognizes the strength of John Paul II's teaching on this and restates this whole line of thinking in *Fratelli Tutti*, encyclical letter (Vatican City: Libreria Editrice Vaticana, 2020), §120.
36. John Paul II, *Laborem Exercens*, §§12, 14.
37. To be entirely clear, I have here replaced every reference to "labor" in the original text with "use."

property is at the service of equitable access to use of the things of the earth, the central principle that animates both the scholastic and the longer Christian tradition on property.

Key theologians have long recognized that at the core of CST's teaching on property is its concern that property of whatever form be instrumental to equitable use. Across several of his writings, Msgr. John Ryan interpreted the natural right to property in Leo XIII by likewise situating it within the broader Christian tradition.[38] To understand the natural right to property in a way commensurate with Christian theology, Ryan argues that we must distinguish between three orders of rights. The first order of rights is characterized by rights to immediate, intrinsic, and necessary goods, the paradigmatic example being the right to life. The second order is goods that are not ends-in-themselves, as life, but that are essential and nonsubstitutable for human welfare, the paradigmatic example being a right to subsistence.[39] The third class of rights, the paradigmatic example of which is the right of private property, "is not an intrinsic good, but merely a means to human welfare, but [unlike the second order of rights] it is not *per se* and *directly* necessary for the majority nor for any one individual." For Ryan, the right to private property is contextually bound: in a society (such as a preindustrial society) where complete or partial collectivism or communalism could secure a just distribution of human welfare, there would be no "natural right" to private property.[40] For Ryan, the natural right to private property only has force in the present industrialized society, as it is so much more capable of securing human welfare than state ownership in such a society.[41]

---

38. John A. Ryan discusses this distinction among rights in several places: John A. Ryan, "Why Private Landownership Is a Natural Right," *Catholic University Bulletin*, 1912, 228–30; John A. Ryan, *Distributive Justice: The Right and Wrong of Our Present Distribution of Wealth*, rev. ed. (New York: Macmillan, 1927), 56–60.

39. I am not entirely sure about the cogency of distinguishing between these first two orders of right. In the second order, Ryan also puts marriage and personal freedom, both of which seem like intrinsic goods and not "means to human welfare." Similarly, though subsistence is a means to an end, it is also one specification of the right to life and a right without which others cannot be enjoyed. There are, I take it, many ways of dividing rights, but the important distinction here is not between first and second but between first/second and third orders of rights.

40. This dovetails with chapter 1, note 69, which points to another example of a natural law (against theft) that only has force in particular contexts (after the establishment of property).

41. This is but one facet of Ryan's balanced approach to economic justice, which focused on security, sufficiency, and status, the latter of which connects with the Hegelian threads

Oscar Romero is much more succinct than Ryan. He makes little of the language of "natural right" and is laconic in his description of the point of the church's defense of property in his second pastoral letter (1977): "Although there have been different ways of stating the church's concern, it has always been to defend the rights of the individual in the use of material goods so that human beings may live with dignity."[42] But despite their different styles, both Ryan and Romero recognize an order to property that places it in service to more basic rights and goods, which for Ryan completely relativizes the naturalness of the right and, for Romero, seems to render the language of natural right superfluous. Situating the right to private property in subordination to other rights and values is also the tack taken by liberation theologians resisting the domination of neoliberal economic and political systems, the backbone of which is an ahistorical and decontextualized assertion of the right to private property.[43] Beyond the conviction that CST's defense of property is focused fundamentally on the right of use or access,[44] which emphasizes the instrumentality of all property regimes and rights, both Ryan and Romero also arrive at the conventionality of property. Ryan does so explicitly, affirming the possibility of other forms of property in other times and places, while it remains implicit in Romero's articulation of CST's central concern.

Even in papal teaching itself, though, property's instrumentality converges with the recognition of the subordination of the economic order to the political order to raise questions about its conventionality and the possibility of forms of property besides private property regimes. Again, Pius XI takes the first step in this direction. Though he clearly maintains property as a natural right,[45] and private property regimes as nonnegotiable, he also notes that given the changing circumstances of society, history proves that the need for the determination of property laws also means that the structure of ownership changes as time and context change, from primitive forms of property ("which may be observed in

---

of CST that I discuss in the next section. Christine Hinze, *Radical Sufficiency: Work, Livelihood, and a US Catholic Economic Ethic* (Washington, DC: Georgetown University Press, 2021), 9–10, 38–39.

42. Oscar Romero, *Voice of the Voiceless: The Four Pastoral Letters and Other Statements*, trans. Michael J. Walsh (Maryknoll, NY: Orbis Books, 2003), 78.

43. David Lantigua, "Liberal Domination, Individual Rights, and the Theological Option for the Poor in History," *Journal of the Society of Christian Ethics* 38, no. 2 (2018): 169–86.

44. See also Ricardo Antoncich, *Christians in the Face of Injustice: A Latin American Reading of Catholic Social Teaching*, trans. Matthew J. O'Connell (Maryknoll, NY: Orbis Books, 1980), 85.

45. Pius XI, *Quadragesimo Anno*, §49.

some places even in our time") to "feudal and monarchial forms down to the various types which are to be found in more recent times."[46] The civilizationalist bent in Pius XI, comparing the property regimes of "rude and savage peoples" with industrialized society, falls out of CST, even as the openness to other property regimes remains. So, for Pius XII, though each person, across time and societies, possesses the natural and fundamental right of use, "it is to be left to the human will and the juridical forms of peoples to set in detail its practical actuation."[47] The positive law of private ownership "may change and more or less restrict its use," but at the least it must prevent the dignity of the worker from eroding into "an economic dependence and slavery which is irreconcilable with his rights as a person."[48] In line with the preceding Christian tradition, the fact that private ownership is a product of positive law does not grant an unlimited scope to political authority in its structure and institution. The limits—in both the tradition and Pius XII's own thought—are moral and political.

John Paul II is the only pope so far to note the possibility of other forms of property explicitly, and the window seems to close on his openness with the fall of the Soviet Union. In *Laborem Exercens* he notes, in agreement with other documents of CST, that a system of private property is preferred, especially in comparison to recent experiments with collectivization.[49] Nonetheless, he recognizes that "for certain well founded reasons exceptions can be made to the principle of private ownership—in our own time we even see that the system of 'socialized ownership' has been introduced." Rather than repudiate the experimentation with other modes of ownership, however, he sets out conditions for the possibility of any such system "to be rational and fruitful." Namely, every "effort must be made to ensure that in this kind of system also the human person can preserve his awareness of working 'for himself.'" The concern with socialized ownership, in fact, is almost exactly the same as prior popes expressed with unregulated industrialization: where the worker feels "that he is just a cog in a huge machine from above, that he is for more reasons than one a mere production instrument rather than a true subject of work with an initiative of his own."[50] The window seems open to consider if and how an alternative property regime might accord with the dictates of a just society, including certain fundamental liberties that pertain to the person as such. In

---

46. Pius XI, *Quadragesimo Anno*, §49.
47. Pius XII, "On the 50th Anniversary of *Rerum Novarum*."
48. Pius XII, "On the 50th Anniversary of *Rerum Novarum*."
49. See, e.g., John XXIII, *Mater et Magistra*, §109.
50. John Paul II, *Laborem Exercens*, §15. A similar concern of capitalism is raised in, e.g., John XXIII, *Mater et Magistra*, §92.

Centesimus Annus, though, this apparent openness is not evident. Though it is possible John Paul II changed his conceptual and moral understanding of systems of property, it seems more likely that a number of other factors, including the changing geopolitical order and the seeming triumph of the private property system associated with capitalism, meant that setting conditions for licitly establishing other forms of property no longer seemed urgent.[51]

To look for CST to advocate for radical alternatives to the current social and economic order is, in any case, misguided. Paul VI articulates the balance appropriate to CST in *Octogesima Adveniens*: the church "does not intervene to authenticate a given structure or to propose a ready-made model, [but] it does not thereby limit itself to recalling general principles." Drawing on applied reflection, the gospel, and its tradition, it nonetheless preserves and points the way to "the daring and creative innovations which the present state of the world requires."[52] The question is not whether CST advocates for concrete radical alternatives, but whether it allows for the possibility of proposing them, as Paul's admonition to seek "daring and creative" innovations suggests.[53] Nonetheless, there is a definitive commitment to avoid prescribing universal solutions. All CST has to be applied to the variety of social contexts in which it is received,[54] and Christians in different social contexts, or with a different set of judgments, can lead to a plurality of legitimate ways of determining legitimate responses to social problems. With respect to property, my claim is that up through today, CST has articulated its principles in such a way that it has steadily preserved space within the Catholic social tradition to articulate more radical approaches to property, as Ignacio Ellacuría does: "If in El Salvador there is no possibility that everyone and each one may get to develop their personal possibilities through the means of one determined form of property, why not think that that type of property is not adequate for the country . . . ? It is one thing to admit that a certain [amount of] property is necessary in order to fully develop as a human person and another, very distinct, to insist that that form of property be private property, such as the Romans understood it and such as Northern and Western capitalism lived it."[55] CST certainly tends

---

51. Jesse Russell, "The Catholic Neoconservative Misreading of John Paul II's *Centesimus Annus* Revisited," *Political Theology* 21, no. 3 (May 1, 2020): 178–79, https://tinyurl.com/upcnfw68.

52. Paul VI, *Octogesima Adveniens*, §42.

53. On the balance between radical and reformist approaches, and the possibility of CST to ground more radical Catholic social movements, see Hinze, *Radical Sufficiency*, 49–53.

54. Paul VI, *Octogesima Adveniens*, §4.

55. Ignacio Ellacuría, SJ, *La lucha por la Justicia: Selección de textos de Ignacio Ellacuría (1969–1989)*, ed. Juan Antonio Senent (Bilbao, Portugal: Universidad de Deusto, 2012), 241.

to be conservative, or, perhaps, cautious, with respect to significant changes to the social order, though at the same time it is able to remain open to even the kind of radical specifications that Ellacuría explores.

There is a balance to be found between CST's practical presupposition of private property regimes and its openness to alternative modes of organizing property. For instance, readings of CST that see in it unequivocally a program of distributivism, a particular approach to capitalist political economy emphasizing the widespread distribution of property, rely on a selective set of texts almost exclusively drawn from Leo XIII's and Pius XI's encyclicals.[56] This selective reading allows the practical presupposition of private property to overdetermine the general theory of property and political economy at the expense, at least, of the principled openness that characterizes the natural law tradition. Nonetheless, those who see a program of distributism in CST are certainly right that the conventionality of property in CST remains almost entirely construed within a more general framework of private property regimes as the norm. That is, the popes usually imagine different ways of structuring private property regimes, instead of entirely different regimes of property.

Where another form of property is not evident, one should not expect CST to advocate for it. It is simply the case that CST does not prohibit utopian and experimental ideas of other forms of property. And this should not be surprising—the conventionality of property in the natural law theory is not aimed at a radical undermining of contemporary social structures, but rather at their legitimation in light of a theological interpretation of nature alongside an openness to emergent forms of property (and other social structures) better suited to technology, economics, culture, and history. A natural law framework can accommodate future shifts in property regimes in much the same way it accommodated the shift from feudal to commercial forms of property, for example, even while it provides criteria to engage critically and constructively with new ideas of property. In this way, one can see Pope Francis's recent engagement with popular movements and his encouragement of a certain radical openness in terms of methods to resolve endemic social and economic problems as an exemplification of the natural law theory itself, which, among the popes, Francis's magisterium most clearly captures.[57]

---

56. Recently, Alexander William Salter, *The Political Economy of Distributism: Property, Liberty, and the Common Good* (Washington, DC: Catholic University of America Press, 2023).

57. Francis, "Address of Pope Francis to the Participants in the World Meeting of Popular Movements," October 28, 2014, https://tinyurl.com/277vzrp8; Francis, "Address of the Holy Father: Participation at the Second World Meeting of Popular Movements," July 9, 2015, https://tinyurl.com/4bsefzzd.

In fact, Francis's approach to property demonstrates the harmonization between CST and the natural law tradition, even while, at the very same time, he makes use of the language of natural right from *Rerum Novarum*. In *Fratelli Tutti*, Francis sets his teaching on the same foundations as the natural law theory: that all thinking about property must take place within a framework of common dominion. This claim derives from the identical sources that led Gratian and the scholastic canon lawyers and theologians to the same framework for property—Basil, Ambrose, Chrysostom, and Augustine.[58] Francis is quite consciously positioning himself within this long tradition, and though he does not do so with the medieval sources, the next section of *Fratelli Tutti* articulates in its own way the scholastic position on property as a convention grounded in the natural law of common dominion.

For Francis, as for the scholastics and his papal predecessors, the implications of the universal destination of material goods and its relation to property are central concerns. The first point he makes, citing John Paul II, is that the common use of goods is "the first principle of the whole ethical and social order" and "a natural and inherent right that takes priority over others."[59] The ability to use the things of the earth is integral to principles of liberty and sufficiency, which, along with moral principles like security, do function as first principles of the ethical and social order. The enjoyment of a flourishing human life and the rights associated with it cannot be practiced without what Henry Shue calls these three basic rights.[60] As with his predecessors, for Francis private property is instrumental with respect to the foundational right of access and use. Private property is *for* the attainment of widespread, equitable access to material (and other) goods: "Private property or any other type of property should—in the words of Saint Paul VI—'in no way hinder [this right], but should actively facilitate its implementation.'"[61] Francis never explicitly calls private property a convention, but he evidently thinks that it is an institution devised for the sake of the attainment of other moral goods, which could also take some other shape or regime. In this, he glosses the positions of the early church theologians in a way that mirrors the approach taken by the scholastic theologians.

58. Francis, *Fratelli Tutti*, §119.

59. Francis, *Fratelli Tutti*, §120. The first is a direct quote from *Laborem Exercens*, §19.

60. Henry Shue, *Basic Rights: Subsistence, Affluence, and U. S. Foreign Policy*, 2nd ed. (Princeton: Princeton University Press, 1980).

61. Francis, *Fratelli Tutti*, §120. The quotation from Paul VI is from *Populorum Progressio*, §22, which in this section likewise places the common use of goods at the foundation of political morality.

He then goes on to describe property as a "secondary natural right." What at first might appear infelicitous in his use of "natural" seems rather to be an ingenious way of utilizing something similar to the scholastic method to appropriate, reinterpret, and unify an earlier body of texts, in this case the texts of papal social teaching. The language of "secondary natural right," I think, would not have been incomprehensible to the scholastics. Indeed, aside from the Franciscans, few of the scholastics would have claimed that since property is conventional it is therefore unnatural. As I have noted, "convention" is a word used by scholars of scholasticism and medieval thought in general to summarize a substantive distinction in medieval social and political thought (and theology) between what is given by nature and what is established through human agency. Conventions can certainly go awry (and become unnatural in a strict sense), as with the systematic discrimination institutionalized in Jim Crow laws, for example. But in their ordinary form, conventions are not opposed to what is natural but are creative extensions and specifications (in Aquinas's language, conclusions and determinations) of what is natural. Even those conventions that the scholastics tended to be most uncomfortable with—property and servitude—were construed in their most negative light as deviations from natural law permitted by natural law on account of the postlapsarian condition of humans. They were interpreted, in other words, as fulfilling the ends of the natural law (and so still not, strictly speaking, unnatural) in societies burdened by the effects of sin.

To call property a secondary natural right, "derived from the principle of the universal destination of created goods," not only emphasizes its intrinsic relationship to the natural law of common dominion but also resonates quite closely with how Aquinas describes property in *Summa Theologiae* II-II 57.3. Recall that Aquinas considers property, in a general sense, to be natural not "absolutely," in the sense of given by nature, but relative to something that follows from it or, one might say, "secondarily." Property (of whatever regime and whatever set of rights that follow from that regime) is, for Aquinas and the other scholastics, conducive to a set of goods natural to the human and the maintenance of society—taking responsibility for material resources and peaceability. In Aquinas's language, a system of property as a principle of stewardship is a conclusion of the natural law, inferred from (or in Pope Francis's language, derived from) an understanding of human nature and more basic moral principles. Even a concrete set of property laws, institutions, customs, or a civil right to private property, which for Aquinas would be considered not an inference from the natural law but a determination of that inference, can be considered secondarily natural to the extent that their determination ought not to contravene the primary principles of the natural law.

Francis's approach is identical in its most general principles to the natural law approach. What is more, he appropriates the language of the "natural right to private property" and reinterprets it to bring some sense of unity to the body of magisterial teaching, while also drawing lines about interpretations of the meaning of the natural right to private property within this tradition that are illegitimate. In accomplishing this task, he brings the whole trajectory of this body of teaching into that great arc of the Christian social tradition that dates to its very earliest centuries. The fact that Francis immediately follows this discussion with a discussion of the rights of peoples only further supports what I have suggested is a natural implication of this idea of property—that it is a proper expression of the political nature of humans and, as such, admits to a variety of forms subject to the same equal respect between peoples as respect for territorial integrity and political sovereignty.

This whole hermeneutical arc brings us full circle, in a way, to *Rerum Novarum*, specifically its first and third (and not final) drafts. Ernst Fortin, one of the first scholars of the Catholic social tradition to document the Lockean argument in *Rerum Novarum*, shows that two of the initial drafts of the document contained something close to the scholastic approach to property. The Jesuit Matteo Liberatore's drafts assigned property to the *ius gentium*, properly understood as positive law and thus not natural law but also not identical with civil law. Liberatore evidently thought that private property followed in some sense by necessity from the natural law, but nonetheless resisted the language and any strict identification of property as a natural right that Leo explicates. Fortin notes that elsewhere Liberatore recognized that the categorization of property under the *ius gentium* and thus positive law had opened the door to an argument that civil authority can abrogate private property. Leo, unwilling to leave this door open, strikes the idea of the *ius gentium* from the encyclical and, in place of the tension that the *ius gentium* preserves between rationality and positivity, collapses the argument for private property into a natural right.[62]

This all suggests that property in contemporary CST is strongly influenced by Leo's rhetorical purpose of stemming the rising tide of communism. Interpretation must be attentive to the social context of the document, including the potential to overstate a position to counterbalance a set of social assumptions or arguments against it.[63] Presenting a nuanced argument, such as one

---

62. Fortin, "'Sacred and Inviolable.'"
63. Though I do not claim they would agree with my position regarding the historical contingency of Leo XIII's formulation of a right to private property, Gerard V. Bradley and

in which property is located somewhere between strictly natural and strictly positive law, might be seen by opponents as a capitulation to the communist position, a weak point around which to sow doubt and confusion. Just as early church theologians must be interpreted in light of the rhetorical form of their arguments, for example, or Karl Barth in terms of the rising misuse of the category of nature to justify the Nazi regime's gravest injustices, Leo must be interpreted in light of his sense of the apparent strength and threat of communism to a justly ordered society and the very existence of the Christian faith. All of this confirms the need for just such a nuanced interpretation of the body of papal social teaching, which the popes themselves conducted across the century and a quarter following Leo, and which I synthesize here. It also strongly suggests that where this tradition stands in Francis is in fact very close to where it began, adding plausibility to the argument that Francis provides a faithful reinterpretation of CST to bring it explicitly into line with the tradition where, for rhetorical purposes, it seemed to have fallen out of step.

Developing the Natural Law Framework

While many scholars rightly recognize the Lockean elements of Leo's thought, a slight but crucial distinction between Leo and Locke forms a point to pivot away from a Lockean account of property in later encyclicals. Leo's theory is a variation on Locke's because the pope emphasizes the opposite direction in the causal effects of one's labor. For Locke, through labor one almost strictly appropriates the external object to oneself, in the sense of attaching that object to the person. The causal effect of labor is to draw the external object within the sphere of what can be considered one's person, for just as anyone has property in her person and actions, by mixing her actions with external objects, she acquires property in those things on par with a property in her person.

Leo clearly emphasizes a different causal effect of this "labor mixing." He

---

E. Christian Brugger foreground historical contingency as a key hermeneutical feature of papal social encyclicals that must be accounted for to interpret the encyclicals well. Gerard V. Bradley and E. Christian Brugger, eds., *Catholic Social Teaching: A Volume of Scholarly Essays*, Law and Christianity (New York: Cambridge University Press, 2019), 3–4. This makes a compilation of social doctrine like the selection in J. Neuner, SJ, and J. Dupuis, SJ, eds., *The Christian Faith in the Doctrinal Documents of the Catholic Church*, 4th ed. (New York: Alba House, 1982), 616, all the more difficult and, to some degree, misleading. The section on social doctrine in Neuner and Dupuis begins with Leo XIII's restatement of a Lockean natural right to private property in *Rerum Novarum*, for example.

glosses his assertion that through labor one "makes his own that portion of nature's field which he cultivates," explaining that this is "that portion on which he leaves, as it were, the impress of his personality."[64] This definition suggests that the important effect of labor runs in a direction not emphasized by Locke. It is not the taking up of external things into the sphere of one's person that is paramount, in Leo's analysis, but the change wrought on external things that expresses some part of the individual who labored. Through this twist on the Lockean approach to property, Leo leaves the door open in subsequent magisterial teaching for a hermeneutical reinterpretation of his thought, one that introduces self-development as an evaluative lens for property regimes.[65] In this way, Leo's encyclical becomes an impetus to a potential development and innovation of the scholastic natural law framework rather than a departure from it. In this section, I trace this innovation, which begins in Pius XI and finds its full expression in Pius XII and John XXIII. This reinterpretation of the Leonine approach construes property as vital for moral and personal development and thus sees a moral imperative for political society to extend property ownership universally, at least where a private property regime is presupposed. This line of papal thought resonates in significant ways with a Hegelian approach to property.[66] After John XXIII, moral and personal development remain a focal point of CST, though such self-development is more closely tied to dignified work than to ownership as such, which suggests that later popes modify this Hegelian line of thought in a way that conforms to the pillars of a natural law theory of property. I begin this section with a brief overview of a Hegelian approach to property. I then trace CST's appropriation and modification of this approach and conclude with some reflections on the meaning of these modifications and objections a Hegelian might raise to them.

For Hegel, property is an essential stage for the moral realization of individual personality and the development of freedom. In working on her own

---

64. Leo XIII, *Rerum Novarum*, §9.

65. Though this pivot likely draws on Hegel as a proximate source, the concern for self-development resonates with themes about dominion that are deeply rooted in the tradition I recover.

66. The two most important intellectual influences on Pius XI and Pius XII with respect to political economy were Oswald von Nell-Bruening, SJ, and Gustav Gundlach, SJ, respectively. It is perhaps notable that a convergence with Hegel's thought on property first occurs in the two papacies that relied heavily on German Jesuits for the drafting of their social thought. See Oswald Von Nell-Breuning, "The Drafting of *Quadragesimo Anno*," in *Official Catholic Social Teaching*, ed. Charles E. Curran and Richard A. McCormick, Readings in Moral Theology 5 (New York: Paulist, 1986), 60–67.

property, the individual develops stability and consistency of will and publicizes herself in the external world in a way that calls forth recognition by others.[67] Without this opportunity to allow one's free will to shape and order the external world, one's free will remains trapped in its interior subjectivity, which is a merely incipient and, as it were, noncommunicative expression of freedom. One could imagine the limit case of the slave, whose use of and labor on external things is entirely a manifestation of the free will of someone else, to see that the slave's bare metaphysical freedom remains trapped in his personal subjectivity. Even if the slave manifests a particular aptitude, say, for carpentry, the fine woodworking about the master's property, though demonstrating the slave's skill, is rather an expression of the master's and not the slave's free will. What the supreme skill of the slave calls forth in terms of recognition is less an analogy to the freedom of the master than the recognition afforded to the supreme skill of other unfree creatures, like the hunting dog or the draft horse. To a lesser extreme, one can see how the propertyless wage laborer might also suffer from an inability to know his freedom external to himself, and for others to recognize and acknowledge him as a free creature, to the extent that the things that he works on and uses are ultimately ordered by someone else's free will and so a manifestation of another's and not his own freedom. Hegel, evidently, thinks both are problematic for society, though it is unclear whether he thinks the modern state has any real capacity to resolve the latter problem of the poor and propertyless. Nonetheless, given its importance to the moral development of the person, and the irreducible importance of the person in Hegel's thought as a concrete instance of the universal Idea, for many Hegelians it follows, as an addendum to his lecture notes puts it, that justice demands "that everyone shall own property."[68]

One can see here a certain resonance with scholastic thinking regarding the principle of liberty and property, and the ways in which freedom requires access to material things to generate the kind of robust autonomy, as opposed to bare metaphysical freedom of the will, that is essential for human devel-

---

67. Hegel's account of property can be found in G. W. F. Hegel, *Philosophy of Right*, trans. T. M. Knox (Oxford: Oxford University Press, 1952), §§41–71.

68. Hegel, *Philosophy of Right*, §49A. Waldron offers the most comprehensive interpretation of Hegel's theory of property in Anglophone philosophy in *Right to Private Property*, chap. 10. Alan Ryan situates it more broadly in relation to utilitarian and self-development traditions as well as Hegel's sociology and philosophy in Alan Ryan, *Property and Political Theory*, chap. 5. Whereas Waldron sees private property as a general right (a right everyone may claim) as a practical implication of Hegel's thought, Ryan thinks just social structures that guarantee everyone social standing (and so not universal ownership) would suffice.

opment.⁶⁹ At the same time, Hegel invests much more than the scholastics in the relationship between freedom and private ownership itself, rather than just access to the material world. Private ownership is so important not because it is the end of freedom but rather because, for external things to be a recognizable expression of one's free will and so bring one into free relations with others, the person must have over them the powers of decision characteristic of private property—exclusive use, development, and alienation. Nonetheless, these first steps toward freedom must be ordered toward integration with the society of which one is a part, and Hegel thinks that this ordered integration into society, where one's decisions, responsibilities, and property are recognized by oneself and by others as ordered toward the good of society, occurs by incorporation into estates/corporations or the public bureaucracy. The ultimate goal of freedom, of which taking public responsibility for one's private property is but a first step, is the exercise of responsibility proper to one's person in and for the state. Whether or not private ownership can be bypassed in this path to responsibility, the exercise of ownership is but a rudimentary exercise of freedom, according to Hegel.⁷⁰

It would be overstating the case to say that CST is "Hegelian," in the sense of explicitly drawing on and translating Hegel's philosophy of right into a Catholic political idiom. Nonetheless, key ideas for this self-developmental idea of property—the moral significance of ownership, its connection to the development of moral agency, and the obligation of political authority to make ownership widely available, to each and all alike if possible—all influence and strengthen across Pius XI, Pius XII, and John XXIII. The close connection between self-development and ownership is jettisoned, however, just at the point when it is clearest in John XXIII, who captures not only the moral significance of ownership for self-development but also the importance of structures that can allow for the personal integration of members of society into roles of responsibility in their place of work and in various levels of government. Though CST after John XXIII sets aside the close connection between self-development and ownership, it retains a special concern that each person be able to exercise responsibility in her various spheres of life and is more

---

69. See the discussion of liberty in chapter 3. Annabel Brett's close examination of liberty, dominion, and poverty certainly captures the same concern about the relationship between freedom and the external world in medieval theology. Annabel S. Brett, *Liberty, Right, and Nature: Individual Rights in Later Scholastic Thought* (Cambridge: Cambridge University Press, 1997).

70. Waldron, *Right to Private Property*, 348. Alan Ryan clearly thinks private property can be bypassed in Ryan, *Property and Political Theory*, 131–32.

optimistic than Hegel about the possibility of extending this participation in responsibility to all classes and all persons in society. More importantly for this section, it also retains a clear focus on the importance of self-development and labor as well as property laws that can afford every person in society the opportunity to know herself in the things she labors on, a point insisted upon with supreme clarity by John Paul II but retained from Paul VI through Francis.

Pius XI begins the turn to a self-developmental principle of property with his avid support of partnership corporations. For Pius, the partnership corporation is a promising way of achieving the goal that each person possess at least "some little property," without which the principles of social and distributive justice cannot be put into practice.[71] While Leo advocated a just wage for providing "non-owning workers" the ability to acquire property "through industry and thrift," Pius XI suggests a more direct route for expanding ownership, anticipating the employee-owned enterprise model today, in which the workers in a corporation own or at least share in ownership of its means of production and other forms of capital.[72] Pius XI introduces the idea of partnership corporations and the ideal of widespread ownership in order to modify the basic institutions of capitalism: the wage contract and the exclusive ownership of the means of production.[73] Pius XI does not yet explicitly invoke self-development, but both the notion of greater workplace participation and widespread ownership anticipate key concerns for the self-development paradigm.

The partnership-contract of Pius XI is also a practical anticipation of the turn to a self-developmental approach to private property, in two ways. First, as compared to Leo's argument that workers should acquire property through

---

71. Pius XI, *Quadragesimo Anno*, §63.

72. Misner writes, "With a bit of good will, one can see [Pius XI's corporatism] as a predecessor of Mondragón-like cooperatives, but it has been most commonly seen as a quixotic attempt to modernize the medieval guilds." In Misner, "Predecessors of 'Rerum Novarum,'" 446. At least in the United States, George E. Schultze, SJ, recounts a history in which Pius XI's thought was interpreted as giving intellectual and magisterial backing to the establishment of work cooperatives and partnership contracts like Mondragón Corporation. See "Worker-Ownership & Catholic Social Thought," *Social Policy* 32, no. 2 (2001): 12–16.

73. John Ryan anticipates this shift and offers a detailed method for instituting partnership contracts: restrict outside investors to interest-bearing bond purchases and issue the shares in a company to its employees, which will distribute to them surplus profits (capital appreciation and dividends). One way Ryan's analysis might be modified is to suggest that employees need only retain a company's voting shares, or even just a majority of those shares, and can sell nonvoting shares to raise capital and encourage fair valuation on a regulated market. John A. Ryan, *The Christian Doctrine of Property* (New York: Paulist, 1923), chap. 2.

CHAPTER FIVE

thrift, it exhibits a more deliberate attempt to ensure that all persons acquire some share in private ownership, since in a partnership-contract ownership is contingent only on employment and not employment plus thrift. Though Pius XI does not argue that political authority ought to guarantee that each person have the opportunity for meaningful ownership (a point explicit in Pius XII and John XXIII), he offers a new approach to try to guarantee ownership to nonowning workers by advocating a structure that makes the worker an owner merely by working.

Second, Pius XI's approach suggests practically that the act of laboring *on* something (a point very important to Hegel) is not ancillary to the moral significance of ownership. Indeed, it is the connection of ownership to labor in the self-developmental model that fully evokes the moral significance of each. Ownership allows moral development and self-expression through the use and deployment of (or labor on) what one owns. And labor becomes meaningful to a person by becoming a vehicle of the concretization and publicization of himself in being subject ultimately to his free will through ownership. This is the self-developmental basis of what Waldron calls a general right to property. It is a point likewise central to Marx. Whereas Marx addresses the problem of "alienation" (the separation of the laborer from what she labors on) by letting the state, as the representative of all, own the means of production, Pius XI suggests addressing it by letting the workers and employees of a particular enterprise share in the ownership of the capital of that enterprise.[74]

Pius XII, whose social teachings are delivered as radio addresses and not as encyclicals, is a key contributor to both the self-developmental turn and the efforts to integrate prior teachings into the conventional framework of property. On the self-developmental line, however, his contributions are mostly mediated by John XXIII's *Mater et Magistra*, which cites Pius XII at length to make several points regarding the moral importance of labor and ownership for personal development. In *Mater et Magistra* §74, citing Pius XII's 1941 address commemorating *Rerum Novarum* at length, John articulates the purpose of the economy in terms of both self-development and securing the common right of use. The national economy "has no other end than to secure without interruption the material conditions in which the individual life of the citizens

---

74. In contemporary socialist thought the centralized collective regime seems to be giving way to regimes centered on employee ownership (worker self-directed enterprises) as alternatives to capitalism. Richard Wolff, *Democracy at Work: A Cure for Capitalism* (Chicago: Haymarket Books, 2012); Richard D. Wolff, "Alternatives to Capitalism," *Critical Sociology* 39, no. 4 (July 1, 2013): 487–90.

may fully develop. Where this is secured in a permanent way, a people will be, in a true sense, economically rich, because the general well-being, and consequently the personal right of all to the use of worldly goods, is thus actuated in conformity with the purpose willed by the Creator."[75] John offers his own gloss on this passage, which affirms the incorporation of a self-developmental approach. He argues that the prosperity of a nation is thus best represented in "the equitable division and distribution" of wealth and property. This equitable division of property is what "guarantees the personal development of the members of society."[76]

For Pius XII and John XXIII, the *telos* of property likewise corresponds with that of the national economy: facilitating use and, through use, the liberty and development of each person. Again citing Pius XII, John writes: "In defending the principle of private ownership the Church is striving after an important ethico-social end." John then clarifies that a part of that ethico-social end is "a guarantee of the essential freedom of the individual."[77] Here one can see in another context the conventional and instrumental character of property as being instituted for an end. In this case, the end corresponds to the principle of liberty, but John goes on to gloss liberty here in terms of public standing and the growth of responsibility that resonate more with the self-developmental tradition. Property serves the freedom proper to individuals by providing an "efficacious means of asserting one's personality and exercising responsibility in every field."[78] The "native right to the use of material goods" served by the institution of property is intimately linked to the dignity of the human person precisely at this point, allowing the person "to rise to the fulfillment ... of his moral duties."[79] And here, John connects the dots regarding use, dignity, and property: human dignity "normally demands the right to the use of the goods of the earth, to which corresponds the fundamental obligation of granting an opportunity to possess property to all if possible."[80] Property is a right that demands extension in practice "to all classes of citizens."[81]

At this point, John XXIII, working closely, almost exclusively, with the social thought of Pius XII, has outlined a self-developmental account of property: property is vital for moral development, responsibility, and one's standing in society,

---

75. The original can be found in Pius XII, "On the 50th Anniversary of *Rerum Novarum*."
76. John XXIII, *Mater et Magistra*, §74.
77. John XXIII, *Mater et Magistra*, §111.
78. John XXIII, *Mater et Magistra*, §112.
79. Pius XII, "On the 50th Anniversary of *Rerum Novarum*."
80. John XXIII, *Mater et Magistra*, §114.
81. John XXIII, *Mater et Magistra*, §113.

and so property is not merely a right for some but, one might say, justice demands "that everyone shall own property." The *telos* of property includes human freedom and self-development and, more specifically, securing human freedom and self-development *by securing the power to use the goods of the earth*, what John Paul II later refers to as the "first principle of the whole ethical and social order."[82]

John reiterates the significance of this self-developmental tradition by explicitly linking work, ownership, and personal development. Though with Pius XI he affirms that partnership contracts ensure a more just and greater share in the profits of a firm for its workers, John also argues that such contracts also ensure the possibility for more meaningful and morally significant work. Partnership corporations encourage a greater sense of community within the corporation, as each partner in the firm takes account of "the needs, the activities, and the standing of each of its members."[83] John notes that by having an ownership stake in the firm, the worker can fulfill what Pius XII calls "the economic and social function" that each person desires, since the worker in some sense can exercise agency in his work rather than his work being "completely subjected to others."[84] Through this freedom to act the workers become more than passive "cogs in the machinery" and have the opportunity "of expressing their wishes or bringing their experience to bear on the work in hand." One can perhaps see here a synthesizing of various Hegelian concerns, where the ownership of productive property in a productive enterprise allows the individual to know and publicize herself in her labor and concern for the commonweal of the enterprise and her fellow employees.

And this, for John XXIII, leads to other forms of the public exercise of free will and responsibility for civil and political society. Though Hegel envisions this operating corporately through the various estates that organize a society's productive endeavors, the end is the same in that it orients the individual exercise of free will not just toward his own good but cooperatively in and for the good of society. As John writes of employee ownership: "All this serves to create an environment in which workers are encouraged to assume greater responsibility in their own sphere of employment," which leads to the opportunity for employees to exercise greater responsibility within civil and political society.[85] Ownership is foundational for the exercise of creativity, the development and

---

82. John Paul II, *Laborem Exercens*, §19.
83. John XXIII, *Mater et Magistra*, §91.
84. John XXIII, *Mater et Magistra*, §92. John XXIII is citing an address of Pius XII given on October 8, 1956.
85. John XXIII, *Mater et Magistra*, §§96–97.

utilization of expertise, and thus the exercise of responsibility that is generated from working on what one (partially) owns. This not only develops moral personality but also generates reciprocal recognition from others (employers, political authority, fellow citizens) through what Hegel might call the publicization of one's responsibility or personality through ownership. John XXIII goes further than Pius XII by arguing that the general right to property based on the moral importance of self-development is a natural right.[86]

The designation of property as a natural right in John XXIII is of interest for a few reasons. First, the right is a general right, along the lines of what Jeremy Waldron articulates in his development of Hegel's thinking on property.[87] Every person has this right by virtue of being human because it is of such significant interest to the achievement of each person's end. This is distinct from the special right that Locke and, perhaps, Leo XIII articulate, where only those who have performed some particular action or set of actions (like laboring on something unowned or purchasing something owned) can claim a right to property. The attribution of a natural right to property to CST is inevitably complicated by this discrepancy: Which kind of natural right? Though both natural, the distinctions between the two are as significant as those between natural and positive rights. Second, though this might raise questions about the reception of the natural law theory of property in CST, this is the last time property is unqualifiedly referred to as a natural right in CST, and when Francis refers to it as a secondary natural right, it rather affirms the reception of the natural law theory. One way of interpreting John XXIII here is that if there is a natural right to property, then it only pertains to a private property system as a specification of the natural right to use. This would preserve space for common property regimes, for example, that would otherwise be ruled illegitimate by their denial of an unqualified natural right to property. This interpretation would conform with how scholastics interpreted the prohibition of theft—it is a natural law that is only relevant once property has been settled by positive law.[88]

Though the focus on self-development continues in CST, it is generalized and almost entirely separated from the question of ownership following *Mater et Magistra*. Indeed, this is the last time the natural right to property as such is asserted by a pope. And though Paul VI retains a clear sense of the importance that work itself be open "to a chance to develop one's qualities and personality in

---

86. John XXIII, *Mater et Magistra*, §§108–110.
87. Waldron, *Right to Private Property*, chap. 8.
88. See note 40 above.

the exercise of one's profession," he never ties this to ownership.[89] Indeed, across Paul VI's magisterium, the only right with respect to material things that he articulates is a right to use,[90] even while he continues to insist on greater responsibilities for all in the political sphere, since "the admittance to responsibility is a basic demand of man's nature, a concrete exercise of his freedom and a path to his development."[91] Paul VI retains John XXIII's sense that this admittance to responsibility is vital in the economic, as well as the social and political, fields, without ever giving ownership the foundational place that John does.

In terms of work and development, John Paul II, Benedict XVI, and Francis all follow Paul VI. John Paul II reaffirms the connection between work and moral development, while clarifying the relationship between work, ownership, and moral development in a way that diminishes the essential role of ownership. With respect to work and moral development, John Paul II only reaffirms or even strengthens the teachings of Pius XII and John XXIII on this point: "work is a good thing for man—a good thing for his humanity because through work man *not only transforms nature* ... but he also *achieves fulfilment* as a human being."[92] He maintains similar implications, affirming the potential of joint ownership and socializing certain industries and the necessity of providing unemployment benefits and a just wage.[93] Benedict XVI has even less to say regarding the personal and developmental dimensions of work, though he affirms it at a few places in *Caritas in Veritate*.[94] And, though Francis restates this conviction with even more force in terms of work's conduciveness to sanctification, the primary contribution he makes is to reiterate the insight that through work one does not merely order oneself to the good (self-development), one also orders the world around oneself to the good. There is a good that the world is ordered to that, while serving humans, does not reduce to its usefulness to humans but rather manifests in bearing witness and praise to God. This apparent resistance to tying the usefulness of work for self-development to ownership too tightly certainly finds its font in the whole inheritance of patristic and scholastic thought. Here in Francis the resistance to making ownership natural draws explicitly on that fundamental theological conviction so central to the tradition's reflections on ownership: "The Earth is the Lord's."[95]

89. Paul VI, *Octogesima Adveniens*, §14.
90. Paul VI, *Populorum Progressio*, §22.
91. Paul VI, *Octogesima Adveniens*, §47.
92. John Paul II, *Laborem Exercens*, §9.
93. John Paul II, *Laborem Exercens*, §§14, 15, 18, and 19.
94. Benedict XVI, *Caritas in Veritate*, §§41, 63.
95. Francis, *Laudato Si'*, §67.

What is one to make of the apparent separation of ownership and moral development in CST since Paul VI? It first should be noted that this separation is entirely commensurate with the scholastic tradition. There is no foundational place for property in the scholastic tradition: what is morally exigent is equitable access to use of the things of the world for the sake of sufficiency and the exercise of one's natural liberty. Moral development, as seems to be the consistent claim, only requires access to make rational and moral use of the things of the world, and not ownership. The generalization here expresses the level of generality that runs through the tradition, which allows for specification given the distinctive contexts in which property regimes must be instituted and evaluated. One way of narrating the progression of teachings from Leo XIII, and especially Pius XII, to Francis, is this: the popes recognize, in a way compatible with the tradition's own theology of dominion and work, that work and ownership can play a significant role in the moral and personal development of each individual. The notion is introduced in a way that seems to be open to an articulation of the connection that makes ownership a natural right due to each person on account of its moral significance. The strong moral connection between development and ownership, however, is weakened in a way that is commensurate with the natural law tradition: private property can play a vital role in moral development, but societies may conceive of other ways to foster the moral development of individuals other than private property regimes, just as they can with the principles of equity, equality, sufficiency, and liberty. It seems, then, that CST as a whole has absorbed contemporary articulations of the connections between work, ownership, and self-development, and then reinterpreted those connections in a way that takes account of the natural law tradition that stretches back to the early church. John Paul II exemplifies this in *Laborem Exercens*: though a system of private property might be preferred as the best way to achieve the moral principles of property (especially liberty and self-development), he does not rule out other property regimes, provided that "every effort be made to ensure that in this kind of system also the human person can preserve his awareness of working 'for himself.'"[96]

It might be objected that this concedes too much to the triumphalist narrative of neoliberal capitalism, where capital pays lip service to moral salubriousness of work as a way of distracting from or even diminishing its pecuniary obligations. In a world of capital and labor, a laborer either participates in the benefits of ownership or suffers the harm of being an anonymous cog in the machine—a virtuous cog, perhaps, but a cog, and not, properly speaking,

---

96. John Paul II, *Laborem Exercens*, §15.

enjoying the development of her powers to full participation in her society. This can only be properly achieved through the opportunity for moral self-development made possible by the exercise of free will and responsibility over her own property and in the various enterprises of which she is a part. The Hegelian ideal of the full integration of each member that orders the free will of each toward the cooperative exercise of freedom in society looks instead, in neoliberal capitalism, like the subordination of labor to the ends of capital, something that has preoccupied papal thought since Leo XIII.[97] Can the concern for self-development and so participation truly be addressed without universal distribution of property and, one might say, the laws and structures to turn the aspiration for universal distribution into a concrete reality?

The scholastic natural law tradition can, I think, offer two responses to this objection. On the one hand, it can look to John XXIII and Francis for inspiration here. While a just society seems to have other means for integrating the freedom of its members in the true exercise of responsibility for the common good without getting mired in the vast complexities that the universal distribution of property would require, it is perhaps nonetheless true that in the absence of a firm, actionable commitment to universal distribution, the tendency in a capitalist system will always be for capital to accumulate more—more access to material goods, more wealth, more responsibility, more power and authority—to itself than is just.[98] Without deeming that private property is a general natural right in an absolute sense, the Catholic social tradition seems to certainly provide grounds to claim that private property is a general natural right in a conditional or secondary sense. And these resources can be found as early as twentieth-century commentators like John Ryan. When a private property regime is in force, then each person possesses a natural right to claim some property as her own. In a world in which life's necessities, social and political power, self-esteem and virtue, and one's public standing are all tightly correlated to property, then the possession of some durable property seems, as Jeremy Waldron claims, to be of such a vital interest to the individual that it is indeed a natural right.

On the other hand, to make private property a natural right in an absolute sense would prejudice the possibility of alternative property regimes, making them either unjust in an outright sense or mere stages on the way to the more

97. Though the question of the "rabble" in Hegelian thought remains, it seems evident that CST is more hopeful regarding a meaningful integration of most members of society. See the introduction to G. W. F. Hegel, *Hegel: Elements of the Philosophy of Right*, trans. Allen W. Wood, Cambridge Texts in the History of Political Thought (New York: Cambridge University Press, 1991).

98. Thomas Piketty, *Capital in the Twenty-First Century*, trans. Arthur Goldhammer (Cambridge, MA: Belknap Press of Harvard University Press, 2017).

rational ordering of a private property regime, as Hegel thinks. This sort of strict moral determination of private property regimes would violate the conventionality of property according to natural law theory as much as an insistence on a Lockean natural right. Though certainly preferable to communist collectivism, regimes organized around the private ownership of productive property still have much to prove to solidify their status as the highest rational ordering for human property relations. And though such regimes might seem evidently to be the best-known option available for large-scale societies, it seems empirically and rationally unfounded to conclude that they are, rationally and morally, preferable for every society, no matter its size, history, environment, aspirations, or cultural inheritance. Indeed, Elinor Ostrom's research on common governance gives reasons to think that common property regimes might be entirely suitable for small societies and ought likely to form a greater part of the way capitalist societies govern some resources.

It is worth, finally, revisiting my earlier claim regarding the conventionality of property. The tradition seems unlikely to abandon the conventionality of property for either a Lockean special right or a Hegelian general right. There are, as I have just discussed, arguments that either approach falls short of justifying its position. There are, however, also considerations regarding the proper place of political self-determination, which, as I have already shown, holds roots deep in the scholastic natural law tradition. The concern for political self-determination and respect for peoples, however, also holds consistently across CST. This is evident with respect to economic realities in the manner in which politics precedes and forms the framework for economics, rather than vice versa. To treat economic realities as something that precedes political realities, and property as something that precedes custom and law, is to deny this very commitment on the part of CST. If politics truly does precede economics, and authority property, then economic and property systems cannot be predetermined by either a special or general natural right to property without risking neocolonialism and the lack of respect for the political autonomy of peoples in their determination of specific economic systems. And, as I turn to in the next section, this would introduce a severe contradiction into CST between putative natural rights concerning property, the priority of politics over economics, and respect for peoples.

Catholic Social Teaching, Property, and the Rights of Peoples

These reflections suggest that the scholastic approach to property has implications beyond the achievement of certain moral and political principles within

CHAPTER FIVE

a society. The generality of these principles and the commitments within this approach to property also reinforce political self-determination, the autonomous exercise of political reason, and the subordination of economic values to political values in relations between states. In this concluding section, I show how these latter political commitments of the scholastic natural law approach converge explicitly with papal teaching. This conception of property reinforces papal international thought, and so here I explicate the significance of a theory of property not just for the internal but also for the international social order.

At least since the popes first turned their attention to the international dimensions of the social order, they have expressed a consistent commitment to the autonomy and self-determination of peoples. Each pope has insisted that authentic development—often referred to as integral or human development—must be more than economic and include the integration, empowerment, and recognition of a people's cultural heritage and political powers as well. In the initial turn to the international order, John XXIII in *Pacem in Terris* insists on the proper autonomy of states and peoples in forming their own internal political orders. Once certain basic rights and duties of the political order are recognized, "it is not possible to give a general ruling on the most suitable form of government, or the ways in which civil authorities can most effectively fulfill their legislative, administrative, and judicial functions." Such determinations can only be made with consideration of the "prevailing circumstances and the condition of the people ... which vary in different places and at different times."[99] We have here the adumbration of a methodological principle that will play a key role in the development and application of CST in different contexts. Right at the outset of *Octogesima Adveniens*, Paul VI reiterates and formalizes this principle: "In the face of such widely varying situations it is difficult for us to utter a unified message and to put forward a solution which has universal validity. Such is not our ambition, nor is it our mission." Rather, it is up to Christians to analyze the social situation in their countries, shed the light of the gospel on them, and draw principles, norms and directives for action.[100] This concrete principle of CST codifies the kind of autonomy for diverse peoples that John XXIII first insists on.

In addition to the proper contextual and thus diverse application of principles, John XXIII also affirms the equal natural dignity between political communities, which entails a right to self-determination.[101] International assistance must be

---

99. John XXIII, *Pacem in Terris*, encyclical letter, Vatican website, April 11, 1963, §§67–68, https://tinyurl.com/8tmv7z6x.
100. Paul VI, *Octogesima Adveniens*, §4.
101. John XXIII, *Pacem in Terris*, §§89, 92.

conducted "in a way which guarantees [peoples] the preservation of their own freedom. They must be conscious that they are themselves playing the major role in their economic and social development."[102] Paul VI in *Populorum Progressio* expands consideration of the question of development to integrate questions of traditional cultures and values. Development does not necessitate a departure from traditional mores and customs; it ought rather to demand the integration of "the older moral, spiritual, and religious values."[103] The protection and promotion of indigenous institutions are part of the best of the missionary impulses of the church and ought to be a constitutive feature of relations between peoples, especially when diverse cultures with differing levels of wealth and technical expertise interact.[104] Technological superiority is distinct from cultural superiority, and convergence in technical development ought not to lead to cultural capitulation but to rapprochement. Technology must be adapted to the cultural circumstances, and not vice versa.[105] The same applies to economic superiority and economic development, a point that each successive pope reiterates.[106]

Each successive pope also demands that politics and political principles, and not economics and economic activity, be the foundations of the international order. Given the dramatic differences in economic power, basing the international order on economic principles and activities "runs the risk of taking up too much strength and freedom."[107] One can indeed think of cases where economic activity has been the grounds for gutting another nation's agricultural economy, creating networks that channel immigrants as cheap labor, and, important for our case, insisting on systems of property that undermine traditional social and economic organization, while primarily benefiting the country that insisted on the importation of that system of property in the first place.[108] "This is why the

102. John XXIII, *Pacem in Terris*, §123.
103. Paul VI, *Populorum Progressio*, §10.
104. Paul VI, *Populorum Progressio*, §12.
105. Paul VI, *Populorum Progressio*, §72.
106. Paul VI, *Octogesima Adveniens*, §§43–46. For example, John Paul II, *Redemptor Hominis*, encyclical letter, Vatican website, March 4, 1979, §12, https://tinyurl.com/yakst7uk; John Paul II, *Sollicitudo Rei Socialis*, encyclical letter, Vatican website, December 30, 1987, §§39, 43, https://tinyurl.com/yuhcua4f; Benedict XVI, *Caritas in Veritate*, §§26, 33; Francis, *Laudato Si'*, §§143–46.
107. Paul VI, *Populorum Progressio*, §46.
108. On agriculture and trade, see Richard Miller, *Globalizing Justice: The Ethics of Poverty and Power* (New York: Oxford University Press, 2010), 145–46. On immigration systems, see Saskia Sassen, *The Mobility of Labor and Capital: A Study in International Investment and Labor Flow* (Cambridge: Cambridge University Press, 1988). On the imposition of property regimes, Jeremy Waldron briefly mentions this sort of worry in *The Rule of Law and the Measure of Property* (Cambridge: Cambridge University Press, 2012), 10–12. A clear

need is felt to pass from economics to politics ... that in the social and economic field, both national and international, the ultimate decision rests with political power."[109] These are the general terms of integral development, which integrates cultural, political, and economic concerns while giving priority to the practical and political reasoning of each state to direct and determine its own course of development. Such an approach is incompatible with the agriculturalist models I discussed in the previous chapter, with developmentalist models that reduce development to economic advancement, and, to my mind, with approaches to politics that insist on a single valid property regime (what I take to be the implications of a general and natural right to property).

Finally, another aspect of magisterial teaching on the international order connects with the notion of directive dominion that I outlined in chapter 3 as well as with the principle of self-development. This aspect concerns the international order but parallels earlier discussions about the domestic order and self-development, especially with respect to laborers. The concern for the domestic economy is not just that workers have the use of material resources, but also that they have opportunities to exercise genuine responsibility in the workplace, the wider economy, and politics. While access to the use of things (and ownership) facilitates this exercise of responsibility, it does not reduce to it. The popes also advocate for work councils and labor organizations as ways for workers to exercise responsibility in the firm and in society. A similar concern animates papal teaching with respect to less powerful peoples and societies. After discussing the need to establish "a greater justice in the sharing of goods," Paul VI demands also "a greater sharing in responsibility and in decision-making."[110] Though Paul VI seems to be focused on the internal order, Benedict and Francis extend this to the international order, in parallel fashion. Mutual assistance, development aid, and international cooperation are all facets of integral development, but integral development also presupposes "giving poorer nations an effective voice in shared decision-making."[111] It is not enough to have things to use; CST insists on structures that enable each people to participate in the decisions and activities, political and economic, of the international order.

This concern for participation has its roots in the Thomistic account of

---

and compelling historical example of the power of economic organization to undermine a society is found in William Cronon, *Changes in the Land: Indians, Colonists, and the Ecology of New England* (New York: Hill & Wang, 1983).

109. Paul VI, *Populorum Progressio*, §46. See also Francis, *Fratelli Tutti*, §177; John Paul II, *Redemptor Hominis*, §16; Benedict XVI, *Caritas in Veritate*, §§24, 35–37, 67; Francis, *Laudato Si'*, §189.

110. Paul VI, *Octogesima Adveniens*, §47.

111. Benedict XVI, *Caritas in Veritate*, §67; Francis, *Fratelli Tutti*, §138.

directive dominion. "Use," the primary power associated with dominion, is a broad term that encompasses activities of directing and ordering the world. One species of this activity is certainly consuming some of the things of the world to sustain and nourish oneself, which within the international order entails a people having enough to nourish and sustain the individuals that compose it and may call for mutual assistance and development aid. Other acts associated with use characteristically pertain to common resources: the division of common goods in the institution of systems of property and the administration, management, and distribution of resources that remain in common. These latter acts are directive acts, in some sense political, that are rooted in the fundamental relationship of dominion that each person exercises over the world. On the international level, it is the latter that is among the most pressing today, which Benedict XVI and Francis express in the need for each people to play a part in decision making at the international level. Without delving into the details, this argument might be applied with respect to common resources like the climate, the open sea, or the deep seabed (or in the future, asteroids). It is certainly laudable to ensure that each people (and through that order each person) may participate fairly in the enjoyment of these resources through mechanisms that distribute their material benefits (as with minerals mined from the deep seabed) or mechanisms that preserve their functioning (as with efforts to control carbon emissions). The popes and the theological conception of dominion suggest more than this, though: each people should have the opportunity to exercise agency in determining, for instance, whether the mining of the deep seabed is an environmental risk worth taking, or whether climate policies ought to give more resource and attention to emissions reductions or adaptation. There is a utopian strain in this line of thinking, which Francis admits, that does not foreclose its pursuit but should temper expectations about its achievement.[112] What I want to highlight, however, is how this demand of papal social teaching at the highest order of society is intelligible in terms of a fundamental theological anthropology that is at the foundations of a natural law theory of property.

Conclusion

The preceding analysis suggests an answer to the question I raised in the introduction to this chapter: What has become of this scholastic approach today, as well as of the longer tradition of which it is a part? One way of answering

---

112. See, e.g., Francis, *Fratelli Tutti*, §190.

CHAPTER FIVE

this question, as the examples in chapter 3 suggest, is that it is alive and well, though articulated within the context of a capitalist and international society. What obscures the contemporary vitality of this approach to property in Catholic social teaching is the expression of a Lockean natural right in Leo and the tendency in secondary scholarship to assume that each time the natural right to property is cited in papal encyclicals, it is functioning in the same way. Once analysis turns from a mere acceptance of the nomenclature to assessing the function of property in papal teaching, one can see expressions of an idea of property that tend to converge with the longer Christian tradition. Indeed, one can find astute expressions of this tradition in some of the great Catholic social thinkers and liberation theologians like John Ryan, Ignacio Ellacuría, and Oscar Romero, and popes like Pius XII, Paul VI, John Paul II, and Francis, among others. Even where the papal tradition seems to diverge from the long tradition, as in John XXIII, I have shown how to interpret those divergences as specifications in light of the present social order.

At the same time, it is not enough that the pillars of a natural law theory—the natural law of common dominion and property's conventionality—are present to show that the tradition is alive and well. It is also a living tradition in the sense that, as I have shown here, it engages critically with new theories of property and develops in response to that critical engagement. In Catholic social teaching, one can see how popes surface and reject a Lockean theory of property, then recognize and incorporate a Hegelian connection between property and self-development even while modifying it to accord with the pillars of the received tradition. The process of engaging with and digesting other ways of approaching the same or similar questions can be quite convoluted and open-ended, which should all the more discourage scholars from treating a single thinker, let alone a single text, as determinative of the tradition's approach. Even the same language of natural right can mean something very different in two different documents written less than a century apart and have vastly different social and political implications. In periods of rapid and significant change, as in the time of industrialization and now globalization, a living tradition brings out of its storehouse what is old and what is new. The process will leave it with some developments, but, if it survives, its pillars will remain largely intact.

Acknowledgments

THIS PROJECT IS THE CULMINATION of several years of work, and I have been enormously fortunate to receive generous support along the way. It has been and remains a privilege to learn from and with mentors and colleagues at the University of Notre Dame and Mount Angel Abbey and Seminary. I owe a debt of gratitude to the theology department at Notre Dame and the administration at Mount Angel Seminary for their institutional support of my research and writing. Both institutional homes have provided invaluable scholarly resources and encouragement, and I would not have been able to start or finish the project without that.

My thanks to those who have read portions of the manuscript either in part or in whole. No doubt all of these readers retain disagreements with what I have written, but this book would not be what it is without their help, and for that I am deeply grateful. This includes colleagues and friends at Notre Dame who read earlier drafts of the manuscript: Carl Friesen, Jimmy Haring, and Nick Ogle. Layne Hancock and Jonathan Ciraulo were instrumental in encouraging me to advance the project to the stage it is now. The Hispanic Theological Initiative provided copyediting for an earlier draft, and the manuscript is much improved thanks to the editorial assistance at several points of Catherine Osborne. Catherine was not only an editorial but also a sympathetic and critical reader. Colleagues at Mount Angel Seminary read and commented on select portions of the manuscript—Justin Coyle, Andrew Cummings, John Rico, and Ted Papa. John Witte Jr. has been a gracious and unfailing source of support through the publication process, and my thanks to Tom Raabe for his editorial assistance in bringing the project to its final form.

I owe special mention of five individuals. Gerald McKenny first provoked my interest in political theology and supported the growth of those interests as they culminated in this project. David Lantigua provided tireless support as

ACKNOWLEDGMENTS

I worked through both early and late scholastic positions on property as well as insight into how to develop the chapter on Catholic social teaching. Paul Weithman was generous with careful and critical feedback and has helped me to sharpen and clarify my argument at several key points. His insights helped me to develop the breadth of engagement with political philosophy that the work reflects. The person to whom I owe the greatest debt of gratitude, for this project and for my development as a scholar, is my doctoral director, Jean Porter. She has helped me to be a better reader of the scholastics and to think through the issues in this book much more cogently and clearly. Her approach to reading Thomas Aquinas in the context of his scholastic contemporaries, and of bringing scholastic thought into conversation with contemporary theology and philosophy, has been an inspiration for the approach I take to the question of property. Finally, for her unfailing fortitude, joy, and confidence, I owe more to Skye de los Reyes than I can express in words.

I dedicate this book to my grandfather, John Thomas Bell. From the time I was a boy he encouraged me to think carefully and critically about the world around me, about science, culture, and, especially, political and economic justice. He died before I graduated high school, but I still recognize his influence in my interest in probing topics related to politics, economics, and justice. For years I received newspaper cuttings in the mail each day with a small note that often concluded with a question, "What do you think?" And for years I remember an attentive and active listener whenever I gave responses. To my first interlocutor, I remain forever grateful.

Works Cited

Alexander, Michelle. *The New Jim Crow: Mass Incarceration in the Age of Colorblindness*. New York: New Press, 2012.
Allen, Douglas W. "Homesteading and Property Rights; Or, 'How the West Was Really Won.'" *Journal of Law & Economics* 34, no. 1 (1991): 1–23.
Anderson, Gary. *Charity: The Place of the Poor in the Biblical Tradition*. New Haven: Yale University Press, 2013.
Andrew, Edward. "Possessive Individualism and Locke's Doctrine on Taxation." *Good Society* 21, no. 1 (2012): 151–68. https://tinyurl.com/342su4kf.
Antoncich, Ricardo. *Christians in the Face of Injustice: A Latin American Reading of Catholic Social Teaching*. Translated by Matthew J. O'Connell. Maryknoll, NY: Orbis Books, 1980.
Aquinas, Thomas. *Aquinas: Political Writings*. Edited and translated by R. W. Dyson. New York: Cambridge University Press, 2002.
———. *Summa contra Gentiles. Book 2: Creation*. Translated by James F. Anderson. Notre Dame: University of Notre Dame Press, 1975.
———. *Summa contra Gentiles. Book 3: Providence Part II*. Translated by Vernon J. Bourke. Notre Dame: University of Notre Dame Press, 1975.
———. *Summa Theologiae [1265–1274]*. 9 vols. Scotts Valley, CA: NovAntiqua, 2010.
Armitage, David. *Foundations of Modern International Thought*. New York: Cambridge University Press, 2013.
———. "John Locke, Carolina, and the Two Treatises of Government." *Political Theory* 32, no. 5 (2004): 602–27.
Arneil, Barbara. *John Locke and America: The Defence of English Colonialism*. New York: Oxford University Press, 1996.
Augustine. *Augustine: Political Writings*. Edited by E. M. Atkins and R. J. Dodaro. Cambridge: Cambridge University Press, 2001.
———. *Sancti Aurelii Augustini in Iohannis Evangelium Tractatus CXXIV*. Edited by Augustino Mayer. Turnhout: Typographi Brepols, 1954.

———. *St. Augustine, Tractates on the Gospel of John 1–10*. Translated by John W. Rettig. Washington, DC: Catholic University of America Press, 1988.

Avila, Charles. *Ownership: Early Christian Teaching*. London: Sheed & Ward, 1983.

Banner, Stuart. *How the Indians Lost Their Land: Law and Power on the Frontier*. Cambridge, MA: Belknap Press of Harvard University Press, 2005.

———. *Possessing the Pacific: Land, Settlers, and Indigenous People from Australia to Alaska*. Cambridge, MA: Harvard University Press, 2007.

Basil. "In a Time of Famine and Drought (Homily)." In *On Social Justice*, edited and translated by C. Paul Schroeder. Crestwood, NY: St. Vladimir's Seminary Press, 2009.

———. "I Will Tear Down My Barns (Homily)." In *On Social Justice*, edited and translated by C. Paul Schroeder, 59–71. Crestwood, NY: St. Vladimir's Seminary Press, 2009.

———. "To the Rich (Homily)." In *On Social Justice*, edited and translated by C. Paul Schroeder. Crestwood, NY: St. Vladimir's Seminary Press, 2009.

Beitz, Charles. *Political Theory and International Relations*. Princeton: Princeton University Press, 1979.

Benedict XVI. *Caritas in Veritate* (On Integral Human Development in Charity and Truth). Vatican, June 29, 2009. https://tinyurl.com/3bwmewjz.

Benton, Lauren, and Benjamin Straumann. "Acquiring Empire by Law: From Roman Doctrine to Early Modern European Practice." *Law and History Review* 28, no. 1 (2010): 1–38.

Birks, Peter. "The Roman Law Concept of Dominium and the Idea of Absolute Ownership." *Acta Juridica* 1 (1985): 1–37.

Birks, Peter, and Grant McLeod, trans. *Justinian's Institutes*. Ithaca, NY: Cornell University Press, 1987.

Bisson, T. N. "The 'Feudal Revolution.'" *Past & Present* 142, no. 1 (February 1994): 6–42.

Bloch, Marc. *Slavery and Serfdom in the Middle Ages: Selected Essays*. Publications of the Center for Medieval and Renaissance Studies. Berkeley: University of California Press, 1975.

Bonaventure. *Disputed Questions on Evangelical Perfection*. Translated by Thomas Reist, OFM Conv., and Robert J. Karris, OFM. St. Bonaventure, NY: St. Bonaventure University, 2008.

Bonnaissie, Pierre. *From Slavery to Feudalism in South-Western Europe*. Translated by Jean Birrell. Cambridge: Cambridge University Press, 1991.

Bradley, Anthony B. *Ending Overcriminalization and Mass Incarceration: Hope from Civil Society*. Cambridge: Cambridge University Press, 2018.

Bradley, Gerard V., and E. Christian Brugger, eds. *Catholic Social Teaching: A Vol-*

ume of Scholarly Essays. Law and Christianity. New York: Cambridge University Press, 2019.

Brett, Annabel S. *Liberty, Right, and Nature: Individual Rights in Later Scholastic Thought*. Cambridge: Cambridge University Press, 1997.

Brock, Stephen L. *Action and Conduct: Thomas Aquinas and the Theory of Action*. Edinburgh: T&T Clark, 1998.

Brown, Peter. *Through the Eye of a Needle: Wealth, the Fall of Rome, and the Making of Christianity in the West, 350–550 AD*. Princeton: Princeton University Press, 2012.

Carlyle, A. J. *A History of Medieval Political Thought in the West*. Vol. 1. 6 vols. New York: Barnes & Noble, 1950.

Carlyle, Sir R. W., and A. J. Carlyle. *A History of Medieval Political Theory in the West*. Vol. 2. 6 vols. New York: Barnes & Noble, 1950.

Cavanaugh, William T. *Being Consumed: Economics and Christian Desire*. Grand Rapids: Eerdmans, 2008.

Chrysostom, John. *St. John Chrysostom on Wealth and Poverty*. Translated by Catharine P. Roth. Crestwood, NY: St. Vladimir's Seminary Press, 1984.

Clement of Alexandria. *The Rich Man's Salvation*. Translated by G. W. Butterworth. Cambridge, MA: Harvard University Press, 1960.

Cloutier, David. *The Vice of Luxury: Economic Excess in a Consumer Age*. Washington, DC: Georgetown University Press, 2015.

Cohen, G. A. *Self-Ownership, Freedom, and Equality*. Cambridge: Cambridge University Press, 1995.

Coleman, Janet. "Dominium in Thirteenth and Fourteenth-Century Political Thought and Its Seventeenth-Century Heirs: John of Paris and Locke." *Political Studies* 33, no. 1 (1985): 73–100.

———. "Medieval Discussions of Property: 'Ratio' and 'Dominium' according to John of Paris and Marsilius of Padua." *History of Political Thought* 4, no. 2 (1983): 209–28.

———. "Property and Poverty." In *The Cambridge History of Medieval Political Thought, c. 350–c. 1450*, edited by J. H. Burns, 607–48. New York: Cambridge University Press, 1988.

Cronon, William. *Changes in the Land: Indians, Colonists, and the Ecology of New England*. New York: Hill & Wang, 1983.

Curran, Charles E. *Catholic Social Teaching, 1891–Present: A Historical, Theological, and Ethical Analysis*. Washington, DC: Georgetown University Press, 2002.

Danilenko, Gennady M. "The Concept of the 'Common Heritage of Mankind' in International Law." *Annals of Air and Space Law* 13 (1988): 247–66.

Davis, Wendy, and Paul Fouracre, eds. *Property and Power in the Early Middle Ages*. Cambridge: Cambridge University Press, 1995.
Day, J. P. "Locke on Property." *Philosophical Quarterly* 16, no. 64 (1966): 207–20.
Duchrow, Ulrich, and Franz J. Hinkelammert. *Property for People, Not for Profit: Alternatives for the Global Tyranny of Capital*. London: Zed Books, 2004.
Dunn, John. "Consent in the Political Theory of John Locke." In *Political Obligation in Its Historical Context: Essays in Political Theory*, 40–44. Cambridge: Cambridge University Press, 1980.
Dworkin, Ronald. *Sovereign Virtue: The Theory and Practice of Equality*. Cambridge, MA: Harvard University Press, 2000.
Dyson, R. W. *The Pilgrim City: Social and Political Ideas in the Writings of St. Augustine of Hippo*. Rochester, NY: Boydell, 2001.
Ellacuría, Ignacio, SJ. *La lucha por la Justicia: Selección de textos de Ignacio Ellacuría (1969–1989)*. Edited by Juan Antonio Senent. Bilbao, Portugal: Universidad de Deusto, 2012.
Filmer, Robert. *Patriarcha; or, The Natural Power of Kings*. 2nd ed. London, 1685.
Finn, Daniel. *Christian Economic Ethics*. Minneapolis: Fortress, 2013.
Fitzmaurice, Andrew. *Sovereignty, Property, and Empire, 1500–2000*. Cambridge: Cambridge University Press, 2014.
Flanagan, Robert J. *Globalization and Labor Conditions: Working Conditions and Worker Rights in a Global Economy*. Oxford: Oxford University Press, 2006.
Fortin, Ernest L., AA. "'Sacred and Inviolable': *Rerum Novarum* and Natural Rights." *Theological Studies* 53, no. 2 (1992). https://tinyurl.com/592etjyv.
Francioni, Francesco, and Tullio Scovazzi, eds. *International Law for Antarctica*. Milan: Guiffrè Editore, 1987.
Francis. "Address of the Holy Father: Participation at the Second World Meeting of Popular Movements." July 9, 2015. https://tinyurl.com/4bsefzzd.
———. "Address of Pope Francis to the Participants in the World Meeting of Popular Movements." October 28, 2014. https://tinyurl.com/277vzrp8.
———. *Fratelli Tutti* (On Fraternity and Social Friendship). Vatican City: Libreria Editrice Vaticana, 2020.
———. *Laudato Si'*. Encyclical letter. Vatican City: Libreria Editrice Vaticana, 2015.
Frankfurt, Harry G. *On Inequality*. Princeton: Princeton University Press, 2015.
Frend, W. H. C. *The Donatist Church: A Movement of Protest in Roman North Africa*. New York: Oxford University Press, 2003.
Garnsey, Peter. *Thinking about Property: From Antiquity to the Age of Revolution*. Cambridge: Cambridge University Press, 2007.
George, William P. *Mining Morality: Prospecting for Ethics in a Wounded World*. New York: Rowman & Littlefield, 2019.

González, Justo. *Faith and Wealth*. San Francisco: Harper & Row, 1990.
Gratian. *Corpus Iuris Canonici: Pars Prior: Decretum Magistri Gratiani*. Edited by Aemliius Friedberg. Graz, Austria: Akademische Druck-U. Verlagsanstalt, 1959.
Gratian and Johannes Teutonicus. *Treatise on Laws (Decretum DD. 1–20) with the Ordinary Gloss*. Translated by Augustine Thompson, OP, and James Gordley. Studies in Medieval and Early Modern Canon Law. Washington, DC: Catholic University of America Press, 1993.
Gregory IX. "Quo Elongati (1230)." In *Francis of Assisi: Early Documents*, vol. 1, *The Saint*, edited by Regis Armstrong, J. Wayne Hellmann, and William J. Short, 570–75. 3 vols. Hyde Park, NY: New City, 1999.
Grey, Thomas C. "The Disintegration of Property." *Nomos* 22 (1980): 69–85.
Habiger, Matthew. *Papal Teaching on Private Property, 1891 to 1981*. Lanham, MD: University Press of America, 1990.
Hardin, Garrett. "The Tragedy of the Commons." *Science* 162, no. 3859 (1968): 1243–48.
Hegel, G. W. F. *Hegel: Elements of the Philosophy of Right*. Translated by Allen W. Wood. Cambridge Texts in the History of Political Thought. New York: Cambridge University Press, 1991.
———. *Philosophy of Right*. Translated by T. M. Knox. Oxford: Oxford University Press, 1952.
Heilbroner, Robert. *The Nature and Logic of Capitalism*. New York: Norton, 1985.
———. *The Worldly Philosophers: The Lives, Times, and Ideas of the Great Economic Thinkers*. 7th ed. New York: Simon & Schuster, 1999.
Hengel, Martin. *Eigentum und reichtum in der frühen Kirche: Aspekte einer frühchristlichen Sozialgeschichte*. Stuttgart: Calwer Verlag, 1973.
Hinze, Christine Firer. *Radical Sufficiency: Work, Livelihood, and a US Catholic Economic Ethic*. Washington, DC: Georgetown University Press, 2021.
Hirschfeld, Mary L. *Aquinas and the Market: Toward a Humane Economy*. Cambridge, MA: Harvard University Press, 2018.
Hoeflich, Michael H., and Jasonne M. Grabher. "The Establishment of Normative Legal Texts: The Beginnings of the Ius Commune." In *The History of Medieval Canon Law in the Classical Period, 1140–1234*, edited by Wilfried Hartmann and Kenneth Pennington, 1–21. Washington, DC: Catholic University of America Press, 2008.
Honoré, Anthony. *Making Law Bind: Essays Legal and Philosophical*. Oxford: Clarendon, 1987.
Huguccio. *Summa Decretorum: Tom. I: Distinctiones I–XX*. Edited by Oldřich Přerovský. Vatican City: Biblioteca Apostolica Vaticana, 2006.
John XXIII. *Mater et Magistra*. May 15, 1961. https://tinyurl.com/294awt43.

WORKS CITED

———. *Pacem in Terris* (On Establishing Universal Peace in Truth, Justice, Charity, and Liberty). Vatican, April 11, 1963. https://tinyurl.com/8tmv7z6x.

John Paul II. *Centesimus Annus* (On the Hundredth Anniversary of *Rerum Novarum*). Vatican, May 1, 1991. https://tinyurl.com/59827buj.

———. *Laborem Exercens* (On Human Work). Vatican, September 14, 1981. https://tinyurl.com/4wmr3htn.

———. *Redemptor Hominis*. Vatican, March 4, 1979. https://tinyurl.com/yakst7uk.

———. *Sollicitudo Rei Socialis* (On the Twenty-Fifth Anniversary of *Populorum Progressio*). Vatican, December 30, 1987. https://tinyurl.com/yuhcua4f.

Kades, Eric. "The 'Middle Ground' Perspective on the Expropriation of Indian Lands." *Law & Social Inquiry* 33, no. 3 (2008): 827–39.

Kilcullen, John. "The Origin of Property: Ockham, Grotius, Pufendorf, and Some Others." In *A Translation of Ockham's Work of Ninety Days*, 2:883–932. Lewiston, NY: Edwin Mellen Press, 2001.

Kopecek, Thomas A. "The Social Class of the Cappadocian Fathers." *Church History* 42, no. 4 (1973): 453–66.

Kuttner, Stephen. "The Revival of Jurisprudence." In *Renaissance and Renewal in the Twelfth Century*, edited by Robert L. Benson and Giles Constable. Toronto: University of Toronto Press, 1991.

Lambert, Malcolm David. *Franciscan Poverty: The Doctrine of Absolute Poverty of Christ and the Apostles in the Franciscan Order, 1210–1323*. St. Bonaventure, NY: St. Bonaventure University Press, 1998.

Landau, Peter. "Gratian and the Decretum Gratiani." In *The History of Medieval Canon Law in the Classical Period, 1140–1234*, edited by Wilfried Hartmann and Kenneth Pennington, 22–54. Washington, DC: Catholic University of America Press, 2008.

Langille, Brian. "General Reflections on the Relationship of Trade and Labour." In *Fair Trade and Harmonization*, vol. 2, *Legal Analysis*, edited by Jagdish N. Bhagwati and Robert E. Hudec. Cambridge, MA: MIT Press, 1996.

Lantigua, David. *Infidels and Empires in a New World Order: Early Modern Spanish Contributions to International Legal Thought*. New York: Cambridge University Press, 2020.

———. "Liberal Domination, Individual Rights, and the Theological Option for the Poor in History." *Journal of the Society of Christian Ethics* 38, no. 2 (2018): 169–86.

Lebovics, Herman. "The Uses of America in Locke's Second Treatise on Government." *Journal of the History of Ideas* 47, no. 4 (1986): 567–82.

Leo XIII. *Rerum Novarum* (On Capital and Labor). Vatican, May 15, 1891. https://tinyurl.com/8t6sxdf4.

Les Glaneurs et La Glaneuse. Documentary. Ciné Tamaris, 2000.
Locke, John. *An Essay concerning Human Understanding*. Edited by Peter Nidditch. Oxford: Clarendon, 1975.
———. *Locke on Money*. Edited by P. H. Kelly. Oxford: Oxford University Press, 1991.
———. *The Second Treatise of Government*. In *John Locke: Political Writings*, edited by David Wootton. Indianapolis: Hackett, 2003.
———. *Two Treatises of Government*. Edited by Peter Laslett. Cambridge: Cambridge University Press, 1960.
Long, D. Stephen. *Divine Economy: Theology and the Market*. New York: Routledge, 2000.
Lower, Michael. *Employee Participation in Governance: A Legal and Ethical Analysis*. Cambridge: Cambridge University Press, 2010. https://tinyurl.com/3pumba7e.
Lustig, B. Andrew. "Natural Law, Property, and Justice: The General Justification of Property in John Locke." *Journal of Religious Ethics* 19, no. 1 (1991): 119–49.
———. "Property and Justice in the Modern Encyclical Literature." *Harvard Theological Review* 83, no. 4 (1990): 415–46.
MacLaren, Drostan. *Private Property and the Natural Law: A Paper Read to the Aquinas Society of London on March 10, 1948*. Oxford: Blackfriars, 1948.
Macpherson, C. B. *The Political Theory of Possessive Individualism*. New York: Oxford University Press, 1962.
Mäkinen, Virpi. *Property Rights in the Late Medieval Discussion on Franciscan Poverty*. Leuven: Peeters, 2001.
Marfin, Catherine. "Texas Prosecutors Want to Keep Low-Level Criminals out of Overcrowded Jails. Top Republicans and Police Aren't Happy." *Texas Tribune*, May 21, 2019. https://tinyurl.com/49znvc4m.
McKee, Arnold F. "The 'Natural' Right to Private Property." *Review of Social Economy* 49, no. 4 (1991): 483–501. https://tinyurl.com/2mjfu9b3.
Merrill, Thomas W. "Property and the Right to Exclude." *Nebraska Law Review* 77, no. 4 (1998): 730–55.
———. "Property and the Right to Exclude II." *Brigham-Kanner Prop. Rts. Conf.* 3 (2014).
Miller, Richard. *Globalizing Justice: The Ethics of Poverty and Power*. New York: Oxford University Press, 2010.
Misner, Paul. *Catholic Labor Movements in Europe*. Washington, DC: Catholic University of America Press, 2015.
———. "The Predecessors of 'Rerum Novarum' within Catholicism." *Review of Social Economy* 49, no. 4 (1991): 444–64.

WORKS CITED

Monro, Charles Henry, and William Warwick Buckland, eds. and trans. *The Digest of Justinian*. Vol. 1. 2 vols. Cambridge: Cambridge University Press, 1904.

Murphy, Liam, and Thomas Nagel. *The Myth of Ownership: Taxes and Justice*. Oxford: Oxford University Press, 2002.

Nell-Breuning, Oswald Von. "The Drafting of *Quadragesimo Anno*." In *Official Catholic Social Teaching*, edited by Charles E. Curran and Richard A. McCormick, 60–67. Readings in Moral Theology 5. New York: Paulist, 1986.

Neuner, J., SJ, and J. Dupuis, SJ, eds. *The Christian Faith in the Doctrinal Documents of the Catholic Church*. 4th ed. New York: Alba House, 1982.

Nozick, Robert. *Anarchy, State, and Utopia*. New York: Basic Books, 2013.

Ockham, William. *A Translation of William of Ockham's Work of Ninety Days (Early 1330s)*. Translated by John Kilcullen and John Scott. 2 vols. Lewiston, NY: Edwin Mellen Press, 2001.

Ostrom, Elinor. *Governing the Commons: The Evolution of Institutions for Collective Action*. Cambridge: Cambridge University Press, 1990.

Otsuka, Michael. *Libertarianism without Inequality*. Oxford: Clarendon, 2003.

Pagden, Anthony. "Gentili, Vitoria, and the Fabrication of a 'Natural Law of Nations.'" In *The Roman Foundations of the Law of Nations: Alberico Gentili and the Justice of Empire*, edited by Benedict Kingsbury and Benjamin Straumann. Oxford: Oxford University Press, 2010.

———. "Law, Colonization, Legitimation, and the European Background." In *The Cambridge History of Law in America*, vol. 1, *Early America (1580–1815)*, edited by Christopher Tomlins and Michael Grossberg, 1–31. Cambridge History of Law in America. Cambridge: Cambridge University Press, 2008. https://tinyurl.com/yrknbp3m.

———. "The Struggle for Legitimacy and the Image of Empire in the Atlantic to c. 1700." In *The Oxford History of the British Empire*, vol. 1, *The Origins of Empire*, edited by Nicholas Canny, 42–47. Oxford: Oxford University Press, 1998.

Parel, Anthony. "Aquinas' Theory of Property." In *Theories of Property: Aristotle to the Present*, edited by Thomas Flanagan. Waterloo, ON: Wilfrid Laurier University Press, 1979.

Patterson, Orlando. *Freedom*. Vol. 1, *Freedom in the Making of Western Culture*. New York: Basic Books, 1991.

Paul VI. *Octogesima Adveniens* (On the Eightieth Anniversary of *Rerum Novarum*). Vatican, May 14, 1971. https://tinyurl.com/4t73t8uj.

———. *Populorum Progressio* (On the Development of Peoples). March 26, 1967. https://tinyurl.com/bdhb37dv.

Phan, Peter. *Message of the Fathers of the Church: Social Thought*. Wilmington, DE: Michael Glazier, 1984.
Piketty, Thomas. *Capital in the Twenty-First Century*. Translated by Arthur Goldhammer. Cambridge, MA: Belknap Press of Harvard University Press, 2017.
Pius XI. *Quadragesimo Anno*. May 15, 1931. https://tinyurl.com/pep49ejv.
Pius XII. "Christmas Address, 1942." Vatican, 1942. https://tinyurl.com/533eah5s.
———. "On the 50th Anniversary of *Rerum Novarum*." June 1, 1941. https://tinyurl.com/2nupwbrp.
———. *Sertum Laetitiae*. November 1, 1939. https://tinyurl.com/ym43ce3t.
———. *The Major Works of Pius XII*. Edited by Vincent A. Yzermans. 2 vols. St. Paul, MN: North Central Publishing Company, 1961.
Pogge, Thomas. *World Poverty and Human Rights*. Cambridge: Polity, 2008.
Polanyi, Karl. *The Great Transformation: The Political and Economic Origins of Our Time*. Boston: Beacon, 1944.
Porter, Jean. *Justice as a Virtue: A Thomistic Perspective*. Grand Rapids: Eerdmans, 2016.
———. *Natural and Divine Law: Reclaiming the Tradition for Christian Ethics*. Grand Rapids: Eerdmans, 1999.
———. *Nature as Reason: A Thomistic Theory of Natural Law*. Grand Rapids: Eerdmans, 2005.
Rawls, John. *A Theory of Justice*. Cambridge, MA: Harvard University Press, 1971.
Reid, Charles, Jr. "The Seventeenth-Century Revolution in the English Land Law." *Cleveland State Law Review* 43 (1995): 221–302.
Rhee, Helen, ed. *Wealth and Poverty in Early Christianity*. Translated by Helen Rhee. Minneapolis: Fortress, 2017.
Risse, Mathias. *On Global Justice*. Princeton: Princeton University Press, 2012.
Romero, Oscar. *Voice of the Voiceless: The Four Pastoral Letters and Other Statements*. Translated by Michael J. Walsh. Maryknoll, NY: Orbis Books, 2003.
Rubianes, Eduardo, SI. *El dominio privado de los bienes segun la doctrina de la iglesia*. 3rd ed. Quito: Ediciones de la Pontificia Universidad Católica del Ecuador, 1993.
Rufinus. *Summa Decretorum*. Edited by Heinrich Singer. Paderborn, Germany: Scientia-Verl. Aalen, 1963.
Ruggini, Lellia Cracco. *Economia e società nell' "Italia annonaria": Rapporti fra agricoltura e commercio dal IV al VI secolo d. C.* 2nd ed. Bari, Italy: Edipuglia, 1995.
Russell, Jesse. "The Catholic Neoconservative Misreading of John Paul II's *Centesimus Annus* Revisited." *Political Theology* 21, no. 3 (May 1, 2020): 172–91. https://tinyurl.com/upcnfw68.

Ryan, Alan. *Property and Political Theory*. Oxford: Blackwell, 1984.
Ryan, John A. *The Christian Doctrine of Property*. New York: Paulist, 1923.
———. *Distributive Justice: The Right and Wrong of Our Present Distribution of Wealth*. Rev. ed. New York: Macmillan, 1927.
———. "Why Private Landownership Is a Natural Right." *Catholic University Bulletin*, 1912, 228–36.
Sahaydachny, Antonia Bocarius. "The Marriage of Unfree Persons: Twelfth Century Decretals and Letters." In *De Iure Canonico Medii Aevi: Festschrift für Rudolf Weigand*, edited by Peter Landau, 483–506. Studia Gratiana 27. Rome: Libreria Ateneo Salesiano, 1996.
Salter, Alexander William. *The Political Economy of Distributism: Property, Liberty, and the Common Good*. Washington, DC: Catholic University of America Press, 2023.
Sassen, Saskia. *The Mobility of Labor and Capital: A Study in International Investment and Labor Flow*. Cambridge: Cambridge University Press, 1988.
Scanlon, T. M. *Why Does Inequality Matter?* Oxford: Oxford University Press, 2018.
Schmidtz, David. "The Institution of Property." *Social Philosophy and Policy* 11, no. 2 (1994): 42–62. https://tinyurl.com/mr3m9stb.
Schultze, George E., SJ. "Worker-Ownership & Catholic Social Thought." *Social Policy* 32, no. 2 (2001): 12–16.
Shue, Henry. *Basic Rights: Subsistence, Affluence, and U.S. Foreign Policy*. 2nd ed. Princeton: Princeton University Press, 1980.
Sierra Bravo, Restituto. *Doctrina social y económica de los Padres de la Iglesia: Colección general de documentos y textos*. Madrid: Compañía Bibliografica Española, 1967.
Smith, Adam. *An Inquiry into the Nature and Causes of the Wealth of Nations*. Edited by R. H. Campbell and A. S. Skinner. 2 vols. Oxford: Oxford University Press, 1976.
Soto, Domingo de. *De justitia et jure (De la justicia y del derecho). Lib. IV: De dominio rerum et de justitia commutativa*. Translated by Marcelino González Ordoñez and Venancio Diego Carro, OP. Colección Clasicos Politicos. Madrid: Instituto de estudios políticos, 1968.
Sousberghe, León de. "Propriété de 'droit naturel': Thèse néo-scolastique et tradition scolastique." *La nouvelle revue théologique* 72, no. 6 (1950): 580–607.
Stiglitz, Joseph. *Globalization and Its Discontents Revisited: Anti-Globalization in the Era of Trump*. New York: Norton, 2017.
Suárez, Francisco. "On the Work of Six Days: Book 5, on the State That Wayfarers Would Have Had in This World If the First Parents Did Not Sin; Chapter 7,

What Kind of Corporeal or Political Life Men Would Have Professed in the State of Innocence." Translated by Matthew T. Gaetano. *Journal of Markets and Morality* 15, no. 2 (2012): 527–63.

———. *Selections from Three Works*. Edited by Thomas Pink. Translated by Gwladys L. Williams, Ammi Brown, John Waldron, and Henry Davis, SJ. Indianapolis: Liberty Fund, 2015.

Swanson, Scott G. "The Medieval Foundations of John Locke's Theory of Natural Rights: Rights of Subsistence and the Principle of Extreme Necessity." *History of Political Thought* 18, no. 3 (1997): 399–456.

Tanner, Kathryn. *Christianity and the New Spirit of Capitalism*. New Haven: Yale University Press, 2019.

———. *Economy of Grace*. Minneapolis: Fortress, 2005.

Tate, W. E. *The English Village Community and the Enclosure Movements*. London: Gollancz, 1967.

Tierney, Brian. *The Idea of Natural Rights: Studies on Natural Rights, Natural Law, and Church Law, 1150-1625*. Grand Rapids: Eerdmans, 2001.

———. *Liberty and Law: Studies on the Idea of Permissive Natural Law, 1100-1800*. Washington, DC: Catholic University of America Press, 2014.

———. *Medieval Poor Law: A Sketch of Canonical Theory and Its Application in England*. Berkeley: University of California Press, 1959.

Tierney, Brian, and Sidney Painter. *Western Europe in the Middle Ages: 300-1475*. 6th ed. New York: McGraw-Hill, 1998.

Tocqueville, Alexis de. *Democracy in America and Two Essays on America*. Translated by Gerald E. Bevan. London: Penguin Books, 2003.

Tuck, Richard. *The Rights of War and Peace: Political Thought and the International Order from Grotius to Kant*. Oxford: Oxford University Press, 1999.

Tully, James. *A Discourse on Property: John Locke and His Adversaries*. Cambridge: Cambridge University Press, 1980.

———. "Rediscovering America: The Two Treatises and Aboriginal Rights." In *Locke's Philosophy: Content and Context*, edited by G. A. J. Rogers, 165–96. Oxford: Clarendon, 1994.

Urbino, Francisco Castilla. "El indio americano en la filosofía política de John Locke." *Revista de Indias* 46, no. 178 (1986): 421–51.

Vitoria, Francisco de. *Comentarios a la Secunda Secundae de Santo Tomas*. Edited by Beltran de Heredia. Vol. 3. Salamanca, Spain, 1932.

Waldron, Jeremy. "Disproportionate and Unequal Possession." In *God, Locke, and Equality: Christian Foundations of Locke's Political Thought*, 151–87. Cambridge: Cambridge University Press, 2002.

———. *The Right to Private Property*. Oxford: Clarendon, 1988.
———. *The Rule of Law and the Measure of Property*. Cambridge: Cambridge University Press, 2012.
Ward, Kate. *Wealth, Virtue, and Moral Luck: Christian Ethics in an Age of Inequality*. Washington, DC: Georgetown University Press, 2021.
Waterman, A. M. C. "Property Rights in John Locke and in Christian Social Teaching." *Review of Social Economy* 40, no. 2 (1982): 97–115. https://tinyurl.com/2fh589sb.
Weigand, Rudolf. *Die Naturrechtslehre der Legisten und Dekretisten von Irnerius bis Accursius und von Gratian bis Johannes Teutonicus*. Munich: Max Hueber, 1967.
Wolff, Richard D. "Alternatives to Capitalism." *Critical Sociology* 39, no. 4 (July 1, 2013): 487–90. https://tinyurl.com/36m9yvfw.
———. *Democracy at Work: A Cure for Capitalism*. Chicago: Haymarket Books, 2012.
Zuckert, Michael. *Natural Rights and the New Republicanism*. Princeton: Princeton University Press, 1994. https://tinyurl.com/4yeu7yfm.

Index of Names

Alanus, 64–65, 67, 106
Alexander, Michelle, 62n
Allen, Douglas W., 164n
Ambrose, 21n, 23n, 31, 32–36, 34n, 41, 43, 44, 50, 66–67n, 77, 92, 115, 116, 194
Anderson, Gary, 31n
Andrew, Edward, 97n
Antoncich, Ricardo, 190n
Aquinas, Thomas, 8, 24n, 36n, 46, 49, 55–56, 57, 77–93, 94, 99–102, 109n, 115, 117, 125–28, 160, 169, 179–80n, 181n, 184n, 195
Aristotle, 109n
Armitage, David, 151n, 154
Arneil, Barbara, 150n, 151n, 152n, 154n, 165n
Augustine of Hippo, 18–25, 27, 31–32, 34, 40–41, 48, 50, 63n, 64, 72, 75–76, 77, 117
Avila, Charles, 3n, 23n, 47n

Banner, Stuart, 149n, 160n, 162, 163n
Basil, 19, 21, 28–30, 32, 39–40, 41, 45–47, 48, 50, 72, 92n
Benedict XVI (pope), 187n, 206, 211n, 212–13
Bentham, David, 2

Benton, Lauren, 33n, 140n, 153n, 158n, 159n
Birks, Peter, 73n, 103n, 108n, 137n, 138n
Bisson, T. N., 127n
Bloch, Marc, 61n
Bonagratia, Francisco, 35n, 138n
Bonaventure, 89n
Bonnaissie, Pierre, 61n
Bradley, Anthony B., 62n
Bradley, Gerard V., 196–97n
Brett, Annabel S., 127n, 128n, 131, 200n
Brock, Stephen L., 99n, 101n
Brown, Peter, 27–28, 30n, 31n, 34n, 36n, 40n, 41n
Brugger, E. Christian, 197n

Carlyle, A. J., 22n, 34n, 49n, 104n, 137n, 167
Carlyle, Sir R. W., 104n
Cavanaugh, William T., 3n
Cesena, Michael, 35n
Christensen, Katherine, 13n, 16n
Cicero, 32–34
Clement (pope). See Pseudo-Clement
Clement of Alexandria, 31
Cloutier, David, 3n, 32n, 119n, 123
Cohen, G. A., 100n, 125, 129–30, 147n

INDEX OF NAMES

Coleman, Janet, 99n, 183n
Cotton, John, 155
Cronon, William, 155–56, 168, 212n
Curran, Charles E., 181n, 198n
Cushman, Robert, 153–55

Danilenko, Gennady M., 73n
Davis, Wendy, 127n
Day, J. P., 145n
Duchrow, Ulrich, 4n, 23n, 91–92n
Dunn, John, 97n
Dupuis, J., SJ, 197n
Dworkin, Ronald, 2, 119–20, 123, 124, 175n
Dyson, R. W., 22, 31n, 32n, 48n, 100n

Ellacuría, Ignacio, SJ, 3, 9, 23n, 192–93, 214

Filmer, Robert, 96, 139n, 145
Finn, Daniel, 4n, 23n, 38n
Fitzmaurice, Andrew, 140n, 153n
Flanagan, Robert J., 112–13n
Fortin, Ernest, 182n, 196n
Fouracre, Paul, 127n
Francis (pope), 166n, 177, 180, 186n, 187n, 188n, 193–96, 197, 205, 206, 208, 211n, 212–13, 214
Frankfurt, Harry G., 118, 119, 121, 124n
Frend, W. H. C., 19n

Gaetano, Matthew T., 85n, 116n
Gandulphus, 74
Garnsey, Peter, 24n, 33n, 34n, 43n, 55n, 115n, 157n
Gentili, Alberico, 140, 141, 150, 152
Gerard of Abbeville, 137–38
George, William P., 43n
González, Justo, 19n, 29n, 48
Gordley, James, 13n, 105n
Grabher, Jasonne M., 14n, 16n

Gratian, 13–54, 55, 57, 61, 66n, 70, 72–77, 105, 124, 131–32, 194
Gregory IX (pope), 52–53, 78n, 128n, 132
Gregory of Nazianzus, 29, 48
Gregory of Nyssa, 29, 48
Grey, Thomas C., 168n
Grotius, Hugo, 150, 152–53, 156, 158
Gundlach, Gustav, SJ, 198n

Habiger, Matthew, 179n
Hardin, Garrett, 102n
Hegel, G. W. F., 2n, 11–12, 177–78, 198–209, 214
Heilbroner, Robert, 3n, 112n, 115–16, 118n, 168n, 180–81
Hengel, Martin, 23n
Hinkelammert, Franz J., 4n, 23n, 91–92n
Hinze, Christine Firer, 3n, 124, 190n, 192n
Hirschfeld, Mary L., 4n
Hoeflich, Michael H., 14n, 16n
Honoré, Anthony, 51n, 168n
Hugh of St. Victor, 53, 64
Hugolinus, 103, 104
Huguccio, 55–57, 66n, 69–78, 80, 85–86, 88, 89, 94, 98–99, 101, 105–7, 108
Hume, David, 2

Innocent IV (pope), 132
Irnerius, 103
Isidore, 38, 88
Ivo of Chartres, 64

John Chrysostom, 15–16, 28, 30–31, 32, 39–41, 47, 48, 50, 169
John of Paris, 183n
John of Rochelle, 64–65, 78n

Index of Names

John Paul II (pope), 177, 180, 186n, 187n, 188, 191–92, 194, 204n, 206, 207, 211n, 214
Johnson, William Samuel, 163
John XXII (pope), 35n, 43, 100n, 138–39
John XXIII (pope), 186–87, 191n, 198, 200, 202–5, 206, 208, 210–11, 214

Kades, Eric, 162–63
Kilcullen, John, 43n, 100n, 137n, 139n
Kopecek, Thomas A., 29n
Kuttner, Stephen, 14n

Lambert, Malcolm David, 35n, 137n
Landau, Peter, 14n, 15n, 126n
Langille, Brian, 112n
Lantigua, David, 140n, 152n, 153, 154, 159n, 160n, 161, 190n
Las Casas, Bartolomé de, 161–62
Laslett, Peter, 144n, 151n, 183n
Lebovics, Herman, 151n
Leo XIII (pope), 132n, 135, 143n, 177, 178–86, 189, 193, 196–98, 205, 207
Leo the Great, 30, 31
Liberatore, Matteo, 196
Locke, John, 2–3, 42n, 96–97, 135–75, 183n
Lombard, Peter, 53
Long, D. Stephen, 3n
Lower, Michael, 179n
Ludlow, Morwenna, 17n, 99n
Lustig, B. Andrew, 135n, 179–80n

MacLaren, Drostan, 3n, 87n
Macpherson, C. B., 143n, 166, 174n
Mäkinen, Virpi, 138n
Marfin, Catherine, 122n
Marx, Karl, 84–85n, 146, 180–81, 202
McKee, Arnold F., 135, 179n

Merrill, Thomas W., 167–68n
Mill, John Stuart, 2
Miller, Richard, 211n
Milton, J. R., 151n
Misner, Paul, 179n, 181n, 201n
More, Thomas, 140n
Murphy, Liam, 2–3, 9, 10, 110, 124

Nagel, Thomas, 2–3, 9, 10, 110, 124
Nell-Breuning, Oswald von, SJ, 198n
Neuner, J., SJ, 197n
Nozick, Robert, 2, 52n, 97n, 129–30, 143n, 147–48, 183n

Ockham, William, 17n, 35n, 43n, 100n, 138–39
Olivi, Peter, 35n
Ostrom, Elinor, 10, 79, 84, 102n, 109, 170–71, 209
Otsuka, Michael, 55n, 148n, 175n

Pagden, Anthony, 149n, 151n, 152n
Painter, Sidney, 111n, 112n
Parel, Anthony, 3, 87n
Patterson, Orlando, 58n, 63n
Paul VI (pope), 187n, 188n, 192, 194, 205–7, 206n, 210–11, 212, 214
Phan, Peter, 24n
Piketty, Thomas, 208n
Pius XI (pope), 180, 183, 185, 187n, 190–91, 193, 198, 200, 201–2, 204
Pius XII (pope), 184–85, 186–88, 191, 198, 200, 202–4, 206, 207, 214
Plato, 35, 71
Polanyi, Karl, 142n, 156n
Porter, Jean, 5n, 6n, 13n, 59n, 63n, 88n, 99n, 114n, 126n
Pseudo-Clement, 26, 34–35, 44, 105–6
Pseudo-Isidore. See Pseudo-Clement
Pufendorf, Samuel, 24n, 145

231

INDEX OF NAMES

Raleigh, Sir Walter, 141–42
Rawls, John, 2, 10, 117n, 174–75n
Raz, Joseph, 119
Reid, Charles, Jr., 141–42
Rhee, Helen, 3n, 19n, 28n, 29n, 30n, 40n, 41n, 47n, 169n
Ricardus Anglicus, 65n
Risse, Mathias, 55n, 100–101n, 121n
Rolandus, 65
Romero, Oscar, 190, 214
Rubianes, Eduardo, SJ, 24n, 49n
Rufinus (twelfth-century canonist), 55–56, 57–70, 71, 77–78, 80–81, 94, 99, 101, 106–8, 109n
Rufinus of Aquileia (fourth-century scholar), 21n, 46, 92n
Russell, Jesse, 192n
Ryan, Alan, 2n, 11, 177–78n, 199n, 200n
Ryan, John A., 124, 189–90, 201n, 208, 214

Sahaydachny, Antonia Bocarius, 126n
Salter, Alexander William, 193n
Sassen, Saskia, 211n
Scanlon, Thomas, 118, 119, 124
Schmidtz, David, 143n, 147n
Schultze, George E., SJ, 201n
Sen, Amartya, 2
Seneca, 33n, 115n, 157n
Shaftesbury, Earl of, 151, 153n
Shue, Henry, 194n
Sierra Bravo, Restituto, 24n, 48n
Simon Bisgnano, 67
Smith, Adam, 40n, 116, 181n
Soto, Domingo de, 43, 55n, 161
Sousberghe, León de, 179n, 180n, 182n
Stephanus, 67

Stiglitz, Joseph, 112n
Straumann, Benjamin, 33n, 140n, 152n, 153n, 158n, 159n
Suárez, Francisco, 38–39, 85n, 115–16n, 161
Swanson, Scott G., 49n, 136n

Tanner, Kathryn, 3n
Taparelli, Luigi, 179
Tate, W. E., 142n
Teutonicus, Johannes, 13n, 17n, 67, 105
Tierney, Brian, 16n, 24, 30n, 39n, 51, 59n, 64n, 65n, 71n, 78n, 88n, 110–11, 121, 123n, 131n, 132, 138n
Tocqueville, Alexis de, 163n, 164
Torquemada, Juan de, 49–50
Tuck, Richard, 151n
Tully, James, 144–45, 151n, 155n, 156n, 159n, 163n

Urbino, Francisco Castilla, 151n

Vattel, Emer de, 149n, 159n
Vitoria, Francisco de, 83n, 85n, 161n

Waldron, Jeremy, 2n, 5n, 10, 84n, 96n, 139n, 140n, 143, 145–46, 156n, 158–59n, 168, 173, 183n, 199n, 200n, 202, 205, 205n, 208, 211n
Ward, Kate, 3n, 118–19, 124, 131
Waterman, A. M. C., 179n
Weigand, Rudolf, 38n, 46n, 51n, 55, 62n, 65n, 67n, 71, 73–74, 77n, 103, 104–5, 106n, 126n, 127n
William of Auxerre, 78n
Winthrop, John, 155
Wolff, Richard D., 202n

Zuckert, Michael, 143n, 151–52n, 166, 172

232

Index of Subjects

agriculturalist theories of property, 135–36, 148–66, 212; and Amerindian dispossession, 148–66; Catholic social teaching in opposition to, 150, 160; decolonial critiques of Locke's labor-mixing theory, 148–66; differentiating from scholastic natural law theory, 165–66; enclosure system, 9, 112n, 141–42, 153, 155; English colonizers, 149, 150–66; Locke on land appropriation, 140–42, 147, 171–73; Locke's labor-mixing theory, 135–36, 148–66; Vattel, 149n, 159–60

Albigensian heresy, 24n

alienation (alienability), right of, 51–52, 145, 156, 163, 167, 181, 200

Ambrose, 32–34, 35–36, 41, 50; on common dominion, 41; critique of property, 23n, 32–34, 35–36; material equality and Golden Age thinking, 115; *On the Duties of the Clergy*, 32–34; on slavery, 66n

Amerindians: agriculturalist theory of property and dispossession, 148–66; land tenure, 160–62; property as a power of distribution, 168; territorial sovereignty, 150, 152, 155–59, 163

Aquinas, Thomas, 55–56, 77–93, 94; on common dominion as common possession, 88–89, 101, 102; on common dominion as a judgment of reason, 89–91; on common dominion prior to the division of goods, 8, 83–84, 88–89; and the conventionality of property, 78–87, 94, 195; on directive dominion, 99–101, 212–13; on the division of property, 83–86, 89n, 91; on general principles of natural law, 79–81, 195; on God's dominion, 92; on human law, 81–82, 85–87; on the *ius gentium*, 81–87; on moral precepts of Mosaic law, 80n; on "natural" dominion, 89–91; on natural equality and material inequality, 115–17; and the normativity of common dominion, 87–93, 99–101; positive view of property, 24, 36n; on principle of equity, 107, 109n; on principle of liberty, 125–28; on principle of stewardship (responsibility), 84, 85–86, 87, 160, 195; on the prohibition against killing, 80–81, 83; and property as power of distribution, 169; on slavery and

INDEX OF SUBJECTS

liberty, 126–27; synthetic approach to property, 55–57, 77–93, 94

Augustine of Hippo, 18–25, 108; on common dominion, 40–41; on convention of property, 75–77; on private property, 27–28, 31–32; on property and God's dominion, 18–25, 72; on property as a power of distribution, 48, 50; *Tractates on the Gospel of John*, 20–23, 40–41, 72

Basil, 19, 21, 28–30, 32, 39–40, 41, 45–47, 48, 50; on common dominion, 39–40, 41; on the misuse of property, 32; on principle of God's dominion, 19, 21, 72; on property as a power of distribution, 45–47; on sufficiency and subsistence, 48; on usefulness of property for sustaining society, 28–29

Benedict XVI (pope): and Catholic social teaching, 206, 212, 213; and implications of CST for the international order, 212, 213; on property and moral self-development, 206

Bologna school of canonists, 53, 65, 74, 106. *See also* canonists

canonists: Alanus, 64, 65, 67, 106; Bonagratia, Francisco, 35n, 138n; Gandulphus, 74; Gratian, 13–54, 55, 57, 61, 66n, 70, 72–77, 105, 124, 131–32, 194; Innocent IV, 132; Ricardus Anglicus, 65n; Simon Bisgnano, 67; Stephanus, 67; Teutonicus, Johannes, 13n, 17n, 67, 105. *See also* Bologna school of canonists; Hugolinus; Huguccio; Irnerius; Ivo of Chartres; Rufinus; Weigand, Rudolf

canon law, 10–11, 13–16, 94, 111n, 123, 131–32. *See also* canonists; Code of Canon Law (1917); *Decretals* (*Liber Extra*) (Gregory IX); Decretist texts; Gratian's *Decretum* (scholastic reception of patristic tradition on property); Huguccio; *miserabiles personae*; Rufinus

Cappadocians, 29–30, 48. *See also* Basil

Catholic social teaching (CST), 9, 135, 176–214; and the agriculturalist argument, 150, 160; Benedict XVI, 206, 212, 213; common (or universal) destination of material goods, 72, 73, 177, 180, 183–89, 194–95, 214; conventionality of property, 177, 190, 193, 195, 209, 214; duty of "social justice," 185, 187–88; Ellacuría, 9, 192–93, 214; Francis, 177, 180, 193–96, 197, 205, 206, 212, 213, 214; and Hegelian approach to property, 11, 177, 198–209, 214; how the natural law framework developed in, 197–209, 214; instrumentality of property, 177, 183, 188, 190; John Paul II, 177, 180, 186n, 188, 191–92, 206, 207, 214; John XXIII, 186, 198, 200, 202–5, 210–11, 214; liberation theologians, 9, 190; and Locke's theory of power as personal use, 167, 174–75; misread as an economic theory of distributivism, 178, 193; misread as introducing a Lockean natural right of appropriation, 178; and natural right of use, 186–89, 206, 213; and partnership contracts/corporations, 185, 201–2, 204–5; Paul VI, 192, 194,

234

205–7, 210–11, 212, 214; Pius XI, 183, 185, 190–91, 198, 200, 201–2, 204; Pius XII, 184–85, 186–88, 191, 198, 200, 202–4, 207, 214; principle of liberty, 199–200, 203; property, the rights of peoples, and the international order, 160, 209–13; property and moral self-development, 11–12, 177, 198–209, 212, 214; property as a "secondary natural right," 195, 205; property as power of distribution, 182, 184–89, 193; and radical alternatives to current social and economic order, 191–94, 208–9; reinterpretations of Leo XIII's *Rerum Novarum* and Lockean approach to property, 135, 143n, 177, 178–86, 196–98; right of sufficiency, 124, 194, 207; Romero, 190, 214; Ryan, 124, 189–90, 201n, 208, 214; and taxation, 186

Centesimus Annus (John Paul II), 186n, 187n, 192

charity, 30, 32, 49, 136, 170–71, 173, 182, 183–86

Charles II, restoration of, 142

Code of Canon Law (1917), 13

colonialism: English, 149, 150–66; Spanish, 160–62, 164

common (or universal) destination of material goods, 72, 73, 177, 180, 183–89, 194–95, 214; Catholic social teaching, 72, 73, 177, 180, 183–89, 194–95, 214; Francis on, 177, 180, 194–95; John Paul II on, 177, 180

common dominion. *See* natural law of common dominion

common governance regimes, 8, 102n, 209

common possession: Aquinas on common dominion and, 88–89, 99–100, 101, 102; Huguccio on common dominion and, 98–99, 101; and open access regimes, 101–2, 108, 121; Rufinus on common dominion and, 99, 101

common resources, 73, 84, 123–24, 137, 213

convention (concept of), 6–7

conventionality of property, 6–7, 26–37; Ambrose's critique of property, 23n, 32–34, 35–36; Aquinas and, 78–87, 94, 195; Augustine on private property (possession), 27–28, 31–32; Basil on hazards of property, 32, 45–47; Basil on usefulness of property, 28–29; Chrysostom on hazards of property, 32; Chrysostom on usefulness of property, 28, 30–31; Huguccio and, 75–77, 85, 94; patristic tradition and, 26–37; Pseudo-Clement, 26, 34–35, 44, 105–6; Rufinus and, 57–69, 94; and the scholastic natural law theory of property, 56, 57–69, 75–77, 78–87, 94, 195; and tension between possession and sin, 26–37; on usefulness of property for sustaining society, 28–31, 36–37

CST. *See* Catholic social teaching (CST)

Decalogue, 59–60, 80n

Decretals (Liber extra) (Gregory IX), 52–53, 78n, 132

Decretist texts: *Summa 'Antiquitate et Tempore,'* 71; *Summa Aurea*, 78n; *Summa Halensis*, 78n; *Summa Lau-*

INDEX OF SUBJECTS

rentius, 71; *Summa Lipsiensis*, 65n; *Summa Monacensis*, 73–74; *Summa Parisiensis*, 71, 73; *Summa 'Queritur,'* 71

Decretum. *See* Gratian's *Decretum* (scholastic reception of patristic tradition on property)

directive dominion, 99–101, 212–13

distribution, power of (property as), 167–75; Amerindian societies, 168; Aquinas, 169; Augustine on, 48, 50; Basil, 47; Catholic social teaching (distributive duties and responsibilities grounded in), 182, 184–89, 193; charity and, 170; Christian tradition, 167–75; Chrysostom and stewardship of possessions, 47, 169; communal property regimes and, 170–71; and contemporary bundle of property rights, 51–52; and duty of "social justice," 185, 187–88; and the goals of property law, 50–52; John Paul II on natural right to use, 188–89; John XXIII on distributive duties, 186; John XXIII on natural right to property and natural right of use, 187; misreading of CST as economic theory of distributivism, 178, 193; patristic tradition and property in Gratian's *Decretum*, 44–52; Pius XII on distributive duties, 184–85; Pius XII on natural right to use, 186–87; and property as a power of personal use (Locke's labor-mixing theory), 167–75; and the tension between property and theft, 44–52; and theological critique of Locke's labor-mixing theory, 166–75

dominion (concept of), 7–8, 17n, 98–103. *See also* natural law of common dominion

Donatist controversy, 19–20, 22–23

Edict of Unity (405), 19–20

enclosure system, 9, 112n, 141–42, 153, 155

equality, principle of, 95, 114–20, 132–33; Aquinas on natural equality and material inequality, 115–17; and civic equity, 114; contemporary political thought on, 114–20; and differential levels of freedom, 132–33; Dworkin on inequality, 119–20, 123, 124; Frankfurt on wealth inequality and principle of sufficiency, 118, 119, 121, 124n; Heilbroner on wealth and inequality, 115–16, 118n; and open access regimes, 115–16; property and state of innocence, 115–17; Rawls on wealth inequality, 117n; Scanlon on wealth inequality, 118, 119, 124; Suárez on property and state of innocence, 115–16n; sufficiency and, 118, 119, 121, 123–24; Ward on morally deleterious effects of material inequality, 118–19, 124

equity, principle of, 95, 103–14; Aquinas and, 107, 109n; canonist tradition, 103, 105–7, 110–11; equality and civic equity, 114; and exercise of self-direction, 111–13, 114, 121; and feudal peasants' subsistence lifestyle, 110–13, 121; Huguccio and, 105–6, 107, 108; laws and conventions that depart from, 108–11; natural and civic equity in the Roman tradition, 103–5; and open access regimes, 7, 108, 109–13; Rufinus, 106–8, 109n;

wealth, income, and taxation today, 110
Essay concerning Human Understanding, An (Locke), 144–45
exclusivity, right of, 42–44, 45, 52, 115–16, 129, 144–45, 156, 167–68, 180–81, 200

feudal society, 110–13, 121–22, 123, 126–27, 167
Francis (pope): and Catholic social teaching, 177, 180, 193–96, 197, 205, 206, 212, 213, 214; on the "common" or "universal" destination of material goods, 177, 180, 194–95; CST and the international order, 212, 213; *Fratelli Tutti*, 188n, 194, 212n, 213n; on property as a "secondary natural right," 195, 205; on right of sufficiency, 194; on work and self-development, 206
Franciscans: on dominion and poverty, 42, 124–25, 127–28; Gerard of Abbeville's criticism of relationship between use and ownership, 137–38; Michaelist controversies, 35, 35n, 41, 43, 136, 138
Fratelli Tutti (Francis), 188n, 194, 212n, 213n

globalization of capital, 112n
Glorious Revolution of 1688, 142
God's dominion, principle of: Aquinas on, 92; Augustine on, 18–25, 72; Basil on, 19, 21; Gratian's *Decretum*, 17–26; Huguccio on, 72–75; and tension between the natural and the conventional, 17, 19, 24–26, 53
Golden Age: in Ambrose, 33–34; Locke's description, 157; Seneca and Stoic idea of, 33–34, 41, 115, 157n

Gratian's *Decretum* (scholastic reception of patristic tradition on property), 13–54, 72–77, 131–32; Gratian's systematization of canon law, 13–15; Huguccio on, 72–77, 105–6; poverty and liberty, 131–32; principle of common dominion, 37–44, 46, 72–77; principle of the conventionality of property, 26–37, 77–78; principle of God's dominion, 17–26; principle of property as power of distribution, 44–52

Hegel, G. W. F., 2n, 198–209; Catholic social teaching and Hegelian approach to property, 11, 177, 198–209, 214; property and principle of self-development, 11–12, 177, 198–209, 214; relationship between freedom and private ownership, 200–201
Homestead Acts, 164
Huguccio, 55–57, 69–78, 94, 101, 105–7, 108; and Aquinas, 85, 86, 87–88; on common dominion and framework for human social life, 70, 74–75, 88, 98–99, 101; on conventionality of property, 75–77, 85, 94; and the dominion of God, 72–75; on Gratian's *Decretum*, 72–77, 105–6; on natural law of common dominion as ethical mandate, 70–74; on natural law of common dominion as theological framework, 69, 72–74, 98–99; on normativity of common dominion, 87–88; *Summa Decretorum*, 69–78

imago Dei, 90, 101
Institutes (Justinian). *See* Justinian's *Institutes*

INDEX OF SUBJECTS

John Chrysostom, 28, 30–31, 32, 39–40, 47, 50, 169; on common dominion, 39–40; on hazards of property, 32; on property as a power of distribution, 47, 169; on stewardship of possessions, 47, 169; on usefulness of property for sustaining society, 28, 30–31

John Paul II (pope): and Catholic social teaching, 177, 180, 186n, 188, 191–92, 206, 207, 214; *Centesimus Annus*, 186n, 187n, 192; on the "common" or "universal" destination of material goods, 177, 180, 204; *Laborem Exercens*, 180, 187n, 188, 191, 194n, 204n, 206n, 207; on natural right to use, 188–89; on property and moral self-development, 204, 206, 207

Johnson v. M'Intosh (1823), 163

John XXIII (pope): and Catholic social teaching, 186–87, 198, 200, 202–5, 210–11, 214; on distributive duties, 186; on employee ownership, 204–5; *Mater et Magistra*, 186n, 187n, 191n, 202–5; on natural right to property and natural right of use, 187; *Pacem in Terris*, 210–11; on political autonomy and self-determination, 210–11; on property and moral self-development, 198, 200, 202–5; on property as natural right (general right), 205

jus cogens, 103n

Justinian's *Institutes*, 53, 137, 138n

just war, 62, 66–67

killing: Aquinas and prohibition against, 80–81, 83; Gratian and Rufinus on capital punishment, 60–62; Rufinus and prohibition against, 59–62, 65–66

Laborem Exercens (John Paul II), 180, 187n, 188, 191, 194n, 204n, 206n, 207

labor-mixing theory of property. *See* Locke's labor-mixing theory of property

Leo XIII (pope), 132n, 135, 143n, 177, 178–86, 196–98; on causal effect of labor, 197–98; and Locke's labor-mixing theory, 135, 143n, 182, 197–98; and Marxist thinking on private property, 180–81; on property as natural right, 181–84, 196; on relationship of the natural right to private property to other rights and duties, 183–84; *Rerum Novarum* and Lockean approach to property, 132n, 135, 177, 178–86, 196–98. *See also* Catholic social teaching (CST)

liberation theology, 9, 63, 190

liberty (self-direction), principle of, 95, 99–100, 101, 125–33, 199–200; Aquinas on common dominion and, 125–28; Catholic social teaching on property and moral self-development, 199–200, 203; contemporary political philosophers on autonomy and self-ownership, 125, 128–31; *Decretals* of Gregory IX on poverty and, 132; feudal society, 127; and freedom in contemporary capitalist economies, 133; and freedom of the will, 125–31; Gratian's *Decretum* (Distinction 87) on poverty and, 131–32; "hyperagency," 131; and Lockean idea of self-ownership, 97, 128–31, 143–46; medieval mendicants

Index of Subjects

on dominion and poverty, 124–25, 127–28; principle of equity and exercise of self-direction, 111–13, 114, 121; and principle of sufficiency, 121; scholastic discussions, 125–28; and slavery/servitude, 126–27

Locke's labor-mixing theory of property, 2–3, 96–97, 135–75; and agriculturalist theories of property, 135–36, 148–66; analytic critiques (question of coherency), 143–48; and the Carolina colony's *Fundamental Constitutions*, 151–52; common dominion and possession, 42n, 96–97, 138–43; construal of one's relation to one's "person," 143–46; decolonial critiques, 148–66; how movables can go from common to private (appropriated), 138–41, 172; idea of self-ownership, 97, 128–31, 143–46; land appropriation (how immovables can go from common to private), 140–42, 147, 171–73; and Leo XIII's *Rerum Novarum*, 135, 143n, 182, 197–98; and Locke's inherited traditions, 136–38; "mixing" one's labor with an unowned object, 143, 145–48; and money economies, 141, 142–43, 157–58, 172, 173; "no harm" theory of property, 1–3, 9, 147; Nozick's libertarian critique, 147–48; political insulation of property, 96–97; property as power of personal use, 166–75; *Second Treatise on Government*, 42n, 97n, 136–43, 145n, 146n, 147n, 149–59, 165–66, 171n, 172n, 174; sufficiency and spoliation provisos, 141–42, 155, 183; theological critiques, 166–75; Tully's analytic critique, 144–45; Waldron's analytic critique, 143, 145–46

Manichaeism, 22, 24
Massachusetts Bay colony, 155–56
Mater et Magistra (John XXIII), 186n, 187n, 191n, 202–5
Michaelist controversies, 35, 41, 43, 136, 138
miserabiles personae, 132
Mohegan tribe, 159, 162–63
Mondragón Corporation, 201n
money economies, 111n; Franciscans and, 128; Gratian's *Decretum* on, 38; Huguccio on, 72–73; and Locke's labor-mixing theory of property, 141, 142–43, 157–58, 172, 173; and open access regimes, 115–16
moral principles of property. *See* equality, principle of; equity, principle of; liberty (self-direction), principle of; natural law of common dominion; self-development; sufficiency, principle of (right of subsistence)

natural law (definition), 5–6
natural law of common dominion, 7–8; Ambrose on, 41; Aquinas and the normativity of, 87–93, 99–101; Aquinas on common possession and, 88–89, 99–100, 101, 102; Aquinas on directive dominion, 99–101, 212–13; Aquinas on "natural" dominion, 89–91; Aquinas on reason and, 89–94, 99–100; Aquinas on the state prior to the division of goods, 8, 83–84, 88–89; Augustine on, 40–41;

INDEX OF SUBJECTS

Basil on, 39–40, 41; Catholic social teaching on the common (or universal) destination of material goods, 72, 73, 177, 180, 183–89, 194–95, 214; Chrysostom on, 39–40; definition of dominion, 7–8, 17n; Gratian's *Decretum*, 19, 37–44, 46, 72–77; Huguccio on common possession and, 98–99, 101; Huguccio and the normativity of, 69–75, 87–88; Huguccio on the ethical mandate, 70–74; Huguccio on the theological framework, 69, 72–74, 98–99; and Locke's labor-mixing theory of property, 42n, 96–97, 138–43; moral principles of, 4, 7, 56, 94, 95–134; principle of equality, 95, 114–20, 132–33; principle of equity, 95, 103–14; principle of liberty (power of self-direction), 95, 99–100, 101, 125–33, 199–200; principle of sufficiency (right of subsistence), 95, 120–25, 194, 207; Rufinus on common possession and, 99, 101; Rufinus on normativity of, 67–69, 99, 101; scholastic reception of patristic tradition, 37–44, 46, 72–77, 99n; tension between common and private, 37–44; tension between the natural and the conventional, 17, 19, 24–26, 53; tension between property (possession) and sin, 26–37; tension between property and theft, 44–52; two ways a theory of property can transgress the framework of, 134
neoliberal capitalism, 190, 207–8
"new natural law" theory, 5
"no harm" theory of property, 1–3, 9, 147. *See also* Locke's labor-mixing theory of property

Octogesima Adveniens (Paul VI), 187n, 192, 206n, 210, 211n, 212n
open access regimes, 5, 7, 101–2, 108, 109–13, 115–16, 121; and common possession, 101–2, 108, 121; equity and, 7, 108, 109–13; material equality and, 115–16

Pacem in Terris (John XXIII), 210–11
partnership contracts/corporations, 185, 201–2, 204
patristic theologians on property, 7, 13–54; Ambrose, 23n, 32–34, 35–36, 41, 50; Augustine, 18–25, 27–28, 31–32, 40–41, 48, 50; Basil, 19, 21, 28–30, 32, 39–40, 41, 45–47, 48, 50; Chrysostom, 28, 30–31, 32, 39–40, 47, 50, 169; Isidore, 38, 88; principle of common dominion, 37–44, 46, 72–77, 99n; principle of conventionality of property, 26–37; principle of God's dominion, 17–26; principle of property as a power of distribution, 44–52; Pseudo-Clement, 26, 34–35, 44, 105–6; tension between common and private, 37–44; tension between the natural and the conventional, 17, 19, 24–26, 53; tension between property (possession) and sin, 26–37; tension between property and theft, 48, 50. *See also* Gratian's *Decretum* (scholastic reception of patristic tradition on property)
Paul VI (pope): and Catholic social teaching, 192, 194, 205–7, 210–11, 212, 214; *Octogesima Adveniens*, 187n, 192,

Index of Subjects

206n, 210, 211n, 212n; *Populorum Progressio*, 187n, 188n, 194n, 206n, 211, 212n; property and the rights of peoples (implications for the international order), 210, 211, 212

Pelagianism, 24, 27

Pius XI (pope): and Catholic social teaching, 183, 185, 190–91, 198, 200, 201–2, 204; on partnership contracts, 185, 201–2, 204; *Quadragesimo Anno*, 185n, 187n, 190n, 191n, 201n

Pius XII (pope): and Catholic social teaching, 184–85, 186–88, 191, 198, 200, 202–4, 207, 214; on distributive duties, 184–85; on natural right to use, 186–87; on property and moral self-development, 198, 200, 202–4

Populorum Progressio (Paul VI), 187n, 188n, 194n, 206n, 211, 212n

property (definition), 5

Quadragesimo Anno (Pius XI), 185n, 187n, 190n, 191n, 201n

Rerum Novarum (Leo XIII), 132n, 135, 177, 178–86, 196–98; on causal effect of labor, 197–98; Lockean approach to property, 135, 177, 178–86, 196–98; and Locke's labor-mixing theory, 135, 143n, 182, 197–98; and Marxist thinking on private property, 180–81; on property as natural right, 181–84, 196; relationship of the natural right to private property to other rights and duties, 183–84. *See also* Catholic social teaching (CST)

right of use. *See* use, right to

Roman Law: dominion in, 99; natural and civic equity, 103–5; the natural law of occupation (and Locke's theory of property), 136–38; property in, 23, 27, 33n, 73, 137, 138n, 152–53n, 167; *res nullius*, 149n, 152–53n, 159–60; rule of usucapion, 103–4. *See also* Justinian's *Institutes*

Rufinus, 55–56, 57–69, 70, 71, 80–81, 94; on capital punishment, 60–62; on civil laws, 60–69; on commands and prohibitions of natural law, 57–61, 65–66, 68, 80–81; on common dominion and common possession, 99, 101; on connection between justice and demonstrations of natural law, 66–67; and conventionality of property, 57–69, 94; on institution of private property, 57–59; on institution of slavery, 57–68, 106–8; and normativity of demonstrations of natural law, 57–69; and normativity of natural law of common dominion, 67–69, 99, 101; on prohibition against killing, 59–62, 65–66; on property and sin, 77; *Summa Decretorum*, 57–69

scholastic natural law theory of property, 5–6, 18, 55–94, 98–103, 110, 177, 198, 208–9, 210; and Amerindian land tenure, 160–62; applying to Catholic social teaching (CST), 9, 135, 176–214; Aquinas and the synthetic approach to property, 55–57, 77–93, 94; definition, 5–6; differentiating from the agriculturalist approach, 165–66; Huguccio and the social-ethical solution, 55–56, 69–78, 80, 94; implications of recovering,

8–10; moral principles of the natural law of common dominion, 4, 7, 56, 94, 95–134; Rufinus and permissive natural law, 55–56, 57–69, 70, 71, 80–81, 94. *See also* Aquinas, Thomas; Catholic social teaching (CST); conventionality of property; Gratian's *Decretum* (scholastic reception of patristic tradition on property); Huguccio; natural law of common dominion; Rufinus

Second Treatise of Government, The (Locke), 42n, 97n, 136–43, 145n, 146n, 147n, 149–59, 165–66, 171n, 172n, 174

self-determination of peoples, 8, 134, 160, 209–11

self-development: Benedict XVI, 206; Catholic social teaching on property and, 11–12, 177, 198–209, 212, 214; Francis, 206; Hegelian idea of, 11–12, 177, 198–209, 214; John Paul II, 204, 206, 207; John XXIII, 198, 200, 202–5; Pius XI, 198, 200, 201–2; Pius XII, 198, 200, 202–4; and principle of liberty, 199–200, 203

self-direction. *See* liberty (self-direction), principle of

self-ownership, 97, 128–31, 143–46. *See also* liberty (self-direction), principle of

servitude: Aquinas on freedom and, 126–27; and principle of liberty, 126–27. *See also* slavery

slavery: in Ambrose, 66n; Hegel's account of property and self-development, 199; Rufinus on, 57–68, 106–8. *See also* servitude

social justice, principle of, 185, 186–88

Spanish Scholastics, 9–10; 160–62. *See also* Soto, Domingo de; Suárez, Francisco; Vitoria, Francisco de

spoilation proviso, 141–42, 154–55, 173, 183

stewardship, principle of: Aquinas on, 84, 85–86, 87, 160, 195; Chrysostom on, 47, 169

Stoic philosophy, 33–34, 41, 58, 64, 115, 157n

subsistence. *See* sufficiency, principle of (right of subsistence)

sufficiency, principle of (right of subsistence), 95, 120–25, 194, 207; Catholic social thinkers on, 124, 194, 207; Cloutier on, 123; in the contemporary United States, 122–24; distinction between scholastic subsistence and contemporary sufficiency, 120–22; Dworkin on equality and, 123, 124; and "equality of resources," 123–24; Frankfurt on wealth inequality and, 118, 119, 121, 124n; medieval right of subsistence and feudal peasants' lifestyle, 110–13, 121–22; and powers of self-direction, 121; Tierney and, 121; and wealth inequality, 118, 119, 121, 123–24

sufficiency proviso, 141–42, 155, 183

"tragedy of the commons," 102n

use, right to, 4, 22–23, 42–44, 51–52, 145, 156, 181–82, 186–89, 206, 213; Catholic social teaching and natural right of use, 186–89, 206, 213; and Christian tradition of property as a power of distribution, 167–75; John Paul II on, 188–89; John XXIII on natural right to property and,

187; Locke's labor-mixing theory of property (as power of private use), 166–75; Pius XII on, 186–87; usufruct rights, 73–74, 138n, 156, 167

usucapion, rule of, 103–4

usufruct rights, 73–74, 138n, 156, 167

wealth inequality. *See* equality, principle of; sufficiency, principle of (right of subsistence)

Weigand, Rudolf, 46, 55, 65n, 71, 73–74, 103, 104–5, 106n

TITLES PUBLISHED IN
EMORY UNIVERSITY STUDIES IN LAW AND RELIGION

Thomas C. Berg, *Religious Liberty in a Polarized Age* (2023)

Harold J. Berman, *Faith and Order: The Reconciliation of Law and Religion* (1993)

Stephen J. Grabill, *Rediscovering the Natural Law in Reformed Theological Ethics* (2006)

Johannes Heckel, *Lex Charitatis: A Juristic Disquisition on Law in the Theology of Martin Luther* (2010)

Timothy P. Jackson, ed., *The Best Love of the Child: Being Loved and Being Taught to Love as the First Human Right* (2011)

Timothy P. Jackson, *Political* Agape: *Christian Love and Liberal Democracy* (2015)

Paul Grimley Kuntz, *The Ten Commandments in History: Mosaic Paradigms for a Well-Ordered Society* (2004)

Douglas Laycock, *Religious Liberty*, Volume 1: *Overviews and History* (2010)

Douglas Laycock, *Religious Liberty*, Volume 2: *The Free Exercise Clause* (2011)

Douglas Laycock, *Religious Liberty*, Volume 3: *Religious Freedom Restoration Acts, Same-Sex Marriage Legislation, and the Culture Wars* (2018)

Douglas Laycock, *Religious Liberty*, Volume 4: *Federal Legislation after the Religious Freedom Restoration Act, with More on the Culture Wars* (2018)

Douglas Laycock, *Religious Liberty*, Volume 5: *The Free Speech and Establishment Clauses* (2018)

W. Bradford Littlejohn, *The Peril and Promise of Christian Liberty: Richard Hooker, the Puritans, and Protestant Political Theology* (2017)

Ira C. Lupu and Robert W. Tuttle, *Secular Government, Religious People* (2014)

Martin E. Marty, *Building Cultures of Trust* (2010)

R. Jonathan Moore, *Suing for America's Soul: John Whitehead, The Rutherford Institute, and Conservative Christians in Court* (2007)

Joan Lockwood O'Donovan, *Theology of Law and Authority in the English Reformation* (1991)

Jean Porter, *Ministers of the Law: A Natural Law Theory of Legal Authority* (2011)

Charles J. Reid Jr., *Power over the Body, Equality in the Family: Rights and Domestic Relations in Medieval Canon Law* (2004)

Liam de los Reyes, *The Earth Is the Lord's: A Natural Law Theory of Property* (2025)

Noel B. Reynolds and W. Cole Durham Jr., eds., *Religious Liberty in Western Thought* (1996)

A. G. Roeber, *Hopes for Better Spouses: Protestant Marriage and Church Renewal in Early Modern Europe, India, and North America* (2013)

James W. Skillen and Rockne M. McCarthy, eds., *Political Order and the Plural Structure of Society* (1991)

Steven D. Smith, *Pagans and Christians in the City: Culture Wars from the Tiber to the Potomac* (2018)

Brian Tierney, *The Idea of Natural Rights: Studies on Natural Rights, Natural Law, and Church Law, 1150-1625* (1997)

Glenn Tinder, *The Fabric of Hope: An Essay* (1999)

Glenn Tinder, *Liberty: Rethinking an Imperiled Ideal* (2007)

David VanDrunen, *Divine Covenants and Moral Order: A Biblical Theology of Natural Law* (2014)

David VanDrunen, *Natural Law and the Two Kingdoms: A Study in the Development of Reformed Social Thought* (2009)

Johan D. van der Vyver and John Witte Jr., eds., *Religious Human Rights in Global Perspective: Legal Perspectives* (1996)

David A. Weir, *Early New England: A Covenanted Society* (2005)

John Witte Jr., *God's Joust, God's Justice: Law and Religion in the Western Tradition* (2006)

John Witte Jr. and Johan D. van der Vyver, eds., *Religious Human Rights in Global Perspective: Religious Perspectives* (1996)

Nicholas Wolterstorff, *Justice in Love* (2011)